OTHER TITLES OF INTEREST FROM ST. LUCIE PRESS

Organizational Transformation and Process Reengineering

Evolution of Management Theory: Past, Present, Future

Competitive Global Management: Principles and Strategies

Seven Fatal Management Sins: Managerial Malpractice (A Wake-Up Call)

How to Reengineer Your Performance Management Process

Macrologistics Management

Sustaining High Performance: The Strategic Transformation to a Customer-Focused Learning Organization

Exporting: Strategic Plans for Business

Problem Solving for Results

For more information about these titles call, fax or write:

St. Lucie Press
100 E. Linton Blvd., Suite 403B
Delray Beach, FL 33483
TEL (407) 274-9906 • FAX (407) 274-9927

S^t_L

COMPETITION
in the **21**st
CENTURY

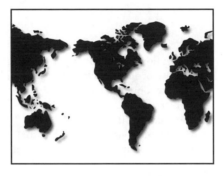

KIRK W.M. TYSON

$S{}^{t}_{}L$

St. Lucie Press
Delray Beach, Florida

Phone: (407) 274-9906
Fax: (407) 274-9927

SᵗL

Published by
St. Lucie Press
100 E. Linton Blvd., Suite 403B
Delray Beach, FL 33483

In Memory of my Father,

George C. Tyson

TABLE OF CONTENTS

PREFACE

I mentioned to a friend of mine, a piano teacher, that I was writing a book on competition in the world of business. She grimaced and said, "I didn't think of you as the type of person to do a book on competition. To tell the truth, I kind of think of competition as a BAD thing." After finishing my own grimace, I told her that, actually, competition is a very good thing. It is a basic economic principle about capitalism and free markets that has actually been the foundation of civilizations throughout history. I was beginning to warm up to the subject.

It creates more choices, more benefits, and more freedom, I went on to say. On a sheer individual level, maximum competition means that consumers like you and I will have the best possible products and services at the best possible prices. And while competition isn't without its upheaval—what with companies that go out of business and jobs that disappear—it is essential in producing the progress and innovations that have benefited our lives. Look at it this way, I said. Standing water stagnates itself; running water revitalizes itself. Pleased at the stand I had taken, I stopped and waited for her acknowledgment. Her response was an unenthusiastic, "Oh." Well, progress is really being made here, I thought. This was a good thing, because business competition has been around since the beginning of time. And that's a long time to be wearing a pained look on your face. In fact, the intensity of competition seems to be the only thing that is changing. The trend seems to be toward more intense competition. As we move out of the information age and into the intelligence age in the 21st century, it seems clear that companies will continue to do battle, especially in global markets.

Now, with the coming of January 1, 2001, we will mark the beginning of the 21st century. So, it seems appropriate that we look back over the last 100 years to get some perspective for the next 100. With that in mind, over the years I have been searching for books on business that put everything into perspective. In other words, where did we come from? Where are we now? Where are we going? What I found was discouraging. It seems we business people are content to look only at the recent past when making strategic and tactical decisions for our businesses. Three to five years of historical information is all that is deemed necessary by many to evaluate the present situation and plan for the future. Unfortunately, it's like preparing a seven-course meal using the history of a three-minute egg as a guideline. The result of such thinking is that company strategic plans lack business intelligence, suffering from a "garbage in, garbage out" mentality. That is unfortunate, because many lessons can be learned from a look further back into history. Such a look provides some surprising things, and, paradoxically, not all of them are new surprises. It appears that the old adage that history repeats itself is true.

This book has some history itself. Ten years in the making, it paints competition of the future based on in-depth research of worldwide business over the last 100 years—its positives and negatives, and its winners and losers. By analogy, it shows business competition in its 19th century childhood, 20th century adolescence, and 21st century adulthood. It shows the geometric expansion of human needs from food/clothing/shelter, and it unveils the evolutionary (and revolutionary) business responses to those needs. It highlights new beginnings—the beginning of the "Intelligence Age," highly networked "MegaStrategic Business Entities," and the need for a "Perpetual Strategy" process. The book provides an "early warning" for executives to change course before it is too late.

That is because business competition has changed—radically! The "shoot from the hip" approaches of the past will not work in the 21st century. To out-think, out-smart, and out-maneuver competitors, business planning and decision making must be based on the global long view rather than a domestic short-term view. And the long view requires a "long" historical analysis of business in each of the major business regions—Europe, North America and the Asia/Pacific region.

In this book, I use the past and present to predict the future of global business competition—what it will look like, how it will operate, and how it got there. Using anecdotal business history as the bedrock, I extend that history to a logical, but often surprising, future. Demonstrations will show that while some business principles evolve, certain other principles are revolving, rather than evolving. That is, they come full circle. So, by applying what we know now, and then comparing it to the past, we can predict the future of business competition around the world.

This view of the future was guided by multiple primary and secondary sources in several arenas, including business, academia and journalism. These sources include senior company management of multinational companies, as well as managers in R&D, marketing, operations, and finance. To that, add professors from the top business schools and business journalists from the leading newspapers. The large business consulting firms also provided vital perspective. Our newfound cyber friends on the Internet were queried, too, for their views on competition. My staff conducted over 4,500 interviews in total over the past 10 years. We also searched newspapers, magazines, trade journals and other reference sources in Europe, North America and the Asia/Pacific region. Literally thousands of published pieces of information provided the starting point for our interviews. Many public relations groups of the large multinational companies provided more information than we could have dreamed of. Many also sent hardbound books of their company history. From all of this data and perspective has come a prediction of the characteristics of 21st century business and competition.

If I have one frustration with this book effort, it is the fact that business history tends to be more art than science. It was not unusual for us to find three to five different dates for an invention or a new product introduction. It was also common to find several companies or countries claiming the same invention. It took much more research and analysis than we would have expected to determine the truth. In a few cases, the differences were not reconcilable, so we applied our judgment based on the available facts. What is personally frustrating is that I grew up believing that most inventions originated in the United States. I remember learning in school that Samuel Morse invented the telegraph, Thomas Edison invented the light bulb, Alexander Graham Bell invented the telephone, Henry Ford invented the car, and Remington Rand invented the computer. Not true. These things were not invented by Americans. They were invented by Europeans. My frustration eased a bit as I discussed this with colleagues around the world that had also experienced nationalistic history lessons in school. I am proud to set the record straight in this book.

This book could have easily been 1,000 pages in length. Since nobody gets very excited about a 1,000-page book, I was forced to leave out many things. In terms of world regions, South America and Africa are noticeably missing. The developing countries and emerging businesses in these regions will play an important role in 21st century business. However, Europe, North America and the Asia/Pacific region will provide the vast majority of the "global" competition. Also, I have covered primarily consumer markets—food, clothing, shelter, etc.—to the exclusion of business markets. I am also sorry to say that the business leaders mentioned in this book are almost 100 percent men. I know this will change in the next century as more and more women rise to the top of multinational corporations.

ACKNOWLEDGMENTS

Because of the sheer volume of research sources, I have purposely not included a bibliography in this book. It would be longer than the book itself. To all of the people we interviewed, to all of the company public relations departments, and to all of the publishers providing background material, I extend my heartfelt thanks. In addition, I would like to thank Sandra Koskoff, my production editor, for her patience and devotion to this project.

I would also like to thank all of the employees of my firm, Kirk Tyson International, particularly Dan Brosnan, Vernon Prior, Todd Kuciunas, Jeff Sienkiewicz, Vic Marriott, John Golde, Tim Powell, Don Ebel, Colleen Brosnan, Tom Kupetis, Wade Hanson, Al Kamienski, Steve Siegel, Jean Phelan, Pat Matoush, David Kalinowski, Gary Maag, and Valerie Fleming.

I would also like to thank my colleagues outside the United States for their global perspective, particularly Daniel Gautschoux, Joseph Rodenberg, Jan Kihlgren, Michael Hass, and Jose-Luis Terricabras.

My biggest thanks goes to Terry Murtaugh of my firm who headed the research team and provided vital editorial assistance. Terry also taught me a writing style which is distinctly different from my previous books. Without Terry, this book would not have become a reality.

INTRODUCTION

Once upon a time, there lived a wise old man who had experienced all that life had to offer.

He was born in the Midwestern United States to parents who had come from Germany just five years earlier. They had originally settled in Germantown, Pennsylvania, near Philadelphia, but soon took a homestead in Missouri.

The old man had a wonderful childhood. His family lived at the edge of town in a white wooden farmhouse. It was rather cold and drafty in the winter, but it was a home warmed by a blazing fire in the fireplace and filled with the perpetual scent of cinnamon emanating from the kitchen. It was a home full of love.

As the old man sat in his rocking chair on the front porch, he remembered his father. His father was a stocky man with a ruddy complexion, who had farmed the land until World War II. Just before the war, his father had given up on farming to take a job as a banker in town. He never forgot that his father came home for lunch every day and tended a small garden in his white shirt and tie.

His mother was a beautiful woman whose light brown hair would turn blonde in the summer. Everyone knew she loved her home and her family. Her life had been difficult, but the journey to America had been a positive event. Even though she had lost a daughter at childbirth, and her second child, a son, at age eight from polio, she always had a zest for life.

1

The old man remembered playing in the hayloft of the grayish red barn, which was badly in need of paint. Horses and cows grazed in the pasture, and the carriage stood ready for his favorite trips to the market. Occasionally, a neighbor came to visit, riding his horse up the dirt road leading to the house. A hitching post stood just outside the house, with fresh water always available for the horses.

The year was 1905, and the old man was then a young five-year-old, the only surviving child in the family. There were no cars and no expressways. Stores were closed at night and on Sunday. Time was available for leisurely strolls in the park. Businesses operated locally to serve the needs of nearby customers.

When they would hitch up the wagon to go into town, they would pass only a few buildings: a bank, a general store, a livery, a tavern, and a church that was an American Gothic style building. He especially enjoyed summers in the town—particularly the Fourth of July. The whole town would come out for a big party. Everyone was dressed in their "Sunday Best" clothes. There would be a parade through the middle of town, with lots of food, candy and ice cream afterwards.

Life continued on in the same way for many years . The old man had wanted to join the army to fight in World War I, but he would not be old enough for another year. By then, in 1918, the war was over. One of his friends, a boy two years older, returned from the war with an idea to start a food processing business. So the two of them did.

The town was starting to change. Model T Fords could be seen making their way down the dirt roads. A few factories with big smoke-stacks had been built near his house. The outdoor smells had definitely changed for the worse.

His business was off to a good start. After two decades of slow but steady growth, the company had become the largest food processing company in the United States. Then America entered World War II, and his factory was pressed into service to make weapons.

After the war, the factory was converted back to its original purpose. The old man was named chairman and chief executive officer. Things started moving faster and faster. The company was selling everything it could produce. But then things changed. Supply started to exceed demand. New competitors from other states were starting to pop up with new products, new packaging and lower prices.

The old man remembered saying, "We will not change our course. We have been successful for 30 years. We will continue to be successful if we remember that 'quality at a reasonable price' is our motto." And he was right. The company continued to grow and prosper. The old man had grown it from a one-room factory to one of the world's largest multinational companies. His boyish grin and easygoing manner had won him loyal friends and customers throughout the world. He suddenly laughed. "I looked a lot like Bill Gates, but food processing wasn't the place to make a billion dollars."

And so it came to be that everything changed dramatically after World War II. In fact, an evil creature had shown its face to challenge the conventional wisdom of the day. The creature said, "Build more factories. Make more products. Grow big companies. Quench the thirst for more consumption. Do it at any cost. Don't worry about the eyesores of industry. Don't worry about pollution. Don't worry about anything. Beat those competitors at any cost...."

And that's how the "COMPETITION MONSTER" got bigger and BIGGER and BIGGER and BIGGER....

Now, as the old man sat in his easy chair, stoking his pipe, he glanced at the calendar. "Darn it, I missed my son's birthday. Oh, well, I'll just send him one of those belated computer cards overnight via UPS." The year was 1996. The old man walked outside and took a look around. My how things had changed. Years ago his parents had left the home to him. He had been forced by the city to sell the majority of his homestead to a land developer. This boyhood home, which used to be on the edge of town, was now in the inner city, along with train wheels screeching, airplanes screaming, the neighbor boy's stereo at full volume, bus fumes, car fumes, chemical plant fumes, sausage plant fumes...yes, things had changed quite a bit in his 96 years.

His wife had preceded him in death. She had developed lung cancer. His own health was failing, but he was bound and determined to make it to his 100th birthday and the turn of the century. The lines of time were written clearly on the old man's face, a mixture of wisdom, worry and concern. His joy in life was his three children, all of whom were healthy, had attended the best universities, and were now happily married with children of their own. Yes, he was a proud father of two boys and one girl, and now a grandfather six times, with three grand-daughters and three grandsons.

The old man had been a former captain of industry, and probably because of this, he was deeply concerned about the future of business. He had seen a lot...steam engines, the cotton gin, small manufacturing operations, Xerox machines, computers, fax machines. He had tried to keep up. One of his grandsons was sending him a weekly e-mail message on the Internet. "But DAMN that Windows 95!" He wished he could go back to the good old days of DOS. But those days were long gone.

He had retired in 1965, a partial retirement where he was still acting as chairman of the company. Then they forced him out in 1975, forced him out of his own company. Can you believe such a thing?

Now, as he sat back in his easy chair reflecting on his business career, he picked up the morning paper. Suddenly, he went numb. Heart pains and angina had become a problem. He grabbed his nitroglycerin bottle, put the small pill under his tongue and tried to relax. This time, however, one pill wasn't enough to do the trick.

The headlines had disturbed him greatly—"downsizing... reengineering...thousands of people out of work...."

He worried about what the world was coming to. Everything in 1996 seemed to be competitive—highly competitive, deathly competitive. Babies competed for birthing rooms. Infants competed at nursery school and kindergarten. Children competed on the sports fields and in the classroom. Young adults competed for their first jobs. Career-minded men and women competed to climb the proverbial ladder of success. Companies competed for customers, and if they couldn't beat the competition, they would buy them, merge with them or run them out of business. Small companies were being swallowed by larger com-panies. Large companies were joining forces to create even larger com-panies. Governments were deregulating and privatizing monopolistic industries such as telecommunications and electric utilities to create competition where none existed before. Sports channels, sports bars, lotteries, and casino gambling had grown to a fever pitch so that com-petition could pervade every waking hour of human existence.

And the COMPETITION MONSTER said, "This is a very good thing!" And, like the Eveready Energizer battery in the television commercial, he kept going...and going...and going...and he got BIGGER and BIGGER and BIGGER....

The old man dozed in his easy chair. His dreams picked up where his conscious thoughts left off.

CHAPTER 1

- - - - - - - - - - - - - -

ON A CLEAR DAY YOU CAN SEE THE 21st CENTURY

The old man continued his dream. He was dreaming of a colorful speech he had given a few years back at an industry association meeting....

So, you say you want to stay in business? Maybe even grow the business. Or maybe you're looking to start a business. Or make your mark in business. Well, in the future be prepared for global competition and more transformations than a chameleon going through a color crisis. And that's if you just want to stay in the game. To really compete successfully, you will need to be the driver of change in your industry. In fact, you're going to have to make changes more often than Clark Kent/Superman does during his peak season...and, oh, by the way, you'll have to be just as dynamic. You know, bend steel wills into compliant minds, leap tall bar charts in a single bound, stop runaway costs with your bare hands.

How do we know that's what the future holds for business competition? Easy. The past predicts it. How so? Well, with each turn of the technological screw, there's been change. Lots of change. And as that screw threads itself faster and faster into the future, there will be even more change, bringing more competition—fierce competition—and on a global playing field.

And just like a centrifugal force throwing things off and away from the force itself, you don't even have to be directly in line with the threads of the screw to get screwed into the ground. Just ignore the competitive changes going on around you and, as sure as you're standing there, you'll find those threads furrowing your head.

Change creates competitive problems, but it also creates competitive opportunities. You pick which set of situations you want to deal with. Take too much time, though, and your only option may be planting corn in that newly-furrowed head of yours.

So take advantage of your competitive change options. You didn't have to be Henry Ford to capitalize on the emerging auto industry, maybe just a realtor with some semi-rural land just outside of town. You know, those high-priced plots of land we now call suburbia. So, maybe you didn't know a spark plug from a fire plug, but if you had the foresight to realize the mobility brought on by the automobile, you would have understood the value of some wide-open spaces at the edge of town.

On the other hand, you could have been the Central Leather Company. Back in 1917, Central was 24th out of the top 100 industrial companies in the United States. They made the finest horse and carriage equipment in America. They also made fools out of themselves by totally ignoring the auto. "Come on, what can come of that newfangled car?", thought management. "It's a toy. It's a novelty." Well, it ended up being the screw that firmly anchored Central to the bottom of anyone's list. It's also a lesson from the past that's just as relevant today—technology creates an evolution revolution. It drives change. It drives competition. Don't let it drive you out of business or steer you in the wrong direction.

Look at Xerox. The bright guys in R&D said, 'Someday there will be a computer on everybody's desk with more power than the large mainframes. Xerox R&D folks invented the first PC, the first mouse, the first graphical user interface, the first laser printer, and the first local area network. Management laughed and said, "Let's concentrate on our areas of core competence." The result? Major global business opportunities lost—forever!

So, that means strong competitors have to be nimble, have to be quick, right? Well, yeah, but let's not imply that being nimble and quick necessitates being small. First, nimble and quick can just as easily pertain to a company's thinking and attitude as much as to its size. There are small, tiny mouse firms that go out of business every day, just as there are big, hulking elephant-size companies that lay down and die. Give most companies enough rope and they'll not only hang themselves, but they'll macramé the noose. So, the companies, big or small, that succeed over time are those who aggressively compete, constantly check out change, adapt to meet the new challenges, and end up with the fewest rope burns.

And just who are some of the best change-challenged competitors around? The big ones. You know—Motorola, General Electric, IBM. And, yes, we're aware of IBM's problems in the early/mid-1990s, but this hasn't been the first time they faced adversity, and there's a good chance they'll be around to face some more.

What the successful big companies have shown, and what small-size firms can learn from, is that it's not size, it's attitude that counts in the global competitive arena. Also, these big companies retain their traumas and triumphs as a sort of corporate consciousness. Essentially, you might say, these elephants—true elephants—never forget.

The lesson to be learned? Competition and change offer the means to grow strong. Just ask some of the elephants...before they trample you.

🐘 🐘 🐘 🐘 🐘 🐘

Really, how different will competition be in the 21st century? When we look at competition in our own local communities, it is not likely to change much. It is when we examine regional and global competition that a picture of change becomes clear. The industry picture of the 21st century can be illustrated as follows.

Food

Ever expanding populations and decreasing farm land will spur new technologies and methods of farming. Consolidation will take place with many more corporate farms and larger meat and poultry firms. R&D will be a big part of costs and sustainable only by large companies. There will be a proliferation of small specialty firms that supply everything from genetics products to hyper-size hydroponic and organic farming systems. People will become comfortable shopping remotely: phone, fax, e-mail, cable TV and network computer. Bulk and specialty food retailers will continue to gain market share at the expense of today's supermarkets. Brand names will win over private labels, with approximately 200 international brands dominating.

Clothing

Clothes will be more expensive because of the costs involved. High-technology and robotics will make most of the clothes by the end of the

21st century because of fewer workers willing to work at lower pay. That's why the "everyday-low-price" stores will continue to flourish. So will the high-end clothes. Mid-level retail operations will continue their fight for survival. As with food, clothes will see steady increases in remote-order as well as video shopping. Yes, there will be malls and hypermarkets. And fashion design will become a global effort.

Shelter and Personal Transportation

Residential dwellings will be smaller and more often in more rural settings. There will be a mix of working at home and working at the office. This will have a decaying effect on cities and suburbs. Corporate-run home maintenance services will spring up to do what we don't have time to do or want to do. Residential homes will remain similar to today's, with the exception of the kitchen which will be much larger. To fill it up, a myriad of new appliances will be available.

Energy

Even more advanced fuel exploration technologies will be invented to find more gas and oil fields as the current ones dwindle. Governments of major industrialized nations will succeed in pushing for alternative fuels. Competition among the remaining fuel-source companies will be exceedingly hot.

Security/Financial

Insurance will be just as important as a financial investment as it is an insurance product. But it will look nothing like it does now. Premiums will vary according to the preventive measures people take to lessen the likelihood of claim filing. Banking and financial investment firms will be allowed to compete freely throughout the world. They will do so fiercely.

Security/Health Care

The health care issue of the 21st century is, "Who will pay?" Nationalized care systems will see people almost revolt, as many of their current benefits are cut or eliminated. Employer-subsidized programs will increase dramatically, while government-supported entitlements will be reduced. Costs will be higher for specific medical treatments, but overall costs will equal today's because of preventive medical advances initiated at birth. Such initiatives cut down on illness and disease in later life. We will also come to rely on a more holistic approach to medicine.

Security/Personal

The same amount of crime will prevail in America, but with more guns. More crime will occur in Europe and the Asia/Pacific region, with just a slight rise in gun ownership. On a per capita basis, US citizens will install a slightly greater number of home security systems than are now being installed. The same will prevail in Europe and the Asia/Pacific region.

Communications

Visual and audio communications will proliferate due to the increase of advanced equipment and systems available. We will have what we have now, more of it, and with even greater technological options. Personal communication numbers will be routine. Cyberspace interaction will increase as the Internet is redefined and reconfigured. It will be regulated and monitored as a system. Books, magazines and newspapers will not disappear. There will be lots of them.

Travel and Entertainment

There will be more professional sports, more and varied entertainment, and the same amount of illicit drugs. A lot more new toys will come on the market, and many of the current favorites will still be around. Travel will be cramped, priced as today and mostly done on airplanes—cramped because airline competition will be heated and plane interiors will continue to be configured for the optimum number of passengers to save costs.

So the industries affecting our daily lives in the 21st century will be much different, except those in our local community. People will be striving to maintain their own space, their own order, as they go through their daily lives. And even though the fate of the traditional nuclear family is unclear, it is clear that human beings require social interaction, social order and security. They will require more of it in the 21st century as populations increase. This will probably signal a trend away from large cities and suburbs back to the rural areas. This will be further encouraged by continuing advances in communications.

So what types of companies will we see in the future? Probably very large companies and very small companies. The large companies will get larger in an attempt to dominate global markets, and the small companies will still be in demand to serve local and regional customers in niche markets. But it will be the large companies, the New Centurions, the MegaStrategic Business Entities (MBEs), that will capture our attention and our investment dollars. Let's take a peek at what these companies might look like.

Characteristics of 21st Century Companies, Leaders and Business Practices

In the past, processes such as product distribution and research and development were kings. They will now be princes. The new kings will be information, intelligence and the concept of perpetual strategy. Add to that a longer view toward the development of business goals and global cooperation through alliances and joint ventures, and you have the road map for business success in the 21st century. All of this will take place within a framework of time-based competition. Products and services will be provided at the lowest price—and provided quickly. The advancement of Information and Communications (Info/Com) technologies will underpin this time-based competitive environment, providing the tools necessary to accomplish the constant change that will be demanded.

Today's current reengineering has created a cost-cutting mentality that will be replaced by growth strategies emphasizing the development of new products and new regional and global markets. Great improvement in productivity will assist in the campaign to conceive these innovative products, while advanced Info/Com technologies will provide the means to identify and exploit new and emerging markets. But somebody will be looking over corporate shoulders. As institutional investors—pension funds, retirement funds, etc.—increase their stake in the financial investment world, they will seek an even greater voice in corporate affairs. And they will get it. Their increasing influence will garner them board seats and more control over CEOs.

Large companies will not have organizational charts. Those command-and-control charts of the 20th century will be replaced by network charts, which pinpoint the different elements that make up the future corporation. Those elements, or nodes, include all the contributors to the output of a company's product or service, inside and outside the corporation. Employees, suppliers, alliance partners and out-sourced vendors are all part of this decentralized organizational structure. Decentralization is a must, because decisions will be made by those closest to the customer. To reach that customer, marketing will once again be asked to do the yeoman's work. This time the marketing package will be tailored explicitly for a particular customer, and not just a market niche or segment. Salespeople will see a whole new world in which they are not asked to sell to people, but are asked to manage the systems that do. Robotics and computer integrated manufacturing systems will increase productivity and efficiencies, while personal computers do the same for the new knowledge workers. Those knowledge workers will have access to the company's knowledge base 24 hours a day. In a day, they will be able to accomplish individually what used to take half-a-dozen employees working a week to accomplish.

Knowledge workers will be asked less "What do you know?" and more often "What else can you learn?" That's because training will be continual, with workers learning more of how to operate in, and with, Info/Com business tools. The training will actually be stimulating and fun, with the lessons relying on virtual reality equipment to clearly and quickly impart concepts. Those workers will receive more from their companies in what are now side issues, such as day care support, office/hour flexibility and true performance compensation systems.

Tomorrow's CEO will be a communicator and network maven. The authoritarian leader, some of whom we see today, will flounder. Their methods are directly at odds with the knowledge system of the 21st century. These new CEOs will leverage information, change and time, using perpetual strategy to constantly evaluate and act on opportunities. Divisional walls will come down as communications and sharing of information become the keystones of a well-operated business. This melding of functions, plus the increased benefits of an improved communications environment, will lead to a continuous process of best-practices implementation.

Why Business Activity of the Future Looks Like the Past

The start of the 21st century will look a lot like the start of the 20th century. In the late 1800s and early 1900s, the trust form of business organizations proliferated. This was a response to the growing size of corporations back at that time. Corporations were growing to meet the demands of the newly emerging markets and the prodigious growth of established markets. Sometimes they couldn't grow fast enough, resulting in marketplaces that were fragmented and disorganized. To capitalize on opportunities and to bring more efficiency to the industry and their own companies, businesses made attempts to consolidate. That attempt resulted in the trust.

It took a great deal of money and deft maneuvering to establish these trusts. It also took a great deal of effort to convince some industry players that it was to their benefit to consolidate. That was because in reality it wasn't always to their benefit to be brought into the trust fold. Sometimes it was, but they still weren't too enthusiastic about their loss of autonomy. Sometimes it was, but the invited party was seeking better terms and arrangements for their inclusion in the trust. Sometimes it was because they were attempting to build their own trust, one where they would dictate the terms. Nonetheless, some very astute business people made some extraordinary moves in order to bring about this consolidation. Andrew Carnegie, Meyer Guggenheim, Edward H. Harriman, Andrew Mellon, J.P. Morgan, and John D. Rockefeller all understood the value and power of the trust. Having built or controlled extremely large companies themselves, they understood the business benefits derived from concepts such as economies of scale, integrated businesses, and the large capitalization needed to build distribution, marketing and production systems large enough to capture and serve vast numbers of consumers.

Tomorrow's business leaders can learn a lot about building today's large corporation from the business leaders of the early 20th century. Today's business environment is striking in its resemblance to the market turmoil that existed back at the turn of the century. Existing markets are exploding in size, new markets are being born at a terrific pace, and consumers are clamoring for new and better products and services (and at lower prices). Market shares are precarious and apt to slip away if not serviced correctly and efficiently. New competitors are popping up, old suppliers are recasting themselves in directly competitive roles, and current competitors are aligning themselves in cooperative arrangements that threaten the very survival of the nonaligned companies. As before, it is ally or die. And if not ally, then merge or acquire. That is precisely the situation that faced those business greats. The threat wasn't from losing market share to a consolidated group of competitors and risk staying small. The threat was losing it all. It will be the same in the 21st century.

Some say there is no relationship to the beginning of the 21st century and the beginning of the 20th century, and that there is nothing to learn from those times but a history lesson. Nothing could be further from the truth. In fact, there are more similarities than there are disparities. We often borrow now what was conceived of then and call it innovation. For example, Kodak's popular disposable camera of today is something that predates 1900, and Kodak popularized the concept back then, too. Xerox's benchmarking process? It was a great new concept, but it wasn't new. It was originally used in a business context in 1913. Computers? The original computer languished, unwanted, in the mid-1830s (yes, 1830s), and the working plans were buried in obscurity. We have borrowed heavily on these ideas, and we will have to do so again. Many processes, methods, techniques, systems, tools and concepts are lying on the business battleground. We just need to pick them up and use them in future competitive battles.

19th Century Childhood, 20th Century Adolescence, and 21st Century Adulthood

Having established that the seeds of success have been planted in the past, it is probably best to take a look at the world as it was back then. What were the forces in play? How was the world evolving? What was at stake?

By casting a critical eye on what has happened in the past, you can identify patterns, trends, and themes that cross all time boundaries. With the analysis of what has happened, you can come to understand what might happen in the future. This book will take a look at business to see how it developed. What were the forces and conditions it encountered and operated within? Business as we know it now began with the

Industrial Revolution in England in the 18th century. It didn't really cross the waters to other locales until the 19th century. With that in mind, we will use the early 19th century as the point that business was up and running, and about to change the world.

There's no doubt that war is often economic in basis, and that still continues today. But for the most part, today's war is about killing a competitor in the marketplace with deft distribution, financial fire-power and salvos of marketing. In most ways, global business was not truly established until competition for commerce was decided—in the main—by business machinations and maneuvering, rather than war. We will cover here what has transpired over the last two centuries and what will transpire in the 21st century by looking at the birth and growth, hopes and dreams in the aging of the Industrial Revolution. Business was in its childhood in the 1800s, in its adolescence in the 1900s, and it will reach adulthood in the 21st century. As a result, the word "competition" may be replaced by the word "cooperation."

Companies That Have Made a Difference in the 20th Century

It is with those companies that have made a difference where we will find most, although not all, of the examples of what companies can do to compete in the 21st century—companies like Nestlé, Siemens, General Electric, Xerox, Matsushita and Evergreen. We will profile 42 in all. By analyzing the events at play in the 20th century we can identify those things—processes, systems, techniques and tools—that can be picked up, dusted off, and adapted for use in the future. As we said before, the 21st century is shaping up as a replay of what has preceded us.

At times we will highlight or analyze companies that may be experiencing difficulties right now or have done so in the past. The reason is twofold. First, by examining what pitfalls have made them stumble, we can attempt to avoid those same set of circumstances or events. Second, by noting the problems, we can study the solutions, so that there is a viable plan or understanding of what is needed to rise up again. Sometimes companies make attempts to avoid problems, but still manage to encounter them.

If you are in business, don't completely discount companies that are currently experiencing problems, especially if they are your competitors. By summarily dismissing them, you could fall victim to their resurgence as they come roaring back with a vengeance. IBM is currently down and bloodied. Many are saying it's over. Back in the late 1940s and 1950s, IBM was badly out-maneuvered by Remington Rand at the birth of the computer industry. IBM righted itself, leveraged its strengths—a great sales force that already had its foot in the door of corporate America—and took the burgeoning mainframe computer market out from under the nose of Remington. In other words, IBM's current situation is the same one it has faced before.

The Hall of Fame of 20th Century Leaders

It takes vision to make a business great. You must have a picture of what you are trying to accomplish. The vision doesn't have to be detailed; in fact, it might be best if it isn't. Situations change and the vision must change with them, because rigid adherence to a vision is as bad as no vision at all. With flexibility you can capitalize on unforeseen opportunities, while avoiding unpredictable obstacles. And all of this continues to be relevant today, with the instantaneous changes now taking place. The business leaders presented here have all shown vision. It might be as simple as providing the everyday low prices, and as complex as building a communications system that spans a nation. But it is a driving vision that these leaders pursued with total abandonment. Some filled in the details as they went along, others knew there were key pieces that had to be in place in order to succeed.

We will profile 36 leaders, including Riboud of Danone, Deterding of Shell, Watson of IBM, Knight of Nike, Fujisawa of Honda, and Nakauchi of Daiei. There will also be examples of how these leaders devised their plans for accomplishing that vision. Studying the strategic tools they devised, how they arrived at them, why they needed them in the first place and what it took to implement them are important steps in understanding their visions and their success. In studying best examples, you acquire strategic plans and machinations that can be used for future competitive circumstances. Some may be lifted verbatim. Others may require some modification or updating before they are applicable. Either way, here is a way to avoid reinventing the wheel in some future situation.

Best Business Practices of the 20th Century

We discussed above the strategic maneuvering of our business leaders. Along with those go the tactics that successfully achieved the strategies. We will profile 23 best practices companies, including Unilever, Electrolux, General Motors, Procter & Gamble, Casio, and Toyota. Our discussion will center on specific examples of the best business practices that proved extraordinarily successful for those who implemented them. Looking at why these practices were needed in the first place—the market events or circumstances that dictated solutions for crushing problems—we will establish a framework of potential problem scenarios that may be facing companies today. There will also be examples of what prompted the actual solution—where it came from, what made them think of it, and how it was implemented.

Just-in-time manufacturing is just one example that will be discussed, but it is a good example of the vision and creativity that is needed to maximize profits and boost a company to world prominence for product excellence. JIT was the solution to a capital expenditure problem of a Japanese automaker. The company needed to compete, but found itself saying, "We don't have the money or resources to handle a large inventory of car parts, so what do we do?" Where did the company find the solution? In an American supermarket. The lesson? The answer is where you look. But looking is not enough. Implementation is key.

Competition in the 21st Century—The Intelligence Age

We are leaving what some have called the Electric Age and others have called the Computer Age. What comes next is something that incorporates those elements, and then takes them to another dimension. The Intelligence Age, or Info/Com Age, will require us to rapidly digest information, analyze it, prioritize it, disseminate it and act on it. And it must be done continually. Not yearly, not quarterly, not weekly, but daily. To not do so—and to not do so well—will severely hamper the success of those companies who fail to make this choice. There is nothing as critical as this ability. Information has always proved to be critical in any business that attempts to cover more ground than had previously been covered by others in the same industry. Early railroads had to develop the first real centralized management systems because their far-flung operations required coordination and information. They looked to technology—the first telegraphs were used heavily by railroads—in order to facilitate coordination and information flow. Without it, freight might be shipped the wrong way, and human lives might be at stake.

We will present a detailed framework for facilitating the rapid intake and output of critical intelligence—the coin of the realm in the 21st century. Employing the management tools of Business Intelligence and Perpetual Strategy will allow companies to match or exceed their competitors as they race to grow current markets and exploit emerging new markets. Perpetual Strategy will force companies to focus on change and the effects it has on a corporation, and it will force companies to do so continuously. It clears the way for management to rapidly respond to opportunities and threats by clearly and quickly identifying them as they emerge, rather than after they have taken their toll or passed the window of opportunity.

The Bottom Line on Competing Successfully

The bottom line on competing successfully depends on making the critical link between intelligence and strategic management. In the coming Intelligence Age, the inability to move intelligence through the management of a company and impose upon it the strategic thinking necessary to move quickly will doom a company. In 1945, Curtiss-Wright was the largest aircraft maker and the largest aircraft engine producer in the world. And the company kept refining that technology. The only problem was that the jet engine, which dictated a specific plane design, was emerging fast. Before they knew it, other aircraft manufacturers had roared by. Curtiss-Wright never adapted, and the company went out of business. That is why the linkage between intelligence and strategic management is so important. Without the linkage, decisions are not only not made, but no one realizes they even should have been made until it is too late.

☞ ☞ ☞ ☞ ☞ ☞

The old man tossed and turned in his sleep.

CHAPTER 2

- - - - - - - - - - - - - -

A PEEK AT THE FUTURE—
INDUSTRIES WITH THE INSIDE TRACK AND
THOSE THAT WILL DERAIL

The old man woke up...or did he?

"What happened? Where am I? This looks like some sort of "Future World" like I saw in the movies last week. What the HELL?"

The old man had been transported to the world of the mid-21st century. He was actually still asleep and continuing his dream cycle.

He walked through his village. His house was no longer on the edge of town as it had been when he was a small boy. It was also not in the "inner city" he remembered from 1996. Instead, he found his house in the middle of a large sports complex, or so it seemed. There were fields for football (soccer), American football, baseball, and other types of fields he did not recognize. They stretched for as far as the eye could see. "What type of sports facility is this?" he wondered. He saw a small building in the distance and decided to walk to it. When he got closer, he found that it was actually a very large building—two stories but probably about 5,400 square meters (60,000 square feet) in size. He adjusted his glasses and could make out the word "school." Oh, this was a SCHOOL, NOT a sports facility! "Looks like school COMPETITION has become more important than education," he complained to himself.

He continued his 21st century journey into town. He saw some of the familiar sites of 1996—the corner grocery store, hardware store, dry cleaners, liquor store, supermarket, theatre, post office, gas station and quick oil change garage.... In fact, many of the signs in the windows looked much the same as they did in 1996—"We will not be undersold" and "We accept all competitors' coupons." But there were some new sites—several large casinos, an off-track betting facility, a sports bar/grill/betting parlor, a "Cannabis & Coffee Cabaret," (what the HELL is that?), a "Touchy-Feely Cabaret" (GOOD GRACIOUS!) and an amateur racing track for cars and motorcycles.

The old man decided he had had enough and headed home. As he turned up his concrete/asphalt driveway, lights along the driveway automatically illuminated, guiding his way. He also noticed that the lights inside his home switched on. Outside the house he saw solar panels on his roof, windmills on his property, and a small one-quarter meter (9.85 inch) satellite dish on his roof pointing to the southern sky. He picked up the daily newspaper (at least some things had not changed). As he came up to his door, he fumbled for his keys. He couldn't find any. Then he noticed an electronic box by the door with a keypad and speaker. He started punching numbers at random. A voice answered saying, "Welcome. Please speak so that I may know you." The old man said, "What the HELL?" The voice responded by saying, "Come in." Obviously, this device had some type of voice recognition system. The voice continued, "I have built a fire in the fireplace and made you some milk and cookies. Is there anything else I can do for you? Anything at all?"

He walked into the living room. Not much change. His beautiful Kawai ebony baby grand piano still graced the room. And the furniture was similar—Queen Anne style but uniquely American. His weekly copies of *Global Time* magazine and *Global Economist* were next to his reading chair. The only thing different was the Sunday *Wall Street Journal* (Sunday?). He was feeling a bit more comfortable. He sat down and gazed at his artwork on the walls, representative of French Impressionism. His beautiful wall coverings remained, as did the various knick-knacks and pictures of relatives and forebears.

The old man got up and walked from the living room to the formal dining room—again, the Queen Anne style dining room table was still there, along with the china, crystal, and sterling silver (or was it stainless steel?). He then glanced into the kitchen. "Wow!" The kitchen had grown to comprise nearly 25 percent of the house. There was an integrated cooking center, with a gas stove, microwave oven, convection oven, indoor gas grill, and a restaurant-style exhaust unit over everything. Next to the integrated cooking center was the food preservation center, which included a large refrigerator, an even larger freezer, and pantry for dry goods. He opened the refrigerator and freezer. "Why so many fresh fruits and vegetables? Where's the beef?" Now that he thought about it, he had not seen a McDonald's on his walk through town, although there was a "McFresh" under the golden arches.

The old man then made his way from the food preservation center to the food preparation center. "Who is going to pay the electric bill for all of this?" he thought to himself. There were an unbelievable number of kitchen appliances, with electric cords either missing or amazingly hidden. Finally, he observed the cleaning and storage area, an integrated facility providing washing, drying, and computer-controlled storage. He had had enough of this!

He proceeded to the family room. The entertainment center seemed a bit more elaborate than the one he remembered in 1996. There was a giant wall with an integrated flat screen TV and music system. Again, no visible wires, not even behind the console. (The old man remembered watching his son hook up a crude entertainment center in 1992—must have been a thousand wires behind it!). Next to the entertainment center was the JAVA-GATES network computing center. He turned on the machine. "Where is the C-Prompt? Where is the software?" he mused. Obviously, personal computing had advanced significantly. Next to the network computing center was the reading and craft center.

Just one last thing to examine—a look in the garage. The garage had also grown—big enough for three cars now, although there were only two there. The small car looked almost like a golf cart and appeared to be battery operated. Must be an in-town vehicle. Then his eyes widened and a big smile erupted. There in front of him was the latest Mercedes S Class car. "Ah, some things never change...."

From all of this, the old man concluded that industry must look quite different now. And indeed it WAS quite different in the 21st century.

The man went back to the living room and picked up the copy of *Global Business Week* magazine. It was a special annual issue with industry updates. He read the magazine from cover to cover, and dozed off. When he did awake, he was back in 1996. "Wow," he thought, "some industries will change quite a bit in the 21st century, and some will not change much at all." The old man began to write down his findings so he would not forget. There were many times these days that he could not even remember his own name. Here is what he wrote.

Food

Retail/Remote Order

Retail food competition in the 21st century will look very similar to the way it does today. The trend toward large local and regional grocery stores will continue. However, small grocery stores, auto convenience marts, and specialty food stores will also continue to proliferate. Consumers will want both the price advantages associated with bulk shopping and the convenience and/or food freshness associated with the small store. More and more consumers will shop remotely, ordering by phone, fax, computer, cable TV or network terminals. Specialty foods in all categories will still be in demand, and they will continue to command premium prices.

☞ *The global challengers: Carrefour, A&P (Europe); and Safeway, Kroger (North America)*

☞ *The globally challenged: All other national retail supermarkets*

A&P has had its ups and downs over the years, but the 21st century is clearly up for this company, thanks to German ownership which is expected to increase to 100 percent in the first part of the century. Safeway, a strong brand name in America, will also dominate in the 21st century. Kroger will be a major challenger because of its decentralized structure allowing local customization of product offerings. These stores will change drastically in appearance in the 21st century as more and more customers will order their groceries remotely for later home delivery. Carrefour of France is the company that introduced the hyper-market and now has over 200 of them. Innovative, experienced and already active in South America and the Asia/Pacific region, this company can and will expand much in the 21st century.

Agriculture, Dairy and Meat Packing

The trend toward giant corporate farms, dairies and meat packing plants will continue, and companies will still compete primarily on the basis of price. Existing operations will grow and consolidate, and new operations will emerge. Weather and soil problems will be solved with new forms of irrigation, sprinkler systems, and natural soil additives. Animal health problems will be solved by new preventative implants. Operations will tend toward full computer control to increase yields. Meat packing plants will both expand and consolidate based on consumer preferences for leaner meat. Despite these efforts, meat consumption and production will continue to decline in the 21st century. Farm equipment suppliers will continue to add features which reduce the overall time and cost of production. Hydroponic farming and other forms of organic and biotechnical farming will grow significantly in areas that do not lend themselves to traditional farming.

- ☞ *The global challengers: Danone, Associated British Foods (Europe); IBP, ConAgra, Tyson Foods, Land O'Lakes, Mid-American Dairymen (North America); and Meiji Milk Products (Asia/Pacific)*

- ☞ *The globally challenged: Sara Lee (North America), and Nippon Suisan Kaisha (Asia/Pacific)*

IBP and ConAgra will dominate the meat industry in the 21st century. While the domestic market in North America will decline, exports will increase, primarily to the Asia/Pacific region. Eventually, these two companies will expand their operations in both Asia/Pacific and Europe. Sara Lee's processed meat business, including Hillshire Farm and Jimmy Dean sausage as well as Ball Park hot dogs, will decline as IBP, ConAgra and others move onto their turf. Tyson Foods (no relation to the author) will continue to dominate the poultry business and will slowly grow its other meat product businesses. Associated British Foods has a vast array of diversified food products divisions that are held together by an extremely efficient central management system. That will work to their advantage as they continue their global expansion.

In the dairy business, Land O'Lakes, Mid-American Dairyman and Danone of France will grow at a rate consistent with the growth in population. This will be at the expense of smaller producers, because the market for dairy products will decline on a per capita basis in the 21st century due to health/nutrition concerns. Meiji Milk Products is Japan's milkman, a shrewd performer at home with innovative R&D and a willingness to do business with non-Japanese companies. They will leverage all of that to secure a nice global niche in the coming century.

Japan's Nippon Suisan Kaisha is a fishing concern that will find it difficult to operate with the industry's increasingly thin profit margins and growing environmental pressure to net less fish.

Food and Beverage Processing

Food and beverage competitors will provide an even wider variety of nutritional foods to serve different tastes.

- ☛ *The global challengers: Grand Metropolitan, Danone, Nestlé, Unilever (Europe); and Campbell Soup, Heinz, Coca-Cola, Gerber (North America)*

- ☛ *The globally challenged: Kraft, Ben & Jerry's, Pepsi (North America)*

In ice cream, Häagen-Dazs of Grand Metropolitan in the UK will dominate in the 21st century. In frozen yoghurt, Dannon of the French group Danone will continue to be a leader. The popular Ben & Jerry's ice cream products in North America will be copied by competing companies, both large and small, making it difficult for their global expansion. However, their emphasis on supporting social causes will make them a leading company no matter what their revenue numbers show. Historical top cheese producer Kraft will struggle to maintain its dominance in a field where local and regional brands will grow in popularity. In canned soups, Campbell will dominate as it keeps in step with health-conscious customers. The trend toward lower fat and salt content will continue. In baby foods, Gerber has a name and reputation that, barring the unexpected, should keep the company feeding the world's babies well into the 21st century. The canned fruits and vegetables market will be led by Heinz, who is also very strong in ketchup. The leader in frozen fruits and vegetables, again, will be Heinz. Green Giant will continue to look for cost efficiencies that will allow it to expand in international markets.

In frozen concentrated orange juice, Minute Maid by Coca-Cola, Citrus Hill made by Procter & Gamble, and Tropicana by Seagrams will dominate well into the 21st century.

In the continuing global cola wars, Coca-Cola will win.

Snacks and Candy

Snacks and candy competition will continue to grow, particularly in chocolate and salty snacks. This growth will come despite health warnings.

- ☛ *The global challengers: Nestlé (Europe), and Frito-Lay, Nabisco (North America)*

- ☛ *The globally challenged: Cadbury Schweppes (Europe), and Mars (North America)*

The UK's Cadbury Schweppes has a few bright spots, but overall its line of confections are beginning to look tired and worn. Mars has a terrific line of products, including Snickers and M&M's, but the Mars family is suspicious of non-family managers, which has created high management turnover. Their outlook is suspect. Nestlé, with its worldwide distribution network, appears to be the best bet to emerge as the global candy company. Frito-Lay places a lot of emphasis on operational efficiency and product innovation. They will continue to dominate markets. Nabisco is finally coming off the effects of the RJR/Nabisco LBO. It must leverage the recognition of its brand names to boost sales, which would allow it to capitalize its plants with updated equipment. The prognosis is good despite some obstacles.

Clothing

Retail Clothing

Retail clothing competition will be most intense at both the low and the high ends of the market. This trend will follow the increasing gap between rich and poor. At the low end of the market, stores such as EuroMart, Wal-Mart, and Daiei will dominate in Europe, North America, and the Asia/Pacific region, respectively. However, intense competition will come from a large number of other local and regional clothing stores. At the high end, new global boutiques will emerge to challenge each other. At the very high end, shops will be few in number and local to cater to their exclusive clientele.

☞ *The global challengers: EuroMart (Europe); Cifra, Wal-Mart (North America); and Daiei (Asia/Pacific)*

☞ *The globally challenged: K-Mart (North America), and Seibu (Asia/Pacific)*

EuroMart (not yet formed at this writing) will benchmark the successes of Wal-Mart and Daiei to launch its own successful operation. Wal-Mart and Japan's Daiei could almost be one and the same (they are not) given the similarities in their operations. Tough on vendors, they squeeze out the best buys and pass the savings on to customers. Backroom operations are spartan and super efficient, serving as a model for other companies. K-Mart tried to move upscale to get away from Wal-Mart and nose-dived. Mexico's Cifra is considered one of North America's best-managed companies, and it will come into prominence in the 21st century. Wal-Mart recognized their expertise and has set up joint ventures that have proven to be very successful for both companies. Japan's Seibu department stores always seem poised to move up, but something often happens to drag them down. Part of the problem is an affinity for the "retail trend of the month" syndrome. The company constantly tries to take wildly innovative steps. Some ideas work, some do not, and that is a drag on their momentum.

Remote Order Clothing

Clothing competition in mail/TV markets will increase as additional mail order catalogs and home shopping channels become available. Busy people will want to do more and more remote shopping for basic items, while cutting down on their visits to local and regional shopping malls. Do not worry about the shopping malls, though. They will continue to be a major entertainment source for kids and adults alike.

- ☞ *The global challengers: Lands' End, Home Shopping Network (North America)*

- ☞ *The globally challenged: All other regional and national companies*

Lands' End thrives on customer service, even more so than Wal-Mart. Management is good, but humble. When customers drifted away a few years ago, saying the fashions were stale, the company jumped right on it and won the market back. There is more to the Home Shopping Network than what customers see on television. The company is actually a holding company with interests in electronic retail sales, mail order and telemarketing. They have had ups and downs, but skirting the traditional modes of retail selling puts them in position to capitalize on future shopping trends.

Clothing Manufacturing

Competition in apparel manufacturing will be more fierce than ever. European designers will still be out in front, but they will be chased by, not leading, the growing number of designers from North America and the Asia/Pacific region. Thousands of manufacturers will compete for shelf space, similar to the shelf space competition in supermarkets today. The manufacturing base will shift from the Asia/Pacific region to developing countries. As world economic conditions improve, wages rise, and the number of low-paid workers dwindles, high tech and robotics will be applied to the apparel industry. It will add to the cost of clothes. Only high-priced goods will be handmade, and they will fetch even higher prices. Because of that, accessories will become more important as a less expensive way to build a wardrobe.

☛ **The global challengers: Benetton, Gucci (Europe); Calvin Klein, Nike, Warnaco, Levi's (North America); and Teijin (Asia/Pacific)**

☛ **The globally challenged: Fruit of the Loom (North America)**

Italy's Benetton may have gotten too advanced with their recent rounds of social conscious-raising advertising (and too loose with operations), but their hearts are in the right place. They will slow down, and the customers will catch up. Then people will like the clothes and the message. Gucci and Calvin Klein—their name is everything. Nike likes to think their product is about performance, not image. It is image—and people will continue to love it. Fruit of the Loom has been distracted by too many side issues—financial, lawsuits, etc. for too long. Getting back on track is not a question of tinkering here and there; it will take a while to right all the things that have gone sour. Warnaco has gone up and down over the years but for this industry that is not too unusual. They have always gotten back on track. Aggressive management now stays very focused and will continue to do so. Levi's has a global product and the marketing to match. It will not stop. Teijin is like most of the big textile makers in Japan; they are looking to enter markets other than clothing. The difference is they will diversify, rather than move into new fields, as they abandon textiles completely. They will take the lead and keep it in the influential Japanese textile industry.

Shelter and Personal Transportation

Real Estate and Construction

Real estate and construction competition will continue to be local in nature, with a trend toward smaller homes, condominiums and apartments. The demand for real estate will increase greatly in the rural areas, as more and more companies move away from the large cities. Advances in communications will also make it easier for employees to work remotely, although the trend will be toward an equal mix of at-work and at-home time. Large national and international construction companies will continue to grow, offering home buyers more features and affordable prices. Builders at the high end of the market will continue to be based locally and regionally. Solar power heating will increase substantially. It is not the concept that really bothers people, it is the obtrusive equipment. People deem it unsightly. The problem will be fixed by clever integration with residential construction techniques. While most building will remain with smaller operations, one-fifth of residential construction will be done by large Japanese companies. The Japanese construction companies will spend lots of money on R&D! They will be global leaders in residential construction.

☞ **The global challengers: Centex (North America); and Shimizu, Sekisui House (Asia/Pacific)**

☞ **The globally challenged: All other national and regional companies**

Japan's Shimizu does commercial and residential construction. They are consistently among the top companies in new orders, work completion rate and profit, and they will stay that way. The biggest home builder in Japan, Sekisui knows consumers very well and will find expansion easy. Centex has shown itself to be a well-constructed company by consistently weathering US home-building downturns through their team-based management. They build a good product and do so at a profit.

Household Appliances

Competition in household appliances will intensify as companies battle for this booming 21st century market. European products from Electrolux and Braun will dominate, although the products will actually be manufactured in the Asia/Pacific region and emerging South American and Eastern Bloc countries. Booming product areas will be kitchen appliances, followed by lawn and garden tools.

☞ **The global challengers: Braun, Electrolux (Europe); and Whirlpool (North America)**

☞ **The globally challenged: Maytag, White-Westinghouse (North America)**

Sweden's Electrolux is always coming out with innovations, and their marketing and sales efforts are top-notch, a trend that will continue. Braun of Germany (and a subsidiary of Gillette) gets good marks for design and product engineering. That is a well-balanced combination for the 21st century. Whirlpool has taken its efficient management, great product engineering, and innovative design and invaded the European market. They will succeed there and in the United States. Debt, bad acquisitions, diversification problems and mismanagement plagued Westinghouse to the point that it was better at handling the next catastrophe than it was at handling the appliance business. This business requires global focus, and White is still stumbling in their own backyard. Maytag can produce a quality product, but well-executed expansion into the much needed global markets might be beyond their capabilities.

Home Maintenance

Competition in home maintenance services will be among large integrated service companies. In addition to providing service on household appliances, they will also begin to offer maintenance services related to electrical, plumbing, and HVAC systems.

- ☞ *The global challengers: ServiceMaster (North America)*
- ☞ *The globally challenged: All other local and regional companies*

ServiceMaster is a natural for this emerging market, and they have begun moving in, picking up plumbing businesses and a home warranty business. Look for them to create the global market.

Other Household Products

Competition in other household products will be strongest in hardware and cleaning supplies. Competitors will strive to provide the most effective product that is the most environmentally friendly.

- ☞ *The global challengers: Henkel (Europe); Rubbermaid, S.C. Johnson (North America); and Kao (Asia/Pacific)*
- ☞ *The globally challenged: All other national and international companies*

At this writing, Rubbermaid was experiencing a dip in demand and sales. That will smooth out, and its fortunes—along with its typical product innovations—will rise again and throughout the 21st century. Henkel turns out great products, dumps unprofitable operations without sentimentality, and is environmentally aware. Consumers and investors will continue to love them. S.C. Johnson keeps the product pipeline flowing with a strong commitment to R&D. This course has served them well in the past and will do so in the future. The Japanese company Kao spends a lot on R&D, but their marketing will need work to achieve global status. One marketing idea was to take their laundry soap product, called "Attack," to Hawaii. It did not occur to them that they might need to change the name.

Auto

Auto competition will intensify globally. European markets will increasingly accept the Japanese cars. This will put pressure on the European manufacturers to provide more features at a lower price. Japanese markets will gradually accept more American cars, especially when the steering wheel is put on the right side of the car. All manufacturers will strive to develop new cars that are more safe and fuel efficient, with some beginning to use alternative fuel sources.

- ☛ *The global challengers: Mercedes-Benz (Europe); Ford, Chrysler (North America); and Honda, Toyota (Asia/Pacific)*

- ☛ *The globally challenged: Saab, VW/Audi, Renault (Europe); General Motors (North America); and Hyundai (Asia/Pacific)*

Germany's Mercedes-Benz cannot be out-engineered, although Japan's Toyota and Honda are right behind them. Ford and Chrysler have been on a product innovation roll that will continue, although they have to watch prices. Lee Iacocca's loud reign was a wake-up call that startled Chrysler into action. GM's slump will not improve for a while; their corporate culture—which is hidebound—is too ingrained. Saab is produced for a market that does not exist anymore. VW/Audi has a very future-oriented car philosophy which is both user-friendly and environmentally friendly. Their challenge will be to sell the concepts outside Europe. In the 1980s, Renault's work force was bloated, and the cars were poorly designed. Substantial improvements were made in the 1990s, but it might be difficult to compete on a global scale. South Korea's Hyundai needs better engineering and design if they truly want to sell outside the Asia/Pacific region and North America.

Energy

Electric

Competition in the electric utility industry will be fierce. The biggest competition will appear first on a local and regional basis. It will then become a global battlefield. Who would imagine that electricity in Chicago or Tokyo could be sold by a company in Paris? Add to that the thousands of independent power producers that will decide to generate their own electricity. Toward the end of the 21st century, look for stand-alone home generating units using natural gas, solar power or wind power.

☞ *The global challengers: EDF (Europe); and Entergy, Southern (North America)*

☞ *The globally challenged: Commonwealth Edison (North America), and other local and regional providers*

EDF has had its share of nuclear power and debt problems, but they have weathered them and now have some of the lowest rates in Europe. As the global competition to sell electricity heats up, they will be there to take advantage of the situation. Commonwealth Edison overbuilt in the nuclear power age's zenith, and now they are suffering from its backlash effects. On top of that, their power infrastructure is suspect; competition is heating up, and they have one of the highest rate structures in the United States. The company seems slow to react. Both Entergy and Southern have had problems in the past, but so have the rest of the industry players. The question is, who is doing something to position themselves for the 21st century? The answer is—Entergy and Southern. As the electric utility industry enters a new age of national and global competition, these two companies have recognized and prepared themselves for it.

Oil and Gas

Oil and gas competition will be severe in the first half of the 21st century as the known supplies begin to dwindle. New discoveries will, of course, be made through new technologies. However, the world will finally wake up to the fact that alternative fuel sources must be found. Governments of major industrialized nations will force the issue. The result will be a new kind of competition not experienced in more than a century.

> ☞ *The global challengers: Royal Dutch Shell (Europe), and Amoco (North America)*

> ☞ *The globally challenged: BP (Europe)*

Royal Dutch Shell, the UK-Netherlands oil king, has a reputation as a long-time global competitor. That will be upheld in the 21st century; they are just too tough to beat. It is better to partner with them. Amoco has the same stature and ability as Shell, with a marketing knack that is top notch. British Petroleum will be too worn out fighting Amoco and Shell to really get things going.

Security/Financial

Insurance—Home/Auto/Life

People will continue to demand better financial results from their life insurance policies. A proliferation of financial products—such as mutual funds—has conditioned people to expect more from any investment. Life policies have proven to be dismal in return on investment, and consumers have borrowed from the policies to invest elsewhere. More companies will enter the industry in an attempt to exploit that weak point. There will be an increase in innovative policies that mirror other types of investment and lure back what people have withdrawn. While the price of policies will not come down on home and auto insurance, companies will increase their value-added aspect. They will do so by giving higher discounts for good driving records, and annual structure and safety inspections for the home. Prevention will pay.

☞ **The global challengers: Allianz (Europe); American Re-Insurance, Travelers, State Farm (USA); and Mitsui (Asia/Pacific)**

☞ **The globally challenged: Lloyd's of London, General Accident (Europe); Prudential, CIGNA (USA); and Sumitomo (Asia/Pacific)**

Prudential wants to be in both insurance and finance, but is serving neither market well. It needs to give better attention to the insurance side first, or it will lose brand name power. Travelers Insurance is creative when it comes to insurance products and knows how to stimulate the market, a perfect combination for the 21st century. Germany's Allianz management knows Europe and will frustrate US companies not only there, but in the United States as well. CIGNA has what it takes, but never quite grabs the brass ring. It looks to flounder through the early part of the 21st century. Mitsui has slipped in the recent past, but it is financially strong and starting to play the alliance game well. It looks to regain in the 21st century what it had lost in the latter half of the 20th century. The best kept secret is that State Farm does a lot more than auto insurance (they are the eighth largest US life insurance company and third largest health insurance company). The cat will come out of the bag as the company gains more market share in the 21st century. Japan's Sumitomo Life has a conservative style that is great for keeping cash reserves strong, but with little imagination, its marketing efforts will suffer. The UK's General Accident might become a casualty itself if management does not tighten the operations and prepare not only for an open European market, but an overseas assault. Lloyd's is operating in the past; American Re-Insurance is poised for the future.

Banking and Investment Services

The consumer can count on computer banking in the 21st century. While still in a fledgling state, home computers and their use will increase in the 21st century. ATM machines and other teller-less transaction systems, plus the growing use of software programs like Quicken, will allow people to become used to the concept.

With home computers the rule in the early part of the 21st century, making the switch from ATM-type machines to using the computer at home will be almost effortless. The line between banks and other investment providers like traditional stockbrokers and mutual funds will blur. Brokers will battle bankers for the consumer's investment money. Bank mergers and alliances will proliferate as individual banks attempt to compensate for their weaknesses with the complementary strengths of another bank. With the decline of pension plans and other traditional retirement investments, people have had to learn the basics of investing, most often from mutual fund investment. That education trend will continue and other types of investing will see an increase due to consumer awareness, understanding and need.

☞ *The global challengers: Citibank, Chase Chemical, Fidelity Investments (North America); and Fuji Bank, Dai-Ichi Kangyo Bank, Sumitomo Bank (Asia/Pacific)*

☞ *The globally challenged: Lloyd's of London (Europe); BankAmerica, Dean Witter (North America); and Mitsubishi Bank (Asia/Pacific)*

Citibank will make market share inroads by boosting its credit card business overseas. Currently, it is the largest such provider in the United States. Chase Chemical will rely on its current strength and its international presence to bootstrap itself. While Chase Chemical is a large bank in the United States, it does not reach into the top ten globally, so it cannot muscle the market, and finesse will be required. Fidelity Investments has the power, size and savvy to make and take markets from competitors. Dean Witter is big with the retail trade, but it does not leverage much outside of that. BankAmerica needs focus and will struggle. Japan's Mitsubishi Bank, a risk-averse plodder, holds a strong hand in a very important market—corporate finance—but will have trouble taking advantage of its position. Both Sumitomo and Dai-Ichi of Japan will learn how to play a deft international game, leveraging their new skills with a large financial base. The question is whether they can muscle past one of their own—Fuji Bank. It is one of the world's most powerful banks, and they are going to be tough to beat because their international division is outstanding.

Accounting and Tax Services

This industry is highly fragmented with many local service providers. No one company has sufficiently consolidated a number of smaller players into a larger, full-service organization that incorporates all accounting and tax services under one roof. The average consumer may turn to a tax preparer for filing their tax returns, and then turn to the neighborhood accountant to help audit and plan their family finances. Occasionally, one firm may grow larger by exploiting a particular niche—like the US company H&R Block with tax returns—but even they are an exception to their industry niche.

☞ *The global challengers: None*

☞ *The globally challenged: All*

Legal Services

As with accounting and tax services, there are no large firms specializing in serving the average consumer. There are many small law offices, and large ones, too, but none are positioned to give full attention to all the needs of the average client. There are a couple of reasons. Small firms can only wear so many hats. They do not have the full compliment of skills and experience to handle all of the legal questions that can arise. Large companies may have the necessary expertise, but their overhead demands that those services are paid for handsomely. The key to combining rests both with an organization that can leverage the concept of alliances or a management that can successfully combine technology's efficiency with today's effective cost-conscious measures.

☞ *The global challengers: None*

☞ *The globally challenged: All*

Security/Health Care

Health Care Plans

Managed health care is in a state of global flux that has consumers the world over concerned. Some countries support government-sponsored systems from cradle to grave (e.g., France). Others opt for a mix of government-supported services and privately managed systems (United States). The underlying conflicts are between the pure government-supported systems that tax heavily to support the health care infrastructure and more free-market systems that rely on business to offer employees medical benefits. These are often additional to government support for special segments of society. This conflict will continue into the 21st century, compounded by advances in medical treatment and techniques. Those advancements are much more costly. The questions will focus on who gets the care and at what level of treatment, and who pays the costs. The United States will see backlash by consumers toward health care providers, the medical system and employers. Employers will be caught between their employees and the health care system and will resent it, their positions as middlemen earned only by default. The government-supported systems will find the added cost of medical treatment to be a severe drain on government coffers—cutting services means angering citizens; raising taxes means, once again, angering citizens.

- ☞ *The global challengers: KaiserPermanente Health Plan, United Healthcare (North America)*

- ☞ *The globally challenged: Blue Cross and Blue Shield (North America)*

The French health care system is wonderful, but the French economy cannot carry the burden of so many social services. As with other government-supported services, the health care system will be cut in size, with programs eliminated or downsized. The Blue Cross and Blue Shield system will have a tough time. It was caught off guard by the whole health care issue and red-hot competition. The real problem was that it was even surprised by the market's direction; it should not have been. Kaiser has captured some large accounts in the past—including CHAMPUS for US military dependents and retirees—and it will grab more. United Healthcare will continue its stream of innovative services and a healthy appetite for acquisitions, both at the expense of its competitors.

Physician/Dentist/Veterinary

Here is a market that suffers from fragmentation, with consumers having to rely on local service providers for all their needs. While hospitals, health care organizations and insurance companies have organized on a national basis, the direct providers of health care have done no more than organize locally. The definition of full-service for these providers consists of associating themselves with others in their specialty, and perhaps hooking up with a local lab for testing services. A national affiliation (other than a professional association) of doctors and dentists representing all specialties and running full administrative and laboratory services would be incredibly efficient and profitable.

- ☞ *The global challengers: None*

- ☞ *The globally challenged: All*

Pharmaceuticals/Biotechnology

Vaccines that prevent not only illnesses, but also life-threatening diseases, will be produced in ever larger numbers. Consumers will not have to pay prices out of line with today's prices. That is because fierce competition from mainstream manufacturers, plus the pressure brought on by governments, generic drugmakers and health care organizations will prevent price hiking. Consumers will be directed to non-traditional pharmaceutical outlets such as remote-order (mail and phone) and super-drug stores. People will become more sophisticated about pharmaceuticals, in part because pharmaceutical companies will advertise more heavily and directly to potential customers. The biotechnology sector will explode after a number of decades, the obstacles to its early growth being high start-up costs, primitive methodology and hidden drawbacks to early formulations. Expectant mothers in the future will have their fetuses tested for more potential diseases and other health problems. Treatment will increasingly rely upon biotech techniques. Along with that, potential parents wil! be tested and treated biotechnologically to eliminate or limit transmission of disease. Biotech measures will also be able to arrest diseases that have already appeared in patients.

☞ **The global challengers: Glaxo-Wellcome, Hoechst Marion Roussel, Roche (Europe); and Genentech, Merck (North America)**

☞ **The globally challenged: Ciba-Geigy, Pharmacia, Upjohn (Europe); and any pharmaceutical company in Japan (Asia/Pacific)**

Much of Glaxo-Wellcome's success can be traced to mergers and revenues generated by its drug Zantac. The company's management will leverage that into a powerful global position from its UK base. Merck's old drugs are still selling well; it has more in the pipeline, a fanatical commitment to R&D, a seasoned and motivated sales force, and a strong interest in biotech—the very thing that may trip them up. The burgeoning biotech market will bring about just as many obstacles as opportunities, and could mire a company in unforeseen problems. Roche of Switzerland has traditionally been big on R&D, and that will benefit them greatly in the 21st century. Part of the payoff comes from their controlling interest in the biotech pioneer Genentech, one of the few biotech firms to show extended life and profit. Hoechst Marion Roussel's R&D strength will have the same effect, and this German company will make inroads on its competition with the addition of Marion Merrill Dow. Switzerland's Ciba-Geigy is not sure of its direction. Is it a drug company marketing chemicals on the side, or vice versa? Their position is tentative for the 21st century unless they play their biotech card aggressively. The Upjohn side of Pharmacia and Upjohn has had trouble getting the steam up since its R&D pipeline dried up. It looks to limp along in the early 21st century, unless Pharmacia of Sweden can breathe some new life into it. The Japanese insular market is supported by the government to the extent that it fosters domestic pharmaceutical production and consumption, while excluding outsiders. Although they have increased their drug patent output, and their pharmaceutical manufacturing operations are world class, Japanese drugmakers have no marketing muscle, and not one has cracked the top ten list of big companies (strange for a country known for manufacturing). The 21st century will be a long, tedious uphill struggle for them.

Retail Medicines/Vitamins/Herbs

This segment will show explosive growth in the 21st century. Self-medication with over-the-counter medicines will be one of the results of consumers trying to beat the health care system. People will benefit from increased competition. Mass marketers, such as Wal-Mart and supermarkets, will continue to align themselves and buy into the drug retailers, cutting heavily into their market. Drug store chains, and the larger independents, will counter with around-the-clock hours, phone and mail order, and home delivery programs. Vitamins and herbs ride that same wave of self-preservation with a holistic backlash toward the health care system's localize-and-treat practices. Consumers will increasingly visit stores that cater solely to nature's remedies and cures, along with a growth in the remote-order business of those products.

☛ *The global challengers: Boots (Europe); General Nutrition, McKesson, Johnson & Johnson, Walgreen (North America); and China (Asia/Pacific)*

☛ *The globally challenged: All other regional and national companies*

In addition to making and marketing drugs, the UK's Boots Company also runs an efficient retailing operation. On top of that, it knows how to bloody the noses of American drugmakers on their own turf. They will be very prominent in the future. General Nutrition will increase its vitamin franchise operation throughout the world. McKesson will leverage its position as the largest US pharmaceutical distributor into a global position by capitalizing on its extensive network and distribution skills. Johnson & Johnson takes an ethical outlook that consumers like. This will be a plus in the 21st century when people cynically judge the coming advertising onslaught. Walgreen will rev up its expansion plans and enter overseas markets. The real excitement of this segment will come from a Chinese company that is not yet formed. Centuries of R&D related to natural remedies will be channeled through one Chinese company. This company will revolutionize the global market.

Security/Personal

Home Security Systems

The home security market will see steady, but not spectacular, growth outside of the United States. Within the United States, sales and service have been growing quickly. However, while most people fear burglaries or home invasions, their perception of crime is that it happens, for the most part, out on the streets and away from their homes. The impetus to install such systems for one's well-being is weak as compared to the economic motivation to spend on health care insurance premiums.

> ☛ *The global challengers: Britannia Security Group (Europe); and ADT, Brinks (North America)*

> ☛ *The globally challenged: Rollins (North America)*

In the US's highly fragmented market, ADT is a leader. Using acquisitions, an effective marketing campaign aimed at the home-owner, and cost-cutting measures, the company has boosted revenues and profits even in down markets. Britannia Security of the UK, an ADT subsidiary, has added to ADT's good fortune by giving the firm a global foothold with a well-run organization in the UK. So here are a couple of slick organizations operating in a fragmented industry on two continents; they will sprint through the beginning of the century. Brinks entered the home security system in the mid-1980s and is already a top player. They will continue to track well in the future and will lock horns with ADT throughout the next couple of decades. Rollins diversified and picked up a couple of home security firms. Questions still remain as to whether they are serious or just trying to play what they think is the corporate empire-building game.

Communication

Education

Students will focus on more math, science and high-technology courses. They will receive more coursework in problem solving,

decision-making, communication and "managerial" type instruction. This will be true even in the early education years. There will
be an attempt to shed an Industrial Revolution-influenced education for an Info/Com one. This updated education will allow students to work in an increasingly abstract world. Students will hone
those new skills with specialized instruction at the college level.
Colleges will also prepare students with a keener eye on commerce
and the skills needed to operate in such a world. While students will
not neglect the arts and sciences, they will increasingly be taught
within a concept of commerce and Info/Com. Do not worry exces-
sively about the combination of commerce with the arts. Commerce
has historically been the initial link between different cultures, and
it has always brought art right behind it. MBA degrees will be even
more popular, becoming the equivalent of undergraduate degrees
today. Focused master's degrees in subjects such as marketing and
finance will increase. As a teaching aid, virtual reality systems will be
an incredible tool. It is not that they will revolutionize education, but
they will be used to demonstrate concepts and theories with a
clarity and quickness we could never hope to duplicate now.

- ☞ **The global challengers: INSEAD (Europe); and University of Chicago, MIT, Stanford (North America)**

- ☞ **The globally challenged: Oxford (Europe), and Harvard
(North America)**

Oxford and Harvard still provide their MBA graduates with a
superior education for today's market. They will continue to be
highly respected institutions, but tradition will go by the wayside.
More and more business leaders will choose the programs at INSEAD,
Stanford, MIT, or the University of Chicago, which will focus more
on global business and perpetual strategy. France's INSEAD is the
only true global education center in the world. A large portion, if
not the majority, of their teaching staff and students are from other
countries. This is where some of the best global business thinking
of the future will originate. MIT will continue to engineer a future for
itself. The University of Chicago's rapid-fire collection of economic
Nobel Prize winners may dip in the near future, but that is just

because they are reloading. Stanford is a sleeper in a lot of ways. The global wake-up time for them will be in the 21st century.

Radio/Television/Stereo/Phone/Fax/Computer/Modem

People will have radio well into the future. Its simple concept— transported sound—can be matched, but not beaten. Television will be transformed, reshaped and retrofitted, and it will still be filled with Saturday morning cartoons. Television gives people the chance to sit back and take in what others have programmed. It provides a certain amount of the unexpected. The all-in-one phone, TV, computer, fax, modem, VCR, Internet interface machine will gain in popularity in the mid-21st century. People will talk to others over the phone—stationary, cellular, car, etc.—and the video-equipped computer if they would like a little more eye-to-eye contact with their callers. We have the technology now, but the global culture is not comfortable with it just yet. And, yes, you will have a personal phone number that follows you everywhere. CDs will be old hat. What will really be exciting are the audio speakers that will be invented, the current stumbling block to hearing great sound.

☞ *The global challengers: Canal Plus, British Telecom, Philips (Europe); AT&T, Compaq, Sun Microsystems, Microsoft, Motorola (North America); and Nippon Telegraph and Telephone, Sony (Asia/Pacific)*

☞ *The globally challenged: France Telecom, Deutsche Telekom (Europe); and Apple (North America)*

The Netherlands' Philips is a big, lovable electronics lug. It does not always do well or come in first, but it does it, year in, year out. And it will do it in the 21st century, too. Canal Plus in France will continue to wow Europeans and north Africans with its imaginative cable programming, aggressive production maneuvers, and the inroads it has made into Hollywood's circle. It will push out globally from there. British Telecom is positioned to take advantage of the booming communications market, especially against late starters like Deutsche Telekom and nonstarters like France Telecom. Apple's computers have always been innovative and useful; its management has not, so they will struggle or dismantle the company. Sony has a sustainable beat that will carry it far into the 21st century—product innovation—and it is almost unbeatable. Look for Sony computers to capture the imagination, and pocketbooks, of consumers. AT&T has survived its breakup, with the "Baby Bells" trying to eat its lunch and numerous other competitive attacks. In the 21st century, AT&T will rise to greatness. Japan's Nippon T&T will ring the Pacific Rim and will not let anybody in. Microsoft has Gates, and he will take them into the early part of the 21st century. After his retirement, they will glide for another decade or so, after which they will be in for the fight of their life. The forecast here is that they will survive and continue to be a global challenger. IBM has the potential to be a challenger, but needs a perpetual strategy process so that it can more quickly recognize market changes. Compaq's high quality and low price strategy will continue to give it dominance. But look for Sun Microsystems, with JAVA and its network computing strengths, to be the rising star of the industry.

Post/Courier/Messenger

People will come to rely on the quick transmission of documents. With that, services such as overnight delivery, efficient postal systems, and same-day messenger services will increase. This increase will come despite a trend toward more electronic transmission of letter and reports. There will not be a rush of new players into this industry because of the immense financial and logistical considerations. With that in mind, the consumer will not benefit from cutthroat price-cutting competition, but they will have access to a number of different levels of delivery services. Consumers will tailor their mailings or posting according to the importance of the document and pay for delivery accordingly. On top of that, customers will benefit from a variety of services, including staggered delivery times corresponding to price, temporary warehousing or storage of mail, and just-in-time delivery programs. When governments finally relinquish control of national postal systems—done in small increments over a number of years—it will be too late. Consumers will have been happily lured away by better alternative services.

- ☞ **The global challengers: DHL International (Europe); and United Parcel Service, Federal Express (North America)**

- ☞ **The globally challenged: All other regional and national companies**

DHL International of Belgium is one of the largest overnight express services in the world, but it will continue to struggle for market share in the United States. United Parcel Service and Federal Express have their respective markets locked up in the United States, but seem to have more difficulty handling packages in markets like Europe. But do not feel sorry for them—each is a king in their particular market, and overthrowing them will be extremely difficult. Look for two of these three players to hook up via a merger or alliance by the first couple of decades in the 21st century. Most of the government postal authorities suffer from a lack of competition (protective regulations impede competition) and a lack of incentive (they are state-mandated, so even if they lose business, they will not go out of business).

Travel and Entertainment

Internet/On-Line Computer Services

When telephones first came out, it was difficult to use them. You had to shout to be heard and strain to hear. That is what on-line services and the Internet are like now. By the first quarter of the 21st century, we will have the equivalent of speed dialing. Regulation will come to the Internet because disciplined markets are the ones that will be preferred by most people. Structureless markets are messy and hard to use. Because of that, consumers will only use such markets when all other avenues are closed to them. The Internet will change, not the people. There will be a continuing boom in computer productivity in the 21st century, especially during the first 25 years. That is because today's children will be tomorrow's businesspeople. Those same people will use the Internet and on-line services much like we use the telephone today. Some say the trend for on-line services is to peak right around the turn of the century and then experience subscriber declines. That will not be the case. The Internet will eventually outshine anything commercial on-lines can do, but the on-line firms will shift gears and become the support and service sector of the Net. By mid-century they will be members in a consortium that helps run a regulated Internet. Governments will control the airways, and they will do the same in cyberspace.

☞ **The global challengers: Internet, America On-Line, CompuServe (North America)**

☞ **The globally challenged: Prodigy (North America)**

They are hyping the Internet now, but that is just journalists jostling for column space. It is only hype. Wait until you see the real thing in the 21st century. America On-Line and CompuServe do not have it down pat just yet because the Net keeps changing. The reason they will make it is because they keep trying to change with it. Prodigy is so stodgy and backward-thinking already that if they do not move quickly, they are gone.

Alcohol/Recreational Drugs

Beer companies are "Budweising" up to the fact that microbreweries are cool and here to stay, but to truly go global, they will have to make alliances and tap into the local expertise for production, marketing and distribution savvy. Beer lovers' tastes have changed. They have less local allegiance and are willing to try other country offerings. Wine was once monopolized by France, Italy and Spain. Now wines are produced in North America, South America and Australia, and people are drinking them. In fact, in the late 1980s through the mid-1990s, wine imports to the United States dropped as California wines increased in sales. While liquor (distilled alcohol) consumption will increase in the 21st century, that will be due to population growth and not per capita consumption. Overall, people will drink less, out of concern for health and safety. Look for a continued increase in the sale of nonalcoholic beers. Illegal drugs, on the other hand, will continue to grow, but in a haphazard fashion, with declines in some decades and increases in others. The Netherlands' relaxed view toward marijuana will creep into the rest of Europe and then the United States, but hold there. The Asia/Pacific region will continue to outlaw all nonprescription, illicit drugs.

- ☛ *The global challengers: Grand Metropolitan, Heineken (Europe); Miller, Seagrams, Budweiser, Mondavi (North America); and Kirin, Foster's (Asia/Pacific)*

- ☛ *The globally challenged: French vineyards (Europe)*

Grand Metropolitan's International Distillers & Vintners unit markets with a vengeance. Note the names—Smirnoff, J&B, and Bailey's Irish Cream, and it has Jose Cuervo under a subsidiary. There will be more from this UK company. The Netherlands' Heineken can be found anywhere and that will not change in the future. Miller and Budweiser will continue to battle it out in their domestic market and abroad; the competition will keep them sharp, and both will be winners. Seagrams has the spirit and great brand names. The only question is their MCA acquisition. Japan's Kirin is looking to open up the Asia/Pacific market by winning China. They will. Foster's is darting all over the place and aligning themselves with some interesting partners. French wines are still the best in the world, but they will suffer market share loss just like the beer and liquor markets did. Less drinking and foreign wines will be the forces at work there. Look for Mondavi to be the dominant global player in wine in the 21st century.

Personal Care Products

People will continue to request environmentally safe (or "green") and nonanimal-tested products. A parallel issue is natural ingredients. Consumers have come to love natural ingredients in their care products and will see more of them. Such products imply health and simplicity. People will use the personal care product category as a target for their own cost-cutting measures. They will purchase lots of generic or knock-off products and brand names that are on sale, taking advantage of the super or warehouse retailers. However, consumers will spend money on a few premium items as a way of pampering themselves. Manufacturers will be reluctant to put brand names on sale too often. It diminishes their profit margin and the allure of their product. Counterfeit products will proliferate as the industry grows.

☞ **The global challengers: L'Oréal, Unilever (Europe); Procter & Gamble, Mary Kay (North America); and Kao, Shiseido (Asia/Pacific)**

☞ **The globally challenged: All others**

France's L'Oréal has had a long and successful tradition as an international player and that will continue well into the 21st century. Unilever, the UK-Netherlands company, plods along, taking hits from competitors along the way, but it never stops—in fact, it has been picking up speed lately and will move quickly into the 21st century. Procter & Gamble is a juggernaut, a bruising competitor that will push its way into the future with the same success it has had in the past. Mary Kay has a formula that will continue to work even without the flamboyant founder. Kao will move out from its successful market in Japan, relying on its fanatical R&D (four years were spent collecting dirt from around the world in order to find a specific enzyme) to pave the way. Japan's Shiseido has a history of incorporating health aspects into its beauty products, which creates a perfect position for it in the 21st century.

Games and Toys

We will continue to respond to ever increasing marketing as toymakers campaign hard to maintain razor-thin profit margins. They will see increasingly aggressive marketing as their only option. Consumers will be receptive and will respond. Computer games will improve, but they will not change drastically. That is because virtual reality systems will take over the audio/video venue, making computer monitor sales as flat as their screens. Educational toys will grow in popularity, but they will enlarge the market rather than take market share away from standard toys. Which means we will be spending even more. Board games will continue to sell. Once again, they are based on a simple concept that can hold its own against technology because of the human interaction. And action figures will continue to appeal to kids.

☞ **The global challengers: Lego (Europe); Hasbro, Toys 'R' Us (North America); and Sega, Nintendo, Sony (Asia/Pacific)**

☞ **The globally challenged: Brio (Europe); Mattel (North America); and Chiyoda's Hello Mac (Asia/Pacific)**

In the 1990s, Lego's building blocks could be found in an astounding 80 percent of European homes with children and in 70 percent of US homes. It is an imaginative toy that will continue to be marketed well beyond the company's Danish base. Hasbro's product line is very diversified—a particular product can slump without killing the company—and will grow in the 21st century by building on that. Japan's Sega and Nintendo benefit from fierce competition between them. Hypersensitive to lost market share, both companies will constantly innovate to stay competitive. Look, however, for Sony to make giant strides against the two of them in the 21st century. Mattel has a couple of killer products—Barbie and Hot Wheels—but they need to expand into new lines, and not just extend the old ones. They are vulnerable to slumps without them. Brio is pricey and a target for knock-offs. Toy's 'R' Us attacked the huge Japanese toy market and won, beating the likes of Chiyoda's Hello Mac stores. They will not be playing around in the 21st century, either.

Restaurants/Coffee Houses/Bars/Nightclubs

Remember "cocooning?" That was to be the phenomenon where people would hibernate in their homes surrounded by lots of consumer goodies and services. It did not happen, and it will not. Sure people bought lots of products and signed up for cable TV, but they still spent billions on outside stimulation. They will continue to do both. Coffee houses will evolve as people get tired of the same old thing. Look what happened to McDonald's. Instead of playgrounds, though, coffee houses will have live entertainment. It will give a more health-conscious society a place to entertain and socialize. Restaurants will not change much, except for an overall improvement in the quality of food. That will be a response to internal industry competition and the supermarkets' attempt to sell better quality and more varied foods. People will want more variety. The restaurant chains that have expanded internationally will bring back local hits and add them to their home country's menu. Ethnic foods will include those from the Middle East and South America. Cafeteria-style restaurants will grow in response to consumers' desires for something more than fast food, but less than sit-down dining establishments. Price will be a factor, too. Nightclubs are just starting to see successful chains for the first time; they finally have the formula, which surprisingly has nothing to do with liquor.

- ☞ *Global challengers: Hard Rock Cafe International (Europe); McDonald's, Starbucks Coffee (North America); and Karaoke bars (Asia/Pacific)*

- ☞ *Globally challenged: Kentucky Fried Chicken (North America)*

Hard Rock Cafe (based in the United States, but owned 100 percent by a UK firm) found the secret to a successful nightclub chain—place no emphasis on the liquor, but hype the excitement to no end. McDonald's secret is to expand, but that is everybody else's secret, too. McDonald's second secret is knowing how to execute. And that effectively whittles down the "competitor" list. Starbucks is young, but already savvy. They will keep the coffee house concept fresh at least into the early part of the 21st century. Collectively, karaoke bars opened up a strong niche. Their expansion overseas will continue for some time. Kentucky Fried Chicken—somebody will eat their lunch if they do not start innovating. Following the crowd is chickening out.

Sports and Concerts

Sports will grow in the 21st century. This may surprise American fans who are slowly becoming exasperated by high ticket prices, player-owner greed and the perception that they are not getting value for their dollar. Americans will not give up their sports. They will just change the level of competition they follow or develop interest in new sports that are gaining in popularity. On the other hand, European, South American and Japanese fans will see a pronounced increase in sport leagues, teams, and sporting events, as evidenced by the current increase in television's contracting for televised rights. Improved home satellite systems will increase that market. One industry niche to profit will be those who insure high-price athletes, selling policies paid by the clubs as safeguards for expensive player contracts. Concerts will change little. Classical music will continue to stage roughly the same number of events as it does now. In popular music, some periods will see more concert events, some periods less. Prices will depend on the popularity of the music at that time, economics and the suitability of the music to hold large events.

- ☛ *The global challengers: FIFA (Europe); NBA, International Management Group (North America); and J League (Asia/Pacific)*

- ☛ *The globally challenged: National Football League (North America)*

FIFA will be in the perfect position to capitalize on football's (soccer's) increased popularity from its globally televised games. The NBA has a fast-paced, easy-to-market franchise with a built-in advantage; basketball does not require large numbers of players, which limits payroll. Shrewd marketing is also a hallmark of theirs, and they are a slam dunk success for the 21st century. Japan's J League is another basketball triumph. Their key was to do away with the traditional system where Japanese companies sponsor teams named after their corporation. Instead the teams are stand-alone businesses named after cities. Fans took immediately to the idea of rooting for a particular region, rather than a company. That new market will grow tremendously for a number of years. The US sports "conglomerate," International Management Group, will continue to juggle sports-product marketing, player representation and the staging of sporting events without dropping anything. The race is on. Who will succeed first in popularizing their sport on the other organization's home ground—FIFA's football (soccer) or the NFL with American football? FIFA. Soccer has millions of tiny ambassadors on all those US youth and school teams. The NFL (American football) makes attempts to sell their game through sheer "excitement" marketing. Globally, it will not work in the long term.

Airlines/Trains

Passenger trains will not make a comeback in the United States, although there will be passenger train service. A comparable train system, serving all the points US airlines do now, would cost more than the airline system. Distances are too great, and Americans want to spend as little time as possible traveling. Asia/Pacific and European travelers, on the other hand, will continue to use train services heavily. Japan and Europe have shorter destination points, Australia has fewer routes to cover, and China's social and political infrastructure will hamper air travel for some decades to come. No matter what, flying will be a commodities game. Pack them in, move them out. Airline travel conditions will not improve much, nor will prices be lowered. Airlines will continue to be expensive and competitive businesses to operate. Those expenses will show up as cramped seating (more passengers per plane, more money) and healthy prices (to cover costs) in order to show a paper-thin profit.

- ☛ *The global challengers: British Airways (Europe); United, Southwest (North America); and Singapore Airlines (Asia/Pacific)*

- ☛ *The globally challenged: Aeroflot (Europe), and Amtrak (North America)*

Southwest Airlines will continue to mean lower prices and absolutely no frills, but they ease the cramped seating with a great dose of customer service. Someday they will figure out how to make it work internationally. They will be the first. United is owned by its employees, and those people are hungry. Slowly but surely, they will learn how to work together. Add to this their alliances with Lufthansa and other airlines, and you have a strong global player. Singapore Airlines' world renowned comfort and service calls for a premium price, and there will be enough customers to pay for it—especially since they fly those long, tedious routes. British Airways will consolidate the European market by staying cost-conscious and eager to acquire weaker airlines. Russia's Aeroflot does not have the capitalist infrastructure to take off from, and it will be at least a quarter of a century before it finds the power. Amtrak will fail nationally before it even thinks about international business.

Hotels/Resorts

People will find that hotel accommodations will continue to be uneven for most of the 21st century. In all major cities of the developed countries, luxury, mid-price and economy hotels will exist, and in abundance. Even in less populated areas the accommodations will be plentiful and appealing. As in the past, less developed countries will still support only a few hotels that would barely pass muster elsewhere. Chains will multiply, and the business traveler will be specifically targeted for amenities like a mini-office section of the hotel (separate from the residential section). This will provide a professional and supportive setting in which to conduct business. Not only will chains categorize themselves as luxury, business, tourist and economy, but they will specialize even within those classifications. Consumers will find it easier to book rooms through universal reservation systems like American Airlines' SABRE. Resorts will begin their service right at your door, trying to extend the resort feeling. They will take care of every detail, right down to the chauffeur who whisks you to and from the airport.

☞ *The global challengers: Forte (Europe), Radisson (North America), and Accor (Asia/Pacific)*

☞ *The globally challenged: Holiday Inn (North America)*

The UK's Forte runs an eye-opening array of hotels and dining operations—everything from five star hotels to TraveLodge. They may merge or be acquired, but their standard of excellence will be seen well into the 21st century. Accor in France is like a mirror of Forte, right down to the success. Look for the two to battle or merge within the next 20 years. Radisson is aligning with European partners, and it will pay off in the future. Holiday Inn is tired and didn't answer the wake-up call. As a result, their vision was blurry and opportunities were lost—forever.

Gambling

Bet on this: Gambling will always be here. Mind you there will be tide-like decreases and increases in the level of participation, acceptance and government tolerance, but even governments have a hard time keeping out of the gaming industry. People will find more ways to gamble. A number of national and smaller governmental bodies hold lotteries and will continue to do so. The trend here is for more government-sanctioned gambling, not less. Even in some regions where religion has raised concerns about such activity, such as in the United States, gambling operations have increased. That trend, too, will continue, with the bar on the level of tolerance being raised. People will not have to travel as far to gamble. Gambling will proliferate by the establishment of smaller venues, but in more locations. Even with the smaller venues, service will be attentive and the excitement level kept high, at least in the gaming areas. Successful gambling operations depend on it. To lure more gamblers, credit policies will be relaxed.

- ☛ *The global challengers: Holland Casinos (Europe), and Harrah's (North America)*

- ☛ *The globally challenged: All others*

Holland Casinos will apply The Netherlands touch to operate well across their borders. They are a sure bet for the 21st century. Harrah's will continue to move quickly in establishing gaming operations throughout the United States and will then expand internationally.

☛ ☛ ☛ ☛ ☛ ☛ ☛

The old man was tired from his writing. He had not done this much writing since he struggled with his autobiography in 1975. He slowly got up from his chair and ambled off to bed.

"What a day! What a dream!" he thought as he lay in bed. He now knew that he did not want to be alive when his grandchildren's children were born. He had experienced enough in the good ol' 20th century. His chest started to hurt again. He put another nitroglycerine pill under his tongue and went to sleep.

CHAPTER 3

The New Centurions—
A Business Smorgasbord of Successful Companies,
Leaders, and Business Practices of the Future

Continuing his mid-21st century dream, the old man noticed another magazine—*Global Fortune* magazine. It was the annual issue featuring the most admired corporations. He quickly glanced down the list.

He recognized some old names, companies that had been around when he was growing up as a kid in the early 20th century—Nestlé, Shell, AT&T, and Coca-Cola—and some like Sony that appeared just before his retirement. But there were new ones as well.

The article sounded as if practically the whole world was a market economy, with open competition regulating supply and demand of goods. It also appeared that there were fewer companies competing.

He noticed an article on notable business leaders. They seemed different. Their background was not sales, marketing, finance or operations. It was "information," or "intelligence," with the other functional experience picked up through a planned management rotation program.

Business practices were highly streamlined and automated, with a perpetual strategy process guiding them all. Business schools had changed to meet the demand for knowledge workers, and many more trade schools had popped up to train the service workers. "Gosh, Peter Drucker was right!"

To facilitate this knowledge revolution, or "intelligence revolution" as it would be called, the entire learning process from birth to death was forecast to change in the late 21st century. The idea was, when babies were born, they would be injected with a small (harmless) implant, a chip no larger than the head of a pin which would contain over 1 billion microprocessors. The intention would be to provide the new baby with 12 years of basic knowledge on day one of its life. The traditional schools, then, would spend their 12 to 18 years working with young people in the "application" of that knowledge. This new approach would allow each human being to actively use 85 percent of his or her brain capacity, a new record!

In the meantime, in the archaic mid-21st century, business managers and educators were forced to use the crude technology of the day, expert systems and artificial intelligence, for planning and decision-making processes.

So what types of companies will we see in the future? Probably very large companies and very small companies. The large companies will get larger in an attempt to dominate global markets, and the small companies will still be in demand to serve local and regional customers in niche markets. But it will be the large companies, the New Centurions, the MegaStrategic Business Entities (MBEs), that will capture our attention and our investment dollars.

These business entities are in a global competitive race to incorporate the services and technology demanded by the consumers—and to do it with simplification and speed, another demand by consumers. Appearing to mirror the business trusts at the beginning of the century and the conglomerates of the 1960s, with their mish-mash of unrelated companies, these new alliances and partnerships will forge what seem to be incompatible businesses into seamless MBEs.

The old man thought for a moment. His creativity was flowing. He said, "How about a company called GERLINGEN, a powerful health care trust that would fuse together GNC, Merck, SmithKline Beecham, Genencor and 437 lesser entities. Shelter and subsistence could be covered by HAWAN, which would include Wal-Mart, ConAgra, Nestlé and, for the first time, the nonprofit Habitat for Humanity International. There could also be SAIRAH, which would be the leisure and communications conglomerate of Sony, AT&T, IBM, Philips, Harrahs and others. These global giants would align in order to exploit every market—no matter how insignificant its value. They would be able to substantially reduce costs, focus on growth, and not just survive on competition, but thrive on it." He was now convinced that competition and change offer the means to grow strong.

All of this was logical, he thought. In the mid-1990s, almost every daily newspaper brought news of another merger or acquisition. For awhile, the old man thought he was starting to get senile in his old age because he could no longer remember all the new names. What was even more frustrating, he was beginning to have trouble remembering their corporate genealogy. "Did Philip Morris always make Jell-O? Does Campbell Soup really own Godiva Chocolate, or was that just a fish story? Are Disney and ABC really teaming up? I must be one confused old man," he thought to himself.

But it was not the old man. These things were true. His memory was not any worse than business men and women 40 years his junior. Upon picking up the paper on any given morning, the business world had changed again, sometimes changing the structure of an entire industry. Companies were trying to grow, to become stronger, to acquire new products or technologies— to become bigger global players. And everyone seemed to be in on the act—even "Ma Bell," AT&T, and those little "Baby Bells." Look what happened in 1996 after the US government further deregulated the telecommunications industry. Talk about merger mania!

"Yes, there will be plenty of changes in the future," mumbled the old man in his sleep. "Global changes, country changes, company changes, changes in business leaders and business practices—all of which will have an impact on company employees and consumers."

Global Changes

Europe, North America and the Asia/Pacific region will dominate the business world in the 21st century.

The Industrial Revolution was born in Europe in the 19th century. In the 20th century, North America exploited technology, manufacturing, distribution and MARKETING. Also in the 20th century, the Japanese rose to a position of dominance. They focused on a few industries, applied manufacturing, distribution and marketing, and accomplished the same feats as North America—only faster, better, and cheaper. The 21st century will be more of a level playing field, with the only question mark being China. Will China rise in business stature the same as Japan, or will politics slow their rise to business power? It is clear that manufacturing will shift beyond the three major business regions to developing and emerging countries. The remaining countries will play a role as suppliers.

Almost all countries of the world will gravitate toward democracy and capitalism.

After the apparent collapse of communism in the former Soviet Union and the decay of socialism in many countries, the message has become clear. Any country looking for the successful benchmark will conclude that some combination of democracy and capitalism is the right system for the 21st century. Almost all countries in Europe, North America and the Asia/Pacific region will move toward a market-based economy. As a result, we will see even more deregulation of industries and privatization of state-owned companies. In democratic systems, citizens will have more access to their government leaders via fax and e-mail.

Europe will finally become one unified force, politically and economically.

To become an effective global competitor, the individual countries of the European Union (EU) will finally put away their differences and stick to an agreed timetable for union. The final stumbling block will be the Euro, the common currency for the member countries.

Global productivity will rise; business regulations and tariffs will gradually disappear.

"Why fight them when you can join them?" This will be the motto of country politicians as they gradually dismantle regulations and tariffs related to domestic and international business. Governments will become partners with business. Countries will exploit their industry strengths internationally to maximum advantage. In some rare cases, such as casino gambling, governments may nationalize the industry in an attempt to control it.

The world will start to become one.

Local cultures will slowly fade away as people attempt to become world citizens. The approximate 4,000 languages of the world will be reduced to about 400. English will become the world language, first for business use and then for personal use. People will begin to think more globally in their daily lives.

Population will shift back to rural areas.

After decades of gravitation from rural areas to the cities, the opposite will occur in the 21st century. The original migration was due to the decline of small farming, together with the increase in the jobs which came from massive industrial buildups. This started during the Industrial Revolution and continued through the beginning of the Information Age. As we move forward to the Intelligence Age—brought about by revolutionary changes in information and communications technology—company employees can now contribute without physically being in the office. In addition, large companies will continue their migration from the cities to the suburbs, to the exurbs, and into the rural areas. What will happen to the city skyscraper? It will become smaller and smaller. For example, in 1995, the tallest skyscraper under construction in all of the United States was only 30 stories. Contrast that with the behemoth now under construction in Kuala Lumpur.

Living standards will rise worldwide.

All of the people of the world will be richer by today's standards. Unfortunately, the gap between very rich and poor will become much greater. However, the typical 21st century community will be of more help to the poor in providing them with a better standard of living.

The environment will be a major world issue.

Global warming, deterioration of the ozone layer, and the disposal of nuclear waste will continue to be issues. The difference in the 21st century will be that real progress will be made toward solving these problems. All manufacturing industries will eventually internalize the problem and self-regulate their continuous clean-up efforts. All citizens of Europe, North America and the Asia/Pacific region will also become personally responsible for their own waste reduction and recycling.

Change will be a constant—and constantly faster.

Technological development was not new in the 20th century. Change was not new. But the pace of change will be new and different in the 21st century—occurring at warp speed. At the end of the 20th century, the last 20 years of technology development produced more advances than in the last two centuries. At the end of the 21st century, the 20:2 ratio will be much greater. In 1946 there were approximately 8,000 TVs in homes; in 1996 there were over 900 million. When music CD players were introduced, there were millions sold within just one year. Technology changes in less entertaining fields will require companies, employees and consumers to adapt—and quickly.

Info/Com (information/communications) technology will be the biggest area of change.

Information technology will actually become a positive thing in the 21st century. It will be more user friendly, and it will allow people more time for thinking and networking with colleagues. Staying close to the customer will be easier, and the company knowledge base will be accessible to all employees at any hour, anywhere in the world. Growing professions will include advanced Dis-Net (distributed/networked) computers, optical data storage, lasers, fiber optics, satellite communications, expert systems, and artificial intelligence. Info/Com products will continue to be smaller, cheaper and faster. Suppliers of Info/Com products and services will continually consolidate and merge in the 21st century.

Biological technology will score major advances.

In the 21st century, the gene structure of the human body will be fully mapped. Not only will medical professionals understand all gene functions and their roles in diseases, but they will be able to administer short- and long-term gene therapy. This will lead to longer lives, more nutritional food, higher quality products and a cleaner environment. Growing professions will include genetic engineering and advanced biochemistry.

Energy technology will make strides.

The biggest energy complaint of the 20th century was nuclear power. Finally, in the 21st century, scientists will discover how to make fusion reactors which emit only helium rather than radiation. In addition, the wider use of clean natural gas will lead to the conversion of power plants away from "dirty" coal or oil. Alternative energy sources such as photovoltaics, low head hydro and ocean thermal energy conversion will increase in popularity. The most fascinating advance, though, will be the introduction of stand-alone home power stations which handle non-peak electric loads for the home.

Changes in Characteristics of Companies, Leaders and Business Practices

The bottom line—information, knowledge, intelligence and perpetual strategy.

In the past, companies with strong marketing and product distribution were king. In the future, those with the most knowledge and intelligence distribution will rule. Combine this with a company culture of perpetual strategy, a view to the future and global cooperation—and you have the overall formula for success in the 21st century. Companies will recognize information as a corporate asset of the company.

Time-based competition will be the rule of the day.

Companies will thrive or die based on the clock. They will be expected to provide better products and services at the lowest price— and quickly. Fortunately, advancements in Info/Com technology will facilitate this.

Growth strategies will replace cost cutting strategies.

The emphasis in the 20th century was on cutting costs. Every company wanted to be the low cost producer. If they were the low cost producer, it meant that they would be more price competitive. Benchmarking studies and reengineering efforts of the late 20th century narrowed the cost gaps between companies. Growth will be the buzzword of the 21st century. Emphasis will be placed on developing new products and new global markets.

Large companies will be controlled by institutional investors.

The largest stockholders of the largest companies will be institutional investors—institutions investing funds from savings and retirement programs. These stockholders will exert more and more pressure on companies to perform to their expectations. They will control boards of directors and usurp control from CEOs to accomplish their objectives. This will proliferate except where prohibited by law.

Large companies will have smallest percentage of employees.

In the future, the largest number of employees will work for small and medium-sized companies, entrepreneurial growth companies and local "mom and pop" companies. These companies will account for the greatest growth, much of which will come from being a supplier to one or more of the MegaStrategic Business Entities.

Companies will have an organization chart labeled "lean and mean."

Organization charts will have fewer layers and virtually no middle managers. The hierarchical chart of the 20th century is replaced by a network chart. The corporation is leveraged by hundreds or thousands of network nodes—employees, subsidiary companies, strong strategic alliances, and some temporary support groups. There will be continued outsourcing of what are considered to be non-core activities. The network structure will be highly decentralized. Power, authority, and responsibility for planning and decision making will rest with decentralized groups that are closest to the customer. This will also allow the best use of knowledge, intelligence, and strategy processes.

Virtual marketing will be a key company function.

It was marketing that propelled companies to success in the 20th century. The same will hold true in the 21st century. The art and science of marketing will be improved to the point that customized marketing packages can be developed for individual customers.

Salesmen go the way of Willy Loman.

The sales function will change dramatically due to Info/Com technology. The systems will do most of the selling. Expect big changes in ordering and delivery systems. The 20th century saw companies like Procter & Gamble linking computer systems with Wal-Mart to facilitate ordering and delivery. These kinds of strategic systems alternatives were just the tip of the iceberg of what we will see in the 21st century due to advances in computer networking, optical disks and electronic data interchange. Salespeople will become consultants, helping the customer in analyzing sales information.

Operations people will be highly leveraged with automation.

For those companies involved in manufacturing, more robotics will be used as well as Computer Integrated Manufacturing (CIM) systems. For companies in service industries, the desktop computers will allow employees to become true knowledge workers.

Finance will be a reengineered function.

The finance and accounting activities of the company will be dramatically reengineered, and finance professionals will be retrained to focus on intellectual capital. Companies will develop and measure intellectual capital as a key input to long-term financial analysis and planning.

Computers for employee use will leverage their time for knowledge activities.

Every knowledge worker will have 24-hour access to the company knowledge base. They will use the knowledge base for reference, to prepare communications, to share information with colleagues, and to perform analyses in the expert systems or artificial intelligence applications.

Great strides will be made in the knowledge development activity, thanks to advances in parallel processing computers, advanced simulations and digital imaging.

Knowledge obsolescence will accelerate and demand constant retraining.

In the 20th century, company training was on the decline. In the cost cutting era, it was an easy cost to cut. Companies paid a big price for this decline in terms of decreased productivity and cost-competitiveness. In the 21st century, companies will spend two to three times their average 20th century levels for training. The training programs will be much different. Multimedia computers were used in the 20th century for training, but new Info/Com advances will allow training to be personal and customized in the 21st century. In addition to training on the industry, the company, and a person's specific job responsibility, additional training will be customized in the areas of:

- ☞ Communication skills
- ☞ Innovation and creativity
- ☞ Teamwork and empowerment
- ☞ Info/Com literacy
- ☞ Problem solving
- ☞ Decision making
- ☞ Competitive knowledge development
- ☞ Business intelligence
- ☞ Perpetual strategy

Unlike earlier training programs, training will be fun and exciting—fewer facts and more training on how to use the facts, how to analyze and solve problems, and how to make decisions.

Care and feeding of employees will be paramount.

With fewer employees, companies will do a much better job of caring for their employees. In addition to 20th century benefit programs, they will be made to feel part of the team. Internal processes will be more democratic. New compensation schemes will be developed to reward employees with outstanding performance. Offices and hours will be flexible, allowing employees to work at home or in the office during the hours they will be most productive. Additional benefits will be provided in the areas of child care, elder care, banking/investment services, shopping and errand services. For very large offices, small indoor shopping malls with shops and restaurants will be provided.

Company leaders will have different characteristics.

Absolute, authoritarian CEO power will decline. This will be due to the institutional owners mentioned previously as well as a continued decline in respect for leaders of any kind. The 21st century will see more women as CEOs. The trend will start in Sweden and the United States. Companies in Germany and Japan will be the last to accept the trend. Successful leaders will be great communicators and networkers. They will empower their workers and foster intrapreneurship, thereby earning the respect of subordinates. The education and background of the typical CEO will still be a highly regarded business school and rotation through marketing, finance and operations positions within the company. However, there will be one key difference. Those rising to the top will be perpetual strategists, capable of leveraging information, knowledge and intelligence to the company's best advantage.

Best business practices will be more seamless.

Business processes will be highly automated in the 21st century. This will allow knowledge workers to focus on analysis, problem solving, planning and decision making. Organizations will be highly networked, and ad hoc project teams will come together as required to solve specific business problems. The walls that existed in previous hierarchical organizations have come down. Internal cooperation rather than competition will be stressed, as well as creativity and innovation. Processes will change almost daily, and this will be considered routine. Knowledge workers, for the most part, will be performing self-determined activities in pursuit of company objectives and goals. The old departmental divisions of Sales, Customer Service, Technical Service, Public Relations, Purchasing, etc. are replaced by one process: external communications. Functions like personnel, employee benefits, the company newsletter, etc. are also replaced by one process: internal communications. Granted, there are many elements to these processes, but they become highly automated and efficient, allowing the knowledge worker to be that friendly person on the phone that some of us remember from the early 20th century.

🐾 🐾 🐾 🐾 🐾

The old man thought again about the MegaStrategic Business Entities. Extremely large and highly diversified within their industry, or more accurately, their business arena, these 21st century global trusts could take consumers from cradle to grave, particularly with seamless business processes where it took multiple hierarchies before. "This is really exciting," he said. "I cannot stop thinking about the MBE concept. But what about governmental intervention? This would be a different kind of mergers and acquisitions era, with MBEs built on alliances and centered around emerging business synergisms. It is an uncanny reminder of the early 20th century trust period when I was growing up. Economies of scale, integration of resources, service and production capabilities, and segment marketing were the tactics then. It looks like they would be similar in the future. But the feeding frenzy among different business entities, along with the consolidation of many companies into one, might frighten society. I bet governments will attempt to band together in an effort to bust those global trusts. Remember the antitrust period in America in the early 20th century? I bet it will be similar. In fact, I bet a lot of things in the 21st century will be a replay of what happened in the 20th century."

The old man dozed in his easy chair. It had been a strenuous morning.

CHAPTER 4

TIME WARP—
THE GHOSTS OF BUSINESS PAST,
WHY THEY'RE STILL HAUNTING US,
AND
THEIR FUTURE MISSION

The old man awoke with a jolt. "What was this? A cruel hoax? A bad nightmare?" What was this future world he was dreaming about? It seemed so real—and what was all this GERLINGEN stuff? He relaxed a bit. "You know," he said, "basically it actually doesn't look too different from things at the beginning of the 20th century."

"Ah, those were the days—when men were men, and companies were built out of sheer guts and determination—men like Rockefeller, Mellon, Carnegie...."

The old man fell back to sleep. Another dream, a relaxing dream—Yes, Rockefeller, Mellon and Carnegie—now those were REAL men. And the giant business trusts they built in the late 19th and early 20th centuries were REAL companies. They CRUSHED competition with their bare hands and sprinkled the crumbs for all to see. There were actually several men which ran companies that looked amazingly like GERLINGEN of the mid-21st century.

Andrew Carnegie

In 1880, Andrew Carnegie viewed the steel business as fragmented and disorganized. At the time, the United States was home to more than 1,000 manufacturing plants in the steel industry. Carnegie knew that a large, integrated steel producer, formed from the acquisition of smaller companies, would benefit enormously from the associated economies of scale. The producer would have to be involved from the start of the manufacturing process throughout the final delivery. Others, such as J.P. Morgan, came to that conclusion, too. The only problem was that Carnegie had begun to make his move in 1892, whereas Morgan waited until 1897. When the other steel consortiums tried to tie up the industry, only one thing stood in their way—Carnegie. Attempts to broker deals usually ended with Carnegie proposing stiff prices that were deemed too expensive by the other consortiums. At one point, Carnegie's adversaries tried an end-run by refusing to buy the raw materials from Carnegie's steel company, which was also a major supplier to other steel manufacturers. Carnegie stonewalled them by inferring that he would enter their marketing niches and wreak havoc, something the others knew he had the resources to do. In the end, it came down to J.P. Morgan and Carnegie. Morgan, tired of all the machinations, finally asked Carnegie's price. Carnegie's emissary, Charles Schwab, came back with a figure of US$492 million. The price was US$335 million more than Carnegie had demanded from potential buyers just a few years earlier. Morgan paid it.

Meyer Guggenheim

Meyer Guggenheim was a very astute man. This native of Switzerland realized that the key to enormous profits was involvement throughout the marketing and manufacturing processes. He began his empire, with the help of his family, by making shoe polish. Rather than earning 10 percent of a sale by marketing shoe polish, Guggenheim sought the 70 percent which the manufacturer would earn. Guggenheim leveraged that stake into a larger household product line which made him a comfortable sum. Not content with that, he shrewdly played the stock market, piggybacking on railroad trades that Jay Gould, a notorious stock plunderer, was successfully making. Eventually, Guggenheim found himself with ownership of several silver mines, which he worked with his usual proficiency. Employing his seven sons in the operation, Guggenheim consolidated his position, while waiting for the forces that were then putting together a smelter trust, a segment of the mining industry that Guggenheim thought particularly profitable. While others gave in, Guggenheim held out until he was the last, and one of the most powerful, smelter owners around. His position gave him the opportunity to strike a deal which netted him over US$42 million in stock. The earnings enabled him to control American Smelting. Again, Guggenheim was a very astute man.

Edward H. Harriman

While few remember him now, Edward Harriman was a mover and shaker of national proportions in the days when railroads had a corporate power and prestige which equaled that of today's *Fortune* 50 firms. Harriman did not form railroads from scratch. Starting with ownership of a small line, Harriman strung together a series of mergers, acquisitions, equity stakes and squeeze-outs, and came to control the Union Pacific and the Illinois Central. Both the Union Pacific and the Illinois Central were powerhouses which had lost steam. With Harriman at the throttle, both railroads were eventually restored to their original powerful configurations. Harriman showed not only his usual financial prowess, but also an extremely keen operational sense in turning the two around. It is noteworthy that Harriman did all of this during the days of people like John D. Rockefeller, J.P. Morgan, and the Vanderbilts, not to mention slightly smaller but still immensely powerful national figures like Jacob Schiff, the financier; Jim Hill, a railroad magnate; and James Stillman, banker to the Rockefellers. Audacious, tenacious and cocksure, he was perhaps the equal of any of them. Harriman forged alliances with Rockefeller and fought war with Morgan. If nothing else, over the years, Morgan developed a deep respect for Harriman. So great were Harriman's ambitions that at the time of his death in 1909, he had an option on the South Manchurian Railway in China and seemed on the verge of providing a transportation outlet from Siberia to capital cities throughout Europe.

Andrew Mellon

It took Andrew Mellon over 20 years to build the empire which was to be the monopoly for aluminum production we know today as Alcoa. Mellon started his quest in 1888 when he founded the Pittsburgh Reduction Company. The company was founded with the sole purpose of commercially manufacturing aluminum. After the Pittsburgh Reduction Company was established, Mellon acquired additional bauxite ore companies throughout the United States. His most important bauxite venture came with the purchase of General Bauxite company, which he purchased from the General Chemical Company in 1905. The last maneuver in gaining monopoly control of the aluminum industry came in 1909 when Mellon acquired Republic Mining & Manufacturing's bauxite properties. With this, the Aluminum Company of America (Alcoa) had been formed. Alcoa strengthened its monopolistic reign by establishing subsidiaries to control the entire process from raw materials to finished product. Alcoa continued to purchase any company that had usable ore for aluminum, eventually controlling 90 percent of all usable ore. Being a monopoly meant being able to set prices, and Alcoa did just that. Prices were low to promote usage. This was done in conjunction with promotional campaigns to gain a wider acceptance for aluminum products. Lastly, to discourage competition, Alcoa ensured prices of finished products were not much higher than ingots, which eliminated the possibility of someone starting a competing fabricating company. Alcoa kept a constant eye and firm grip on all aspects of the aluminum market from production to sale of products. This, coupled with its deep pockets, ensured Alcoa's monopolistic reign.

J.P. Morgan

Finance has always played a significant role in the development of business. This was especially true during the latter part of the 19th century and the beginning of the 20th century when large corporations depended heavily on commercial bankers to fund company growth. Consequently, bankers were in control of many industries—the greatest banker being J.P. Morgan. Consider that the "House of Morgan" organized and financed the following mergers, forming some blockbuster companies that still exist today:

- General Electric

- US Steel (currently USX)

- International Harvester Company (currently Navistar)

- AT&T

The AT&T deal was not the organization of a splintered industry, but a takeover by a Morgan-led consortium. Morgan took back the company from its original Boston-based investor who was more interested in quick profits than long-term company growth. Morgan reinstated Theodore Vail, the architect of AT&T's monopolistic empire.

On top of those achievements, Morgan was involved in numerous railroad consolidations and mergers, helping to forge the rail's infrastructure. This was an important contribution because the railroads were initiators of modern management techniques. They had to be. Their operations were so far-flung that some sort of centralized command-and-control was required or the systems would fall apart. While not a direct proponent of modern management, Morgan understood the validity of management systems, as indicated by his repositioning of Vail at AT&T.

John D. Rockefeller

Upon his death, Rockefeller left an oil dynasty and a legacy that defined the monopolistic corporation. His development of the Standard Oil voting trust, initiated by a Standard Oil attorney, was a brilliant move, one quickly imitated by a number of other companies within their respective industries. Legislation forced an end to this practice, but Standard Oil quickly countered with a more sophisticated tool—the holding company—a concept still in practice today. By the early 1900s it controlled 85 percent of the US business and 90 percent of the nation's petroleum exports. Tenacious and often ruthless, at times, (Rockefeller forced his own brother out of the oil business), he refined other predatory business practices such as price wars, secret rebates, hostile takeovers and a host of other tactics. Yet, it was the very object of these tactics, Standard Oil's competitors and not the government, that successfully broke the near-strangle hold that Standard wielded. In essence, Standard Oil found it could not be everywhere at the same time in combating competitors' advances. Sometimes it conceded a competitive advantage simply because it was blind to the opportunity, an affliction not always suffered by its competition. So, the competitive arena was successful in stopping Standard Oil even when the efforts of government could not.

☞ ☞ ☞ ☞ ☞ ☞

The old man woke up. "YES! These men could easily handle the MegaStrategic Business Entities of the 21st century," said the old man, "although their methods would have to change a bit. Well, probably quite a bit. But they conceived the concept over a century ago. There is so much that can be learned from men like that. If you look to business history, there is so much that can be learned and used today. So why are businesses always reinventing the wheel?"

☞ ☞ ☞ ☞ ☞ ☞

Reinventing the Wheel

There is something to that old saying that history repeats itself. All around us are some excellent examples of strategies we can use again, product ideas that have life today, and management concepts as original now as they were when they were first implemented. Let's look at some examples.

New Products

When Kodak introduced its disposable fun cameras in the late 1900s, we thought it was the most exciting concept. The camera was an immediate hit with consumers. You would see one sitting on nearly every table at a wedding reception. It invited participants to snap candid shots of people. Those cameras were a great idea. The thing is, though, they were basically the same concept as the original Kodak camera produced in 1888. When Kodak first introduced its camera then, it had film installed by the manufacturer. After taking your pictures, you returned the entire camera to Kodak for film developing—just like the fun cameras of the late 20th century.

New Management Concepts

When the Xerox Corporation popularized the concept of benchmarking in the early 1980s, we thought it was such a novel concept. They said you should pick a functional area of your company, say Customer Service, and then decide which companies in the world provide the best customer service. These companies would be referred to as "best in class" or "best practices companies." Then you would compare your customer service function with theirs, using agreed upon quantitative measures. You would then analyze the results, understand your own strengths and weaknesses, and implement improvements to your own customer service function. What a novel idea. However, in 1913 Henry Ford also wrote about a novel technique he used to develop the assembly-line concept. He called it "benchmarking." He benchmarked the meat packing industry to better understand how to handle high volume production.

New Technology

When the computer was introduced in the mid-1900s in Germany, England and the United States, what a marvelous invention it was. We all had visions of the wonderful things this computer would do. It was rather large and built with vacuum tubes, the technology of the day. But futurists promised that it would get smaller. Companies began to install the contraption, and the typical first applications were accounting functions like customer billing and payroll. It was a marvel—and a curse at the same time. But wait. Charles Babbage, a British mathematician, actually designed the computer in 1833.

What Has Gone Before Us

There may be concepts or strategies that strike us as fresh and innovative, or maybe lead us to believe we are seeing a new twist on an old theme, but a look behind us may reveal something we hadn't seen before or taken the time to notice. When facing a problem and looking for a solution, it would serve managers well to examine the past for any applicable examples.

In most cases, there won't be exact examples, although it wouldn't be surprising to find situations that parallel a particular problem. Remember, there has already been almost 200 years of large-scale business. (Prior to the Industrial Revolution, there were a few large companies, such as trading concerns, but with the onset of the Revolution, there have obviously been many more—and many more applicable—examples.) So there's a good chance that someone before you has encountered a similar problem or set of circumstances. Sometimes, though, the past business event you are studying can provide startling parallels to what you may face today or tomorrow.

When studying past events, clear away any peripheral or extraneous facts that do not pertain, and concentrate on the salient points. People often have the tendency to include everything they encounter in studying an example. It is crucial to remove the clutter in order to see the relevant. So, by all means, disregard the difference in, say, product type, distribution means, and other secondary aspects if they are not germane to that business situation, and if they do not apply in your circumstances.

By using what has gone before, we can often construct the best course of action to take or obtain a better understanding of the forces at play. It might also prevent us from reinventing the wheel. Why labor over a set of problems or plan a strategy when someone has already experienced your predicament? Furthermore, your strategy may contain flaws or be poorly informed as to the circumstances or influences that are out there. By looking at an example that mirrors yours, it allows you to avoid costly errors in thinking that have already been experienced by others in your situation. Sometimes, there is no immediate or pressing need to come up with a solution or strategy. Still, such case studies can serve as a wake-up call. Take a function of your business, say, distribution. Compare what takes place in your company distribution system with distribution systems of the past. Start with identical industries, if possible, then move on to any industry distribution system. Managers can read about a set of business events and recognize their own company's situation, then react.

Now, let's examine some strategies of the past.

Teaming Up

Most managers understand that to create new markets, access remote ones or increase presence in established markets, they can try to
muscle their way in on their own, or they can forge an alliance with a
partner that knows the market well, is closer to it, or has the strengths
to complement their weaknesses in that market. Old hat, right? Well,
you may be surprised at how old that concept is.

Alliances

How about strategic alliances? We have talked about them in the
late 20th century as something new, something different. But alliances,
partnerships and joint ventures have been practiced for centuries in one
form or another. At the beginning of the 20th century, Nippon Electric
Company of Japan celebrated its first anniversary as a joint-stock company with Western Electric Company of Illinois. Western Electric Company was the maker of telephone equipment for AT&T for many
decades in the 20th century. Western Electric owned 54 percent of
Nippon Electric after treaty revisions with western nations encouraged
the influx of foreign capital.

Mergers and Acquisitions

We always talk about the latest wave of recent mergers and acquisitions as if it was the biggest wave yet. The mid-1990s brought a big one
with deals between Disney and ABC, as well as Chase Manhattan with
Chemical Bank. However, the largest merger or buyout, after adjusting
for inflation, was in 1901. US Steel was formed when J.P. Morgan
organized a consortium to purchase not only Andrew Carnegie's then
huge organization, but additional steel makers, suppliers, shippers and
other peripheral businesses. Again, it was the largest of the 20th century.

Comebacks

Failure. Sometimes there is failure in keeping market share. Other
times there is failure in winning market share from stronger competitors.
A look at those who turned around their fortunes may not give an exact
blueprint for a winning strategy, but it can often provide invaluable

insights into the strategic thinking that produces winning moves and upsets the equilibrium of the competition.

Gaining the Lead

Sometimes we look at long and heated rivalries as always having been there, like Coke versus Pepsi. But that isn't always the case. Until the 1950s, Pepsi was a dismal and distant competitor of Coke. Pepsi had a reputation as a poor quality drink. The taste was so poor, the company had to market on the quantity of beverage you got for your money. "Twice as much for a nickel, too," went the jingle. Then new Pepsi management threw the gauntlet down. They improved the formula, changed the bottle design, and sharpened their marketing tactics. They concentrated everything they had on one front—the take-home market. And in that market, they targeted only one particular consumer—the housewife (remember, this is the 1950s). She alone influenced almost the entire take-home market for soft drinks. When Pepsi's fiercely aggressive attack won solid market share there, they moved on to the next battleground—fountain drinks. Then the bottlers. And so on, and....

Making the Switch

Dusty, musty S.S. Kresge was always a perennial number two to the Woolworth variety chain. Then in 1959 Harry Cunningham became president. Cunningham had just finished a tour of all his chain's stores. He saw something others didn't. Discounters were his competition, not the other variety stores. Cunningham opened a new Detroit discount store in 1962. He called it K-Mart. He left Woolworth in the dust, even when Woolworth tried to comeback with Woolco. How ironic to now find K-Mart fighting for its life against deep discounter Wal-Mart. But we issue caution here. Cunningham was only following the path once taken by another S.S. Kresge leader, Sebastian Kresge, who started S.S. Kresge—as a discounter. Could K-Mart come back again?

Hidebound

It is important to note that having a vision and seeing it through to its successful implementation (whether it is a new business, or new product, or an innovative process) doesn't mean the vision is complete. Managers in the 21st century must be on guard to inroads by competitors, events that alter their industry, and new products that can not only take away market share, but even render a company's industry obsolete. Advancing technology, itself, can produce all three of the previous problems on very short notice.

Narrowly Focused

Baldwin Locomotive was probably the top locomotive or engine manufacturer in the United States, a country that was built by the railroads. In fact, Baldwin probably built the best steam locomotive around, and the company was constantly improving the technology. The only problem was that General Electric and General Motors were starting to build the best diesel-electric locomotives around. It was as if Baldwin never saw the new technology barreling down the tracks. The company became history.

Complacency

The International Match company was ranked 42 on the *Forbes 100* list in 1929. Rapid fire technology advances—including products like pilot-lit gas stoves, more reliable cigarette lighters, automatic furnaces— almost rendered the kitchen match obsolete. Over the next three years their market dissipated. By either failing to notice or just discounting these emerging products, the company doomed themselves to oblivion. At the end of that three-year period, they were not only off the top 100 list, they were out of business.

Ill-Advised

Now, for some quick examples of ill-conceived strategies on the part of some short-sighted companies and individuals.

- ☞ In 1977, Ken Olson, President of Digital Equipment, said, "There is no reason for any individual to have a computer in their home." Even though the company later introduced a home computer, they were never a serious contender. They subsequently got out of the business.

☞ When Remington Rand bought the rights to the UNIVAC with the intention of selling it as the first commercial computer, they were advised by marketing people that the company could expect perhaps a dozen sales a year.

☞ In 1981 Osborne Computers aimed for the businessperson when it opened for business and rolled out its portable computer. Loaded with bundled software, including a spreadsheet, the computer was a smash hit. The company skyrocketed for a period and then fell under the weight of mismanagement, finally going out of business in 1983. When an audit was done, it was discovered that the company didn't even have a manual ledger accounting system.

Pleasant Surprises

Thomas Edison said, "The phonograph is not of any commercial value." Thank goodness others in General Electric didn't believe him.

☞ ☞ ☞ ☞ ☞ ☞ ☞

"History does seem to have repeated itself," said the old man. "Why is it that most businesspeople do not remember? First, probably because they were not alive at the time. They have no first-hand recollection. Another reason is that business history is usually not part of any education system or company training program. Yet, there are all those examples that are so relevant to what is going on today."

"Companies focus on only the past three to five years of history for planning and decision making. It is unusual thinking in many ways. If companies intend to stay in business a long time, why such short-sightedness? Of course, there are outside influences, such as stockholder pressures for good quarterly and annual results. Those can very often make companies react short-term, but there is no reason that a short-term plan cannot rest on a long-term strategy."

"We can learn much from a comprehensive study of business history. History teaches us many important lessons. Every day we use our personal history to avoid mistakes and take advantage of opportunities. We would never think of touching again what burned once. What goes around, comes around...and comes around again."

The old man woke up. He was starting to understand his dream. He walked out to his front porch. The fresh air, the bright sun, the smell a mixture of pine and roses. Yes, things were becoming clearer. His dream had shown him there was a natural evolution in business. The 19th century was much like childhood, the 20th century like adolescence, and the 21st century like adulthood.

CHAPTER 5

- - - - - - - - - - - - - - -

THE INDUSTRIAL REVOLUTION AND BUSINESS EVOLUTION— 19th CENTURY CHILDHOOD, 20th CENTURY ADOLESCENCE, AND 21st CENTURY ADULTHOOD

The old man remembered his grandfather's stories of the latter 19th century. It is so often said that life was much simpler then. It was. When the rooster crowed, it was time to milk the cows at sunrise. When the sun set for the day in the western sky, it was time to eat dinner with the family, read the good book by the light of the kerosene lamp, and go to bed. It was a hard life with much manual labor during the day. But it was a very rewarding life, with much quality time for the family.

Business was simpler too. Business was a collection of markets, not subdivided into hundreds of market segments and served markets. The primary consumer markets of the 19th century were limited to food, clothing and shelter, although that began to change.

The old man remembered his grandfather describing the developments in the 1800s. Hans Christian Oersted of Denmark, André-Marie Ampère of France, and Georg Ohm of Germany contributed to the development of electricity in the 1820s. Ressel of Germany invented a screw propeller for steamships in 1829.

In 1830, the first steam railway line operated between Liverpool and Manchester in England. The 1830s brought the telegraph by Wilhelm Weber of Germany, the computer (yes, the computer) by Charles

Babbage of England, the reaper by Cyrus Hall McCormick of the United States, and improved photography by French inventors Louis-Jacques Daguerre and Joseph Niepce.

In 1844, Samuel Morse of the United States installed the first electric telegraph between Washington and Baltimore. His grandfather remembered the first message by Morse, "What hath God wrought!"

The 1850s brought the first successful oil well by Edwin Drake in the United States. In 1860, Lenoir of Germany designed the gasoline engine. In 1861, Reis of Germany constructed an electric telephone. And in 1867, Alfred Nobel of Sweden invented dynamite.

The 1870s brought more inventions and refinements on previous inventions. Alexander Graham Bell of the United States designed a serviceable telephone that could carry speech. Otto constructed the four-stroke internal gasoline combustion engine. Thomas Edison of the United States built a cylinder phonograph and an improved carbon filament light bulb. Edison also created the basis for the power supply system required for electrical household lighting.

In the 1880s, the first electric power plants started operation in London and New York, Hollerith of the United States patented his automatic punched card counting machine, Benz built the first gasoline engine motor car, Coca-Cola was produced in the United States, Berliner of the United States invented the record for phonographs, George Eastman of the United States introduced the first practical consumer camera, and Toynbee introduced the term "industrial revolution" to describe the series of events then taking shape.

The last decade of the 19th century brought the diesel engine by Diesel of Germany, cinematography by Lumière of France, x-rays by Röntgen of Germany, the wireless telegraph by Marconi of Italy, the cathode-ray tube by Braun of Germany, and the first 30-kilometer radio broadcast by Braun and Zenneck of Germany.

When we think about the evolution of business and competition, the Industrial Revolution can best be characterized as "childhood." So many new things were discovered. So much knowledge had been amassed. And so much learning by citizens would need to take place. The business markets were still relatively simple: food, clothing and shelter. But the

Industrial Revolution was providing the tools for further growth. Let's take a look at the evolution of the industries.

Food (19th century)

Most of the world's markets were local. In the early part of the century, businesses that served the markets were also local or certainly within one day's travel by horse. Consumers of the day largely ate what they grew, selling their surplus to the inhabitants of the nearest town in farmers' markets. Most of the population worked on their farms, using rudimentary tools and animal power. In North America and Europe, regional movement of foodstuffs increased in the 19th century with the proliferation of canal systems and other waterway routes, many of which were interlocked with large lakes and rivers. What could be cultivated in New York could be bought in New Orleans. This was also true of the Rhine River in Europe, a critical link to a succession of French and German river towns. Europeans had started developing their systems earlier than the North Americans, with the Asia/Pacific region surpassing all continents throughout previous centuries, before it inexplicably stagnated. Any continent's efforts prior to the mid-19th century were constantly in a state of flux due to war, governance issues, the lack of a managerial class separate from the entrepreneurial one, geographical obstacles, underdeveloped infrastructure, and primitive machinery and equipment to surmount those obstacles.

With the advent of the locomotive and other mechanized improvements, much of that began to change, but it also doomed the waterway system. Who needs better canal mechanization when you can lay railroad track almost anywhere? The chief beneficiary—foodstuffs and all related functions, such as cultivation, harvest, storage and distribution. During the 19th century came the advance of transportation and the increase of regional food processing over the local custom of grow-and-eat. Cattle was moved over great distances for slaughter and processed upon arrival. The dressed carcasses that traveled along the railroad's new refrigerated-car system logged more miles by rail than they ever did by hoof. If it was not refrigerated, it was canned and vacuum packed. Milk received the same treatment—shipped, treated, condensed and shipped again—eagerly awaited by a newly-minted "consumer" market. And even condensing was not always necessary—the refrigeration rail car could transport fresh milk over a distance that would have shown sour results with previous methods.

Farmers dwindled as machinery increased, wheat and farm manual labor being fodder for mechanized reapers. This new machinery increased productivity—much like today's personal computers—reducing manpower needs and allowing one farmer to leverage the amount of land he could cultivate. The instruments that drove farmers off the land were being manufactured in cities, more and more often by former farmers who had now migrated to urban areas for work and food. Global populations began a shift from rural to urban, with their new distribution almost capsizing some social orders (that would come later).

The practice of marketing also began to appear in the United States. In the early 1800s, "branded" meant a red-hot iron applied to identify cattle. Now it was the touting of Armour-labeled beef over Swift, and the importance of the sizzle over the steak began to take root. Budweiser staked a claim to a throne with "The King of Bottled Beers." Europe saw much the same, although there was some drop-off in commercial participation due to the strength of national borders. European companies such as Nestlé lay siege to such imaginary lines as much to push the survival of their fledgling companies as to push their products. Economies of costs for big milk-condensing plants could only be realized by pushing for economies of scale, and man-made boundaries succumbed like their geographical counterparts. Commerce proved to be stronger than national borders.

Strangely, the Asia/Pacific region lagged behind, its formidable trading experiences almost inexplicably dissipating at the very moment in history that they were so relevant. Interestingly, international brands were making their mark in small numbers in the latter 19th century, and even in the Asia/Pacific region one could see the tin containers of Royal Dutch Shell and Standard Oil. Unfortunately, the cans were as valued as their contents, put to use as cooking implements and other everyday utensils, a sign that commerce's progress was still in its infancy here. Years of outside intervention—colonialism—had a damping effect on the generation of a homegrown economy and infrastructure that could support an efficient food chain. Most exporting was done by foreign companies piggybacking on their governments' overseas interventions.

Clothing (19th century)

The 19th century saw clothing as fashion, but that had been the case centuries before. What really began to take place were improvements in the basic machinery used to process fiber into fabric, at least in the early part of the century. These improvements were built on the textile infrastructure brought forth by England's Industrial Revolution. By the 1800s, fabric and the finished clothing produced from fabric had become more accessible and less costly. The only stumbling blocks were an efficient distribution system and the fact that individual nations jealousy guarded the fruits of their textile labor. Machines invented in a particular country and the means to produce fiber, such as the wool-producing sheep, were usually forbidden for export. Only the finished product, fabric or clothing, could be exported.

These efforts were established in order to enhance the profitability of the home country's businesses (why let other countries capitalize on a homegrown invention or resource?). Animal skins and furs were very important during this period, not only for the decorative clothing that could be made, but also for the everyday apparel and other non-clothing items that could be fashioned from the hides. Each nation tried to protect and encourage their respective textile and clothing industries by limiting imports and controlling export of the means to produce competing products and enacting tariffs. England refused to export its machinery, Japan and China their silk worms, Spain its sheep—and they were joined by a host of other countries that banned textile-producing products. These efforts were a failure and a nation's textile "secrets" were most assuredly spirited across borders and oceans. While a country might forbid export of manufacturing methods and machinery or the organic means to produce textiles, it usually did not limit export of fabric or finished products. The one time that actual fiber was embargoed came during the American Civil War, when the North was surprisingly successful in stopping exports of the South's cotton to Europe. This problem was frustrating enough that England, a large importer of American cotton, thought long and hard about supporting the Confederate States with arms and money. In the end it did not, but it is an example of the power of the textile industry in the early years of the Industrial Revolution.

Ready-made clothing was rather pricey prior to the mid-1800s, with most clothing being made by the consumer from textile mill end-product or from fabric. This occurred more often in the rural areas than in urban centers, but even among the larger populations, the making of clothes was a routine chore. Those in rural areas waited for the itinerant peddler to arrive in order to buy fabric. Those close to villages and towns made use of the small municipalities and their conveniences, usually general stores for the fabric and an occasional specialty shop for the more hard to find or ready-made apparels. The specialty shops were especially valued because they carried elaborate items which the consumer had neither the time nor materials to make. Weaving cloth was time consuming, so providing a family with clothing could mean lots of time spent at a loom or spindle. It was better to pay or barter for ready-made fabric and make the clothing from there. With the introduction of the American Singer sewing machine and its imitators, costs and prices began to come down. The Singer machine and its brethren became so popular that clothing manufacturers worldwide purchased them. The majority of the early Singer machines were sold in Europe. Other machines were invented to handle boot and shoe manufacturing. Unlike food production, the Asia/Pacific region was more adventurous in the production of fabric, especially silk. But once again they trailed far behind the rest of the world in textile trade, basically lacking the business infrastructure and motivation to make much impact.

On most continents and toward the end of the 19th century, the cities and large towns usually had everything one could want within reason, and even then it might be ordered from distant cities, especially as telecommunications came into being. The cities were populated with specialty shops, general stores and early versions of the department store. By the end of the century, a good portion of the world's population was wearing ready-made clothing.

Large retail and mail order-generated operations really did not get started until later in the 19th century, when daily life began taking on a more hectic pace and leaving less time to produce homemade clothing. Previously only the fabric needed to make clothes and special items like wedding dresses were reasons to enter a general store or dressmaker. As always, though, people living in urban areas were much more prone to buy apparel from retail operations and did so much sooner than those in the rural areas. This was not the result of a more sophisticated clientele, but merely consumers reacting to opportunity—where retail operations were the most prevalent. The United States led the way for retail chains and mail order, with companies like Sears and Wards pioneering many innovations in the field, but Europe also boasted many large retail stores, such as France's Au Printemps (founded in 1865), Germany's Hertie and the UK's Marks & Spencer, which rivaled the best the United States had to offer. The Asia/Pacific region had to wait until the 20th century before any large retail operations appeared. The small general store or specialty stores held exclusive domain over the apparel business until then. It should be noted that outside the United States, the mail-order catalogs business was practically nonexistent. Sears, Wards and Spiegel overcame customer resistance to buying from distant sellers by guaranteeing satisfaction and by offering easy credit terms. The concept was surprisingly embraced by consumers. The fortunes of all three companies took off. By the turn of the century, consumers were enthusiastically responding to a booming retail atmosphere with all its marketing and financial innovation.

Shelter and Personal Transportation (19th century)

Real estate is the foundation for shelter and personal transportation, both figuratively and literally. Prior to the 19th century, real estate was the object of violence, alliances, exploitation and appropriation—and that was just between neighbors. When coupled with governmental ambitions, the land rushes looked like the wars they really were, with their version of real estate agents wearing lots of braid and leading armies. Prior to the Industrial Revolution, most people lived where they farmed. Sure there were towns and fiefdom centers, where the guild craftsman, local merchants, and local royalty resided. But for the most part, people lived on the farm, first as serfs, later as yeoman farmers. And while the centuries just prior to the 19th century produced more landowners than ever before, it was not until the Industrial Revolution that things really began to change in real estate and shelter. The opening of North America and its flood of immigrants created a real estate shakeup that was unprecedented. Village, town and city land became a vehicle for speculation as land closer to urban areas commanded a high price. Conversely, rural land brought the lowest prices.

With the Industrial Revolution the population shifted from rural areas to urban areas. This migration took place in order to meet the demands of industry's need for workers, and combined with a mechanical revolution on the farm that displaced farmers and farmhands. And while most of these shifts took place in North America and Europe (where the Revolution had its strongest impact), the reverberations were felt around the world, if only because products were beginning to seep into the most remote geographic areas. The Industrial Revolution also changed the face of commerce, encouraging the trade of products and ideas. In fact, it was the expansion of commerce rather than the direct effects of the Industrial Revolution that opened geographically remote areas. The people in those areas might not be able to purchase steel plows, but they could afford simple devices meant for the home or barn.

In the continents that were advancing—North America and Europe—homes went from being crude dwellings roughly made from local materials, such as timber and stone hand-hewn by the homeowner, to more refined dwellings that traded oiled animal-skin windows for glass ones, and fired bricks and sawmill-cut lumber for the structure. Cast iron stoves supplemented or replaced fireplaces as a source for cooking food and warming the residence. At the beginning of the century a good portion of the population cooked in their fireplaces. By the end of the century most cooking was done on a wood-burning or possibly gas stove. This was a result of the population switch from rural to urban, which brought more people into a setting where fireplace-cooking was neither convenient nor safe, and of the march of technology and industry which had just made the older implements obsolete. Even in the rural areas commerce made inroads. While brick or commercial lumber wasn't always available, or even desired (thanks to local materials), rural people would opt for real glass, a luxury trucked in on the wagon of the traveling peddler. As the century wore on, more and more of the urban conveniences and refinements reached the rural areas as a result of infrastructure improvements that included the railroads, as well as traditional roads which carried wagon, carriage and stagecoach traffic. The Asia/Pacific region saw much of the same building refinements, but, at least initially, they occurred almost always in urban centers.

As the 19th century progressed, more improvements came to rural villages and small towns, with iron cooking utensils, handtools and guns being most prevalent for the average family. Local houses of worship and businesses might include glass, decorative pieces and other items not easily made locally. But none of these were readily stocked within any reasonable distance, and required supreme efforts on the part of traders to ship these items into areas poorly served by any infrastructure improvements. Dwellings in these areas, even at the end of the century, often showed no visible improvements from even a couple of hundred years before.

In the early and mid-1800s, all the continents were in the dark when it came to electricity, plumbing and heating/air conditioning, although in some of the most affluent homes, there were primitive plumbing systems that made attempts to supply fresh water and dispose of sewage. Homes and businesses were illuminated by candle, whale oil and kerosene. Then Royal Dutch Shell and Standard Oil began to reach even some of the most remote markets with their distinctively colored 5-gallon cans of fuel. As mentioned before, these cans were not only valued for their contents, but also for the many uses to which the empty cans could be put. By the end of the century the principles of electricity were established, and innovations tumbled forth from Edison, Siemens, Bell, Morse and a host of others. Electric lights became popular on almost every continent, with North America and Europe leading the way—although it was more common to find jet gas illumination in many homes and businesses. Heating of buildings in North America and Europe during the latter part of the century came more and more to rely on coal- and oil-fired boilers, especially in urban areas. Although, once again, the traditional means of heating—wood or gas burning stoves and fireplaces—were still common in the rural areas. The Asia/Pacific region saw less in the way of advancement in heating technology, in part because many regions were heated fairly well year-round by natural solar heat. In those regions that required heat, the vast majority relied on fireplaces and stove.

Ventilation and cooling were, with some exceptions, nonexistent. There were attempts at ice-cooled air conditioning systems in commercial buildings that worked fairly well, but the cost, maintenance and supply logistics involved did not easily justify their construction. So adapting them for home use was considered impossible. Fans were common in commercial buildings, but usually only found in the more expensive homes, if found in residential use at all. Open windows and stiff breezes were still the most common source of both air conditioning and ventilation.

Personal transportation in the early 19th century—by foot, by paddle, or by animal—very often saw the person being transported also being the one providing the locomotion. It was only when one rode an animal (horse, ox, mule, etc.), either saddled-up or in a wagon, that the need for physical strength decreased. On the other hand, the expense and labor involved in maintaining and riding a horse meant a serious commitment. The advantage to an animal over footpower or paddling, however, was that long distances could be covered with less wear and tear on humans. Late in the century, Benz of Germany invented the automobile (1886), the perfect personal transportation vehicle. While it was noteworthy, it would not be until the early 20th century that its popularity as a personal transportation vehicle would be cemented. Most people at the end of the century would continue using the same methods for personal transportation as had been in place since the beginning of the century.

Personal Security (19th century)

Personal security, which included security in personal finance, health care and safety, rested on two things in the 19th century: personal wealth and strength of community. Even then, certain amenities that were not available until the 20th century, like advanced health care and dentistry, meant that everybody, regardless of income or social status, went without adequate treatment or safeguards. With institutions such as insurance companies—and here we have to disregard long-established firms such as Lloyd's of London, which almost wholly insured maritime and property issues of a large scale—individual life or home/personal property insurance really did not feature prominently until the middle of the century. Even then, it was usually held by those with substantial income. The lower classes were fearful of insurance company methods. Those familiar with revenue generation—meaning those who had built their wealth by participating in, or sponsoring, capital ventures—better understood the machinations of such things as insurance and the stability of the companies themselves. On top of that, most people were just too poor to afford insurance.

For those with lower incomes, the support of their community, which included family, friends and neighbors, might mean the difference between ruin and survival in financial, health or property issues. Paradoxically, those in rural or small urban areas who had to rely on community support, fared better than those in large urban areas, where social cohesion was already disintegrating. Thus it was a spirit of community "barn-building" that many had to rely on to see themselves through, and even then the commitment was not always honored.

Banking and investment services mainly catered to the affluent, although most banks would take the deposits of the lower income population and honor them with a small amount of interest upon withdrawal. The real action took place with the affluent. It was with this group that banks and lenders felt comfortable that they would see a return on their loan investment. It was not until much later in the century that banks would more readily lend money to the masses for property or home purchases. Such loan applications were personally submitted to one's bank officers, who checked their ledger, then checked the loan seeker's ledger—and character—before grudgingly approving the loan. Many times, though, they did not approve it.

Investment services were fairly active, if not sophisticated, in the 19th century—their activities used mainly to sponsor commerce and trade. Early stock and bond trading was limited mostly to canal and short-line rail construction, with some trading company issues thrown in. This changed late in the century with the introduction of transoceanic telecommunications, the building of transcontinental railroads, and the financing of large manufacturing processes like steel and meat packing. With those introductions, large-scale investing was carried out on an international basis. The main financial blood sport, at least early on, was to back infrastructure improvements like toll roads (yes, even then), trading company enterprises and those few listed stocks and bonds in canals and railroads.

Health care was rudimentary, practiced by everyone from barbers to doctors, and very unscientific. Improvements were being made, but unfortunately many of those came by trial and error and at the expense of the patient. Basic operating room hygiene resembled slaughterhouse practices and contributed greatly to the demise of those caught upon the operating room table. Routine and serious illnesses were often treated with bottled elixirs that were advertised to cure everything from hangnails to hoof-and-mouth disease. Basically, they were inadvertent painkillers that relied on a generous dose of alcohol or cocaine to achieve their temporary effects. No class of humanity escaped these medical insults. The inept and incapable were practicing at all levels. Even in the cases where the physician was capable and educated, the fault lay not with the person, but with the ignorance of the era.

It was not until the second half of the century that a more formal system began to take root in medicine, pharmacology and dentistry. Advances in painless medicine and dentistry were being made. Earlier medical discoveries were being improved, new discoveries were being made and a more rigorous standard was being applied to all the health care disciplines, with the result that surgical techniques, infection control and microscopic studies were rapidly improving. Louis Pasteur discovered the pasteurizing process that helped to prevent food-borne diseases. Anesthesiology was neither discovered nor perfected in the 20th century. Narcotics had long been experimented with, but serious study was just beginning in the 19th century. As a result, many surgical operations were not without pain. No matter what, any improvements that were made trickled slowly from the originating urban centers to rural areas. The more remote the geographic location, the more it relied upon local remedies and traditional cures derived from local herbs, roots and berries. While some actually worked and would later become the basis for modern medical treatments (e.g., tree bark producing medicines and leeches for wound cleansing and circulation promotion), some were just superstition-based cures that offered no hope for improvement, the patient being happily oblivious.

Health care plans and insurance depended on the wealth of the individual and, in effect, everyone was self-insured. The pay-as-you-go plan depended on the largesse of the medical provider, with the rich getting the best medical treatment of the day (which is not saying much) and the indigent going to hospital poor wards (which says even less). Some employers provided basic on-site medical facilities or clinics, as did some municipalities, but such facilities were a rare find, offering the bare basics in medical amenities, and were always overcrowded. Once again, the community often guided the health care treatment, and the goodwill of family, friends and community neighbors made up the "insurance" that someone would take care of you. Sometimes they did not.

Physical and personal property security rested with the individual for the most part, although many urban centers had some form of police protection. Such forces were usually ill-trained, ill-equipped and ill-managed. Poorly motivated, some members were prone to loafing and moonlighting at other jobs while on duty. They were of little use to the remaining officers, whose numbers were obviously depleted by the defections, making the force less effective. Bribery was rampant. As such, both citizens in rural and urban centers were the first line of defense for the protection of their own well-being, along with that of their property. Locking mechanisms became more sophisticated and effective, due to improved steel manufacturing, design and the increased need that prompted business competition. Since home, life and property security rested with the people, many people owned weapons. A large number of weapons did double-duty as hunting pieces and as deterrents to the wild animals that raided farm stock and crops. Lynch mobs, machete-wielding crowds and others bent on murderous revenge were not unheard of in some geographical areas, especially when justice officials were few in number. Even when the officials were sufficient in number, the result might be the same.

Communications (19th century)

Education in the 19th century was elitist and of suspect quality—elitist because those of the middle and lower classes (the middle class is a misnomer for some regions, there being no middle class) rarely were afforded the opportunities to complete a significant level of schooling. Completing the lower grade curriculums was not common, finishing the higher forms or high school was obviously rarer still, and even attending, much less graduating from, college was almost unheard of. Schooling for the middle and lower classes was typified by overcrowded classrooms, few supplies, and underpaid teachers. Children dropped out of school to help on the farm or to work at jobs in order to help support the family, although it must be noted that many families did not see the validity of further education. Their station in life was fixed at a particular point, and they believed no amount of education would surmount it. In some cases they did not want it surmounted.

Those of higher social classes and means could afford education. While it varied from continent to continent, there were some similarities. Reading, writing, and arithmetic were included, plus a heavy dose of biased history and cultural education. There might have been some specialized training, although often that served as nothing more than further indoctrination in a country's social milieu and cultural comportment. Britain's civil servants and China's mandarins are two examples.

In the highest levels of education, little if anything was provided in the way of business management or practice until the mid-century, although some was offered through the US Ivy League schools and Britain's public universities (actually private institutions). It was not until the latter part of the century that these subjects really got attention. By that time the Industrial Revolution had provided a need for such education. Those of the middle and lower classes could and did attend "business colleges," which basically prepared them for clerical, secretarial and entry-level administrative positions. Rarely did these schools demand prerequisite coursework to enter, only requiring that the student pay the tuition and make an attempt to learn.

Rarely, though, were women allowed to take part in such "strenuous" education. Their educational pursuits were limited to finishing schools where important things like running a home and developing the social graces were taught.

One of the most important elements in any civilization is the postal system, ranking just below a government's treasury and military, and probably equal to its commerce or trade sector. Outside of government, the masses would probably rank it equally at number one with commerce (commerce being the driving force in obtaining food, clothing and shelter). Communications rank high because progress is impeded through ignorance. Even governments recognized this and acted accordingly. Postal systems were vastly improved in the 19th century.

As stated earlier, the incredible discovery of electricity occurred in the 19th century, with many taking part in bringing it to fruition. So many things hinged on this discovery that it outdistanced the automobile in importance, and rivaled earliest man's discovery of fire as the greatest advancement of humanity. One of its first practical uses was in the telegraph, an 1833 invention of Germany's Wilhelm Weber, C.F. Gauss and Carl Friedrich. England's Sir William Feathergill Cooke, Samuel Morse of the United States and others also participated in this development during the 1830s. Werner Siemens began hooking up Europe, while Morse attempted to do the same in North America, helped in part by former US Postal General Amos Kendall. The biggest users of the telegraph were newspapers and those in financial circles. Newspapers mushroomed, thanks both to the news-transfer provided by the telegraph and the invention and improvement of mechanically-produced paper. The typewriter made its practical debut in 1868, aiding reporters and an author who used an early model to write *The Adventures of Tom Sawyer*. Both the typewriter and the book were successes. Photography was perfected and before the end of the century, people could take their own photos, shipping the film—still encased in the camera—to George Eastman, founder of the Kodak Film Company. The telephone made its debut in the latter half of the century and made lots of headway, but it did not really take off until the 20th century. The same was true of Marconi's invention of the radio, patented in 1897 in England.

Travel and Entertainment (19th century)

In the beginning of the century, travel and entertainment were limited, even in urban areas. Early-century modes of travel relied on some form of horse- or oxen-driven locomotion. At the mid-century mark, choices of travel widened to include the locomotive, but that was a bone-jarring experience which was stifling hot in the warm months and bone-chilling cold in the winter months. Climate control consisted of rushing air mixed with smoke and cinders. Overseas travel was slow and cramped until the introduction of the screw-propeller, steam-engine ships. Then travel was faster but still cramped. Of course, there were plenty of board and card games, with the 19th century giving way to people's more playful nature. But there was little organized exercise because it was thought to be somewhat eccentric, although some did get involved. Overnight accommodations varied. There was everything from the rural tavern outpost to the mineral springs resorts. Service was always the same, terrible at the lower end and attentive at the high end.

Most entertaining was done in the home, and this applied to the rich and the poor. Music was provided by musically inclined hosts and guests. Musical instruments were brisk sellers to all classes of people, although the poor and middle class might opt for a violin, with the upper class having both the money and room for a piano. The upper class strongly supported the arts with opera, symphony and theatrical venues, and with hired bands. The rest of the masses would watch a circus or troupe of traveling actors. In the 19th century alcoholic spirits were consumed by almost everyone. So were drugs, although the packaging was different, e.g., Dr. John's Miracle Cure in a bottle. The contents were often the same—cocaine and heroin. Cafes, taverns and restaurants were staples of the century's nightlife, with nightclubs, per se, being virtually unknown. In rural areas, taverns and restaurants became one and the same. Sports began to take hold throughout the century, with football (soccer), baseball, American football, and Japan's sumo wrestling seeing their amateur status exalted or being established as professional enterprises. The Olympics made a comeback in 1896. Horse racing was still a main event both with kings and sharecroppers. And gambling survived and thrived.

The 20th Century

The early part of the 20th century saw a technological firestorm race through the world of commerce. As it whipped across the business landscape, it reduced some older industries to ashes, leaving newer ones in its wake to fill the void. These case studies highlight either management reluctance to confront technology's advance or a management that actively embraced technology, e.g., Central Leather. Central Leather manufactured the best horse and buggy accessories one could find. They once were 24th out of the 100 top American industrial firms. Unfortunately, along came the automobile. Rather than diversify, the company continued on its path—to oblivion.

In the first decade of the 20th century, AT&T was in its first year, along with the UK's Cable & Wireless, which operated the largest telecommunications system in the world, most of it with submerged cables. In addition, the 20th century saw the formation of General Electric, introduction of the escalator by Otis at the Paris World's Fair, the formation of Siemens of Germany, the US Kohler Company's introduction of improved indoor plumbing, Bayer of Germany celebrating the first anniversary of its invention of aspirin, Glaxo celebrating its first anniversary as a UK company, the formation of US Steel, Marconi transmitting his first transatlantic radio messages, the formation of Merck, the incorporation of 3M, the founding of Philip Morris, the first flight by the Wright Brothers, the first motorcycle by Harley-Davidson, the formation of the Ford Motor Company, the incorporation of FMC, the registration of Marks & Spencer of England, the establishment of Rolls-Royce, the first telegraphic transmission of photographs, the discovery and preparation of digitalis by Roche of Switzerland, Einstein's theory of relativity, the invention of rayon, the invention of neon lights, Nestlé's introduction of baby formula, the introduction of Kellogg's Corn Flakes, the formation of Royal Dutch Shell, the invention of a production method for plastics, and the introduction of the Ford Model T.

Between 1910 and 1920, we saw a process for manufacturing aluminum, the invention of synthetic rubber by Bayer of Germany, the world's first commercial air service in the United Kingdom, the first reference to the term "semiconductor," the formation of what would become IBM, the breakup of Standard Oil, the sinking of the Titanic, Henry Ford's development of the assembly line, the first traffic lights, the opening of the Panama Canal, World War I, the formation of Boeing, the establishment of Electrolux, the formation of Rockwell, and the founding of KLM Airlines.

The 1920s brought the establishment of the League of Nations, the formation of FINA, the first vaccine for tuberculosis, Johnson & Johnson's Band-Aid, the invention of refrigerators in Sweden, Fiat's new stress-bearing body, sound films, the formation of the BBC, the invention of television, the first electric shaver by Schick, the first portable radio, Marlboro cigarettes, the formation of Caterpillar, Scotch masking tape by 3M, the first Otis automatic elevators, the formation of Lufthansa Airlines in Germany, the first talking film, the first successful television transmission by AT&T, Lindbergh's Spirit of St. Louis, transatlantic telephone service between the United States and Europe by AT&T, the first color films, the discovery of penicillin by British scientist Alexander Fleming, and the Great Depression.

The 1930s brought 3M's scotch tape, Disney's Mickey Mouse, Motorola's practical auto radio, the invention of the jet engine by Frank Whittle of England, the completion of the Empire State Building, the introduction of brand management at Procter & Gamble, Adolph Hitler as Chancellor of Germany, the first public telex networks by Siemens of Germany, radio telephone service between the United States and Tokyo by AT&T, the first 35mm camera by Canon, the tape recorder by AEG of Germany, the first electric typewriter by IBM, the formation of British Airways, the DC-3 airplane by Douglas Aircraft, the invention of polyurethane chemistry by Bayer, the Disney film *Snow White and the Seven Dwarfs*, General Electric's development of the fluorescent lamp, the invention of the ballpoint pen by Bird of Hungary, the construction of an audio oscillator by Bill Hewlett and Dave Packard in their garage, Nestlé's instant coffee, the formation of Volkswagen in Germany, the introduction of nylon, General Electric's isolation of Uranium 235, the first turbojet-powered aircraft in Germany, and the beginning of World War II.

The 1940s brought Motorola's hand-held two-way radio, the Boeing B-17 Flying Fortress, the Volkswagen Beetle, the first nuclear chain reaction by Enrico Fermi, electrical tape by 3M, the first atomic bomb, the end of World War II, the establishment of the United Nations, the ENIAC computer by the Remington Rand Corporation, nuclear power, tubeless tires by B.F. Goodrich, Chuck Yeager's breaking of the sound barrier, the Marshall Plan, the 33 1/3 record by Columbia Records, the transistor, the introduction of nonwoven fabric by 3M, the anesthetic Xylocaine by Astra of Sweden, Velcro produced by de Mestral of Switzerland, the French bikini, the photograph of the gene, the discovery of Cortisone, and the invention of the Xerox copier.

The 1950s brought the Korean War, color TV, the death of Stalin, the end of the Korean War, the isolation of the first antibiotic (Cephalosporin C) at Oxford University, the first transistor radio by Sony, video tape by 3M, the formation of McDonald's, the Marlboro cowboy, pagers by Motorola, Canon's 8mm cinecamera, the USSR's Sputnik I, the formation of the European Common Market, the Fortran programming language, the Boeing 707 jet, the first integrated circuit by Texas Instruments, stereo records, the plain paper copier by Xerox, and Mattel's Barbie doll.

The 1960s saw the invention of the laser, USSR's Yuri Gagarin as the first man into space, the building of the Berlin Wall, the first American troops in Vietnam, the first Wal-Mart store, the launching of Telstar I (the first commercial communications satellite), the assassination of John F. Kennedy, the self-cleaning oven, the introduction of Valium by Roche, the Boeing 727, the compact cassette by Philips, the IBM 360 mainframe computer, the formation of Nike, the first electronic calculator by Canon, 8-track tape players by Motorola, RCA and Ford, the Boeing 737 and 747 aircraft, the first heart transplant, the first hand-held calculator by Texas Instruments, the IBM System/3 computer, the Internet, and the first man on the moon.

The 1970s brought gene synthesis, the McDonnell Douglas DC-10 aircraft, the videocassette recorder by Philips, 11 Israeli athletes killed at the Olympic Games in Munich, the OPEC oil embargo, the Xerox color copier, universal product codes on products, the formation of

Federal Express, the end of the Vietnam War, the introduction of automatic teller machines, the Viking I landing on Mars, the founding of Apple by Steve Wozniak and Steve Jobs, Concorde supersonic service by British Airways and Air France, the 35mm SLR camera by Canon, IBM's System/34, Glaxo's introduction of Zantac for ulcers, IBM's electronic typewriters with microprocesors, the Xerox Ethernet local area network and information processing system (PC), the first 16-bit microprocessor by Motorola, VisiCalc's spreadsheet software, and the demonstration of the first compact disc (CD) by Philips and Sony.

The 1980s brought 3M's yellow Post-it Notes, CNN, photographs of Saturn taken by Voyager I, the space shuttle Columbia's successful launch into space, the IBM PC, MTV, Microsoft Windows software, Chrysler's minivan, the Apple Macintosh, the AT&T breakup, the Hewlett-Packard LaserJet II printer, 3M's refastenable tapes for disposable diapers, Coca-Cola's Coke (then "New Coke," then "Classic Coke"), the Chernobyl nuclear plant disaster, the formation of Sprint, the Tiananmen Square massacre in Beijing, China, and the fall of the Berlin Wall.

The 1990s brought a reunified Germany, a color version of the HP LaserJet printer, the Persian Gulf War, the start of the unification of Europe, the introduction of Lotus Notes software, the free distribution of Java™ networking software, and the opening of the Eurotunnel.

Business prior to the 20th century was much like a small infant—just beginning to become aware, to discover new things. The 20th century saw business progress through childhood and, toward the end of the century, into its "adolescent stage."

Food

The early 20th century saw some geographic regions sprout a sophisticated food system, with all the elements popping up like some sort of perfect-weather wheat. Innovations conceived and implemented in the 19th century were improved in the 20th century. In Europe and the United States, technology and science played a big part in everything from hybrid seed advances to satellite navigation for farming. Yet, in other parts of the world, the whole cultivate-harvest-storage-and-distribution system moved no faster than the oxen that had traditionally been used for food cultivation.

The United States developed most quickly in adapting technology to food processing, with an accelerated marketing focus accompanying those hard-science advances. Europe lagged behind only minutely, bowing slightly to the effects of a longer history and tradition. The Asia/Pacific region, on the other hand, showed significant reluctance to join the global food fight. And while it was true that urban areas have traditionally reflected the food sector's advances most readily, with rural areas being laggards, the Asia/Pacific region was noteworthy because rural ways have persisted long and extensively even within the cities. It appeared to be a mixture of politics, culture and a lack of capital that caused the Asia/Pacific region to stagnate.

As the United States, and quite often Europe, became populated with motorized John Deere tractors, McCormick reapers and automatic milking machines, the Asia/Pacific region stayed mired in old ways. As Birdseye's frozen foods found shelf space on the ever-evolving ice box/electric refrigerator, Asian meals, especially early in the century, were harvested or purchased the day they were prepared. This is not to say people did not frequent individual specialty shops, such as the butcher, baker, and local grocer, but the number of supermarkets stocked with convenience and packaged goods in Asia could not hold a candle to what was going on in North America and Europe. While North Americans and Europeans might indulge in a quick cup of Nescafé coffee, Asians made theirs from scratch, for the most part. The self-serve grocery shops, and then the introduction of supermarkets, made significant inroads in the United States and Europe. As individual supermarkets became homogenized store chains, individual produce stands, general stores, and mom-and-pop retail food shops began to wane. They operated on razor-thin margins, with the more successful small independents leveraging what promotion cache they had through shrewd niche marketing. But even there they saw competition from the mini-marts and convenience stores. These forms of food marketing are readily seen in the cities and large towns of the Asia/Pacific region now, although much of the rural areas continue the same system they had 100 years ago— open air markets and small general stores.

Fast-food operations made their debut in the 20th century. An American innovation, the fast-food industry relied not on the taste of the food, but on peripheral benefits or motivations—convenience, fun, and quality standards, if not taste. Franchised to optimize growth, it fueled the corporate effort and allowed entrenchment before competitors could respond. The concept branched out globally with companies like McDonald's and Burger King.

Marketing and advertising let everyone know that "Wonder Bread builds bodies in 12 ways." In the 19th century you needed bread. In the 20th century you needed Wonder Bread. Why? Because not only would it fill your stomach, but it had ancillary benefits, not the least of which were the selling points it provided marketers. And while many 19th century products had mottoes or promotional taglines, none were the beneficiary of complete advertising campaigns carried through an assortment of media such as radio and television. Whereas 19th century products were promoted, 20th century products were marketed, and heavily. In fact, marketing as a formal discipline of academic study got its start in 1902 when courses were offered at several American universities. By the following decade it had become a major field of study. However, it did not reach its zenith until after World War II, and even the Asia/Pacific region felt its effects, though less so than the rest of the world.

As the century drew to a close, bio-engineered foodstuffs began to appear, while paradoxically stores sprung up touting the organic naturalness of their foods. Food was seen more and more in the context of diet and health. Yet the sheer eating experience, in which taste and/or the eating environment play a large role, was also on the rise. Food was no longer just subsistence. It was no longer on the list of basic human needs. It was a multifaceted entity that drove social, political, business and cultural aspects way beyond the old war-for-bread and personal pride once taken in national cuisine—a stark contrast to Third World countries with wrecked economies, rudimentary infrastructures and political strife. There, the cultivation, storage, and distribution systems were locked into the local variety of commerce—the system was basically ground-to-mouth, the surplus, if any, sold to other locals.

Clothing

The beginning of the 20th century saw a proliferation of large retail operations throughout the world. The fledgling department stores with tentatively established branch stores in a few select locations were now mushrooming. The flagship stores grew larger, and the number of branch stores multiplied. Economies of scale were now understood almost universally, both by those who employed the business tactic and by those who were the recipients of its effects. Those recipients included the customer, who saw a vast quantity of goods in a central location at lower prices than the specialty and niche shops offered.

More formal credit arrangements began to occur, and the terms were easier to meet, even if the interest payments were not. Revolving charge cards and credit cards facilitated even more consumer credit capabilities, a system laid neatly on top of the already existing credit system. The marketing became more focused, disciplined and pervasive. Seasonal changes and holidays were events that spurred large marketing efforts and advertising campaigns. In the past, the seasons had been just acts of nature that prompted consumers to make sure they had appropriate clothing for the climate. Style had been a low priority, except for those in the wealthy class. Now, styles changed more rapidly, and people of all classes began to take them more seriously. The milestone of fashion controversy—the height of hemlines—set tongues wagging with the flapper era in the 1920s and they have not stopped moving since—the hemlines or the tongues. This is no mere casual development. It indicates the evolution of consumer thinking.

Once fabric quality, a garment's craftsmanship and price had been the benchmarks of good clothing, at least for most people. Now style played a critical role in consumer purchases. With that, France's influential couture houses become even more so, their power to move styles gaining momentum as the century moved on. This was so until, inexplicably, their influence became more tepid and weak in the late 1980s and early 1990s. The result seemed to be an undercurrent of American fashions, with dashes of London's occasional offerings, undermining the usual prominence of Paris. There were also hints that the women entering the workplace in large numbers for the first time had produced a backlash. "Do not tell us what to wear anymore," they said. "We will tell you what to make, and then maybe we will wear it." It was not that fashion was dead. It was just that it was coming from many different sources now, and its prestige was measured in different ways. Levi's and a pair of Nikes, decidedly not high-fashion, became fashion—the world over. While America may dictate an increasing number of the fashion trends, it does not produce the fashions anymore. More and more clothing is being manufactured in the Asia/Pacific region. Cheap labor, textiles and overseas transportation make Asian operations almost unbeatable.

Synthetic fabrics were introduced, with nylon being the most noteworthy and polyester the most notorious. Regardless, synthetics added another dimension to clothing. Clothes, once the domain of nature and farming through the fibers and furs they produced, were now a niche for the chemical industry. Another "synthesis" revolution was the discount retail store. Although E.J. Korvette's was generally regarded as the first in the world to completely and extensively embrace the concept, it was not new. The UK's Marks & Spencer originated with "everyday low prices," and Woolworth, which later became K-Mart, was also founded on selling inexpensive goods. The most successful of the discounters in the 20th century was to be Wal-Mart, which ranked 17 in the *Business Week Global 1000* late in the century. Daiei, called the Wal-Mart of Japan, experienced similar success.

Another concept that appeared to be new, but which began with 1800s retailing, was the specialty shop. The marketing force for the 20th century was market segmentation in which specific price or fashion niches were aggressively exploited and expanded. In the 1800s and early 1900s specialty shops were founded on a merchant's familiarity or expertise with the products sold, or because they had access to particular types of products. In the mid to later 1900s, specialty shops were the result of market research showing growth potential, company expansion or diversification programs looking for the next conquest, with competitive analysis having identified a segment filled with weak competitors.

Shelter and Personal Transportation

The influx of former rural dwellers into cities continued into the 20th century. Most pronounced in North America and Europe, it was also a significant phenomenon even in the Asia/Pacific region. Cities grown to their city limits began pouring people out to the suburbs. In some locations this concentric ring of people was made up of the affluent; in others, it was the site of wretched slums. It was often considered prime real estate for various reasons. For the affluent it was often a desire to escape some aspect of the city such as overcrowding. For the poor it may have been because it was the location of a remote city garbage dump, which offered opportunities for scavenging and, hence, a livelihood.

In the more progressive and technologically advanced countries, suburbia was the result of the automobile. While suburbs existed even in the 19th century—transportation evolving from horse-drawn wagons and carriages to electric trolley systems—it was not until the mass production and popularization of the car that a convenient and reliable means of transportation from cities to outlying areas was provided. Suburbia responded with booming growth. The early auto's biggest champion was probably Henry Ford. His production line assembly methods drastically cut costs and lowered prices. By locating plants throughout the world, his autos could be found in cities and in the rural areas, from the Upper Peninsula of Michigan to the Ural Mountains. Owners used the vehicles not only for personal transportation, but for a myriad of other reasons. Belts and other hardware were hooked up to the car's powertrain for use in running everything from buzzsaws to hayloft loading equipment. Only electricity, and possibly the computer (which ironically needs electricity to function), have had as much impact on humankind in modern times.

In many less advanced areas of the world, transportation meant animal transportation, public transportation vehicles like buses or village trucks, water transport (boats, canoes or other skiff-type vessels), trains and motorbikes. The infrastructure to support these modes of transportation—except for the waterways—was usually minimal and almost impassable during inclement weather. Many times employment was local anyway, so the need for more advanced or reliable means of transportation was not essential, though would be welcomed. Unfortunately, with many national economies, rural employment was dismal or nonexistent, forcing the workers to make attempts at commuting further and further in order to gain employment.

The homes in both city and suburb were the subject of more modern construction techniques from balloon framing—in which a skeleton of wood studs is erected and a sheathing of wood planks or slats fastened to that—to a plethora of modern hardware snaking throughout the subflooring of the house or inside the walls. Even brick homes were now available to lower income families, a material once used almost exclusively for mid- to upper-class homes. Electricity was an urban and rural standard in North America and Europe in the 20th century. In the

Asia/Pacific region, the urban areas were wired and some rural areas received power. In those areas it was just as common to see nonelectrical means of illumination and power. Even in North America and Europe, in 1950 there were still millions of homes without electricity, although almost every home had electricity at the end of the century.

Contemporary plumbing was a step away from the almost universal implementation seen in electricity. While electricity can truly be promoted as one of humankind's greatest achievements, improved plumbing can be credited with practical benefits. Whereas electricity improved lives, indoor plumbing and its associated sewage disposal system saved lives. Numerous life-threatening diseases were borne by the untreated sewage produced by inadequate plumbing and nonexistent sewage treatment throughout the centuries. Epidemics would routinely break out and kill hundreds and thousands of people. Even upscale locations were prone to contamination of their water sources from ill-informed plumbing practices. Outbreaks still occur today, almost always in less developed areas of the world where today's plumbing standards and methods are not widely practiced. Certainly plumbing is standard in the urban and rural areas of North America and Europe, but in the Asia/Pacific region, the greatest concentration of modern plumbing is in the urban areas, with rural areas poorly integrated and prone to outbreak of diseases from substandard or nonexistent systems.

Heating, air conditioning and modern ventilation followed the same pattern as plumbing. In the more progressive areas, heating systems were efficiently served by gas, oil or electric furnaces. Where needed, air conditioning, too, was modern and effective. In less developed countries, heating was rudimentary if outside a tropical zone and nonexistent in tropical zones. The introduction of reliable air conditioning opened areas to population migration and growth because people could now find relief from extremely high temperatures.

In the industrialized countries, homes were very often built by trained tradespersons using manufactured materials that had been standardized. Trade unions very often governed these workers and lobbied for construction standards and methods. Municipal zoning and construction laws also added to the standardization. All of this added up to an ad hoc system that, for the most part, advanced improvements at a steady pace. In the less progressive areas, home-building was still the result of the prospective owner and contributions from friends and family who could be persuaded to take part. While a few manufactured items such as glass, piping and some framing materials might be used, nothing was really standardized, and real estate development was haphazard. This was not so much a lack of ambition on the part of the people or the governments, as much as it was a seeming underlying agreement that other issues were more important, such as having a roof that does not leak over your head.

Whereas once hand-driven mechanical egg-beaters were modern conveniences, motorized beaters became the norm. Even those were replaced to some degree by the microwave oven, which allowed fast cooking of ready-to-eat foods. However, there were still areas in the Asia/Pacific region where meals, and the ingredients used to prepare them, were procured and prepared that day. This is also practiced in Europe and North America, but to a lesser degree. In Asia/Pacific rural areas, daily forays to local markets and one's personal garden provided the foodstuffs, which would then be prepared by hand-powered utensils and cooked in fireplaces or basic stoves fired with wood or canned fuels.

Personal Security

On many continents even the lower classes were now becoming participants in the investing, banking and insurance industries. And industries they were. Once small, elite and exclusive in nature, they became more accessible to populations at large. Although at first all of these sectors were largely driven by institutional forces—international trade, the need for manufacturing capital, infrastructure advancement, and monetary machinations—business had finally found the consumer. As the century progressed, simple mortgage loans, volatile investing margins, rudimentary auto insurance policies, term life insurance, and crude forms of health insurance were all being offered to the masses. The offerings were prevalent more on some continents—North America and Europe—less so on others—always more accessible to urban dwellers than to rural ones. Nonetheless, more and more people were allowed to participate. This was the result of seeing business in a new light: money was never tainted by its previous owner. Rich man, poor man, it was all the same. There was some backlash with socialist revolutions and communist disinvolvement, but enough of the world participated that capitalism and commerce became a global force.

In the 20th century more and more people began to participate in the banking system, and although there were many recessions and some depressions, it was probably the most widely utilized form of financial security in place globally. Even if the common man or woman never invested in a stock or bond, bought insurance, sought legal or tax advice, or mortgaged a home, there was still a good chance they saved their money in some type of banking institution. The principles of accounting took form early in the 20th century, and by 1920, it was an established discipline with standards and accepted procedures. Whereas tax consultation was a privilege once only afforded by the rich, enlightened practices such as accounting and tax planning were now enjoyed by the financially comfortable in North America, Europe and the Asia/Pacific region.

Health care and its related industries were in their renaissance in the 20th century. While not everyone was adequately assured of attentive medical service, more and more people did enjoy improved health care. Government agencies charged with managing medical treatment proliferated; private sector health care plans—whether contracted individually or through one's employer—multiplied and improved in their coverage and scope. A scourge at the beginning of the century—high infant and child mortality rates—was attacked by formal and informal medical agendas. The death rates were reduced in the industrialized countries. The growth of unions produced a benefit as great as increased wages—medical coverage for employees and their families. With the establishment of the United Nations and the World Health Organization, countries began to work together—tentatively—to attack chronic health problems and suppress disease. A global community took shape. Plague outbreaks and disasters were met more often with ad hoc health groups mobilizing to combat those periodic problems. Rural areas, especially in less progressive countries, still lagged behind the urban areas, and even urban areas in less medically advanced countries suffered from an inadequate and aging health system. Health care coverage advanced tremendously in the 20th century, but as for providing one of the "basic needs" in life, it was still thin in many spots.

Curie discovered radium in 1898, and the x-ray showed up early in the 20th century. When polio ravaged populations, Salk and others came through with polio-fighting drugs. Wars tore at bodies, and plasma was produced for their mending. Simple pneumonia killed indiscriminately; penicillin was devised to strike back.

Open-heart surgery, organ transplants, and kidney dialysis all helped to prevent what once would have automatically spelled death. The 20th century was amazing in the number of pure medical advances made. True, there are still many forms of cancer that are deadly and extremely tough to eradicate, and AIDs has been relentless in its death pursuit, but it is not inconceivable that the 21st century will produce encouraging discoveries. But the 20th century also produced some unsettling dichotomies. The tissue from aborted fetuses has medical uses. Should it be used? Then there is abortion itself and all the issues it has raised. The accusation that organ harvesting was taking place among the poor in less developed countries was shocking in its concept. Shock therapy was established, renounced and re-introduced—it caused much debate. The subject of euthanasia refused to die down, and the controversy continues—do we have the right to pull the plug on the terminally ill? Some want to know if anyone has the right to force them to live.

The science of medicine, while advancing rapidly in the 20th century, appeared to move forward at times and then regress. However, a look at history shows uneven gyrations to be true of all disciplines. We really have not even begun to see the implications and issues associated with biotechnology, which was in its infancy at the end of the century. Gene splicing, gene alteration, and gene duplication are concepts that only recently have begun to emerge. And that is just the tip of the DNA chain of future events.

While maybe not an exactly humorous phenomenon, 20th centurions still had their elixirs and cures-in-a-bottle. Pills, syrups and sprays were all used to dispense in-home cures for whatever ailment. For the most part, alcohol played much less of a role in home medicines than in the 19th century (and heroin and cocaine became prescription-only). Surprisingly, some over-the-counter remedies did still contain alcohol, even amid controversies regarding health benefits/risks of alcohol consumption. More importantly, the 20th century's take-home medicines represented a more sophisticated and responsible drug industry. Real efforts were made to discover chemical compounds that were both safe and effective. Rigorous clinical testing was done not only on prescription pharmaceuticals, but also with over-the-counter remedies. Paradoxically, certain prescription-only drugs were dispensed without doctors' orders at the end of the century. Their safeness ascertained, it was deemed acceptable to allow a measured amount of self-doctoring. Of course, little of this was reaching less developed regions of the world where a head cold was of little consequence when people still suffered from rickets.

A more holistic outlook toward health was taken in the 20th century, although it was fraught with contradictions. During the early 20th century, red meat was good; in the late 20th century, red meat was bad, except for very lean cuts. Eggs contained cholesterol and were bad for your heart, said the studies. Later studies said eggs in moderation were OK. Alcohol was bad for your liver, unless it was a glass of red wine at dinner. Then it was deemed good for your heart. Low-fat, low-salt, low-taste products were meant to ensure a healthy diet, if not satisfy the palate. Unfortunately, the content of sugar went up. More sugar in the liver means more cholesterol production, so even the fat-free and low-fat products came under fire. The use of vitamin supplements increased, particularly in North America and Europe, as people tried to balance diet with health. And the use of herbs and herb-based medicines increased as people tried to balance the scientific with the natural. People began to realize that nature was the basis of all science and that maybe it was time to return to those roots.

In many parts of the world, personal and home security still relied on guns and protective neighbors. Sometimes it came down to just the guns. And this approach was not just isolated to Third World countries, as the United States knew so well. Even in regions where guns were less likely to be encountered, there had been a growth market for security devices. Homes and cars were equipped with high-tech crime-deterrent systems. Home motion and sound detection devices that automatically place a warning call to private security services, and sometimes even the local police station, would let the authorities know that something was amiss. Their installation became common. Private communities where the affluent could reside without intrusion had private security officers manning the gates. This was not new, but it was more prevalent in the 20th century than in the 19th century. Pepper and chemical sprays could be carried in purses and pockets, and they were. Crime was on the rise in all regions, or least there was a very strong perception that it was on the rise.

There was a certain irony during the latter half of the 20th century. It became the age of communications and information, but many were leery of talking about it with just anyone. Communications and information were commodities, just like wheat. They were cultivated, harvested, stored, distributed, sold and bought. And people did not like to have these entities pilfered, stolen, manipulated and tainted. Safeguards against such abuses were developed; some were successful, some not. Computers have passwords, signals can be scrambled, and cellular phones can be picked up by nursery room monitors and vice versa; yet communications were so widespread and complex that they were easily electronically collected, stored, tabulated, categorized, transferred and sold to others so consumers could be identified, segmented and marketed to. The problem is that there are few controls over the nature of information traded because individual rights were relinquished in an effort to be heard.

Communications

Education in the early 20th century made incredible advances in the industrialized countries, while preserving the status quo in the lesser developed nations. True public schooling evolved in North America and Europe, with governments encouraging people to keep children in school. By the end of the century, education in these regions was not only encouraged, but mandated. But in a surprising development, many regions in the Asia/Pacific region not only gained on the educational front, but overtook their friends in the West. This surge to educate began at mid-century and accelerated until the end of the century. Rigorous education was seen not only as nice, but absolutely necessary if a particular country wanted to improve its standard of living or at least remain competitive. And it was not just reserved for the elite, because to truly compete, the entire population had to make a mental contribution to the effort. The classic curriculum was still taught, but more emphasis was placed on science and math than had been previously. There was also greater emphasis given to business, as well as science and technology at the college level, so much so that accounting, management, engineering, science and computer disciplines muscled out the classic studies in the humanities for the attention of students. Education meant jobs, even on the farm. Women entered universities in large numbers starting mid-century, and they never looked back.

Regular wireless messages were being sent across the ocean before 1910, and by the 1920s there were broadcast transmissions of popular radio programs. The latest in news, sports, culture and entertainment was made available and for a while, without commercials. Television saw its first practical TV set in the late 1930s, the result of experiments conducted in Europe in the 1920s, but World War II halted further development. At the war's end, the industry took off, the invention capturing audio and video transmissions—and everyone's imagination— in one device. In the United States a whole culture soon began to evolve around it, and US programming was exported.

Telephones were now common everywhere, and if not always found in individual homes, were usually available close by. Their absence was most often due to geographical obstacles such as mountains or deserts, and there they were lacking only at the highest elevations and across the most barren stretches. Soon one could call around the world, admittedly with some trial and error. Physically transported communications also improved immensely. DHL, UPS and Federal Express were just a few of the bigger names who ensured that hardcopy communication made it to destinations quickly.

This was the century for true advancement of civilization. Instant cameras, dry plain paper copier machines, overnight courier, the fax, teleconferencing, cellular phones, satellite communications, camcorders and e-mail all sped the communications age, captured it for prosperity, or both. What was once considered a luxury—fast, efficient communi-cations—was now an accepted and expected norm. A component in many of those communications systems was often the transistor, and its advanced counterpart, the printed circuit. Both items were incorporated into the computer, the 20th century's biggest innovation (which played off the 19th century's biggest applied discovery, electricity). Once a space-consuming, vacuum-tube monster that tended to overheat, it was now sleek enough to fit in a watch. Its capabilities impressive, its potential awe-inspiring, the computer went from computing artillery ballistics to putting a man on the moon.

The computer was so impressive because of its many possibilities. You could create a report while communicating with a colleague in another country. Composing the written commentary together and adding graphics to bring the numbers to life, you and your co-worker could receive information from every part of your organization in any part of the world. Your results could then be immediately transferred to others in the company. Computers were used in every conceivable sector of society. The recently introduced bio-tech tomato is one example. The tomato's genetic makeup had been researched on a computer; the farmer growing it probably used everything from computer-generated spreadsheets and planting plats, while the produce distributor stored, transported and tracked the tomato using computers. When the supermarket received and stocked the tomato, it used computers to do it. Then it was computer-scanned when it was sold at the store. It arrived home in a computer-aided car where a computer opened the garage door. A personal-finance computer program tracked the grocery bill, thus extending the computer chain again. With the tomato pureed and heated in the microwave, the chain continued. The 20th century computer technology influenced nearly every aspect of life.

Travel and Entertainment

Means of travel were vastly improved in the 20th century. Trains were engineered increasingly for comfort. Since they could go longer distances without refueling or watering, they included kitchens and dining cars to satisfy the palate. Of course, with the advent of commercial air travel in the 1920s, their demise as the main mode of extended travel was inevitable. The improving automobile also helped to sink their fate.

Ship travel also saw its operations and offerings improve, but once again transoceanic planes sealed its fate, this time without assistance from the auto. And where to go? Well, international travel was no longer confined to intermittent jaunts by the rich and once-in-a-lifetime trips by the poor (usually for immigration purposes, these trips more closely resembled the wooden-hull boat travel of the 1800s). You could gamble in Monte Carlo or Las Vegas, see wonders of nature once limited to photos in magazines, and on every continent, even the Antarctic. Disney World was available in three host languages. Hotels and resorts ran the gamut from everyday-low-priced to extremely expensive accommodations.

Sure, there was still home entertainment. Games were now on CD-ROM. If not that, they were always available with Nintendo, Sega, or

Sony Playstation video games. There were plenty of computer games. How about a little virtual reality gunfight at a local arcade?

For nightlife there was everything under the sun—cocktails, ballroom dancing, disco, karaoke, clubs, restaurants, cafes, ginmill bars, pubs, microbreweries, country-western, blues, jazz and more. It was enough to make your head spin if you really indulged.

Cuisines crossed oceans. Mexican, Thai, Indian, French, Italian, Chinese, Japanese and American food became available everywhere. So did music. With American rock-and-roll and "the British invasion," even Communist kids took note. And there was the old standby, symphonic concerts, with a hundred or so of the best tuxedo-clad musicians traveling the world to put on a concert anywhere. No concert nearby? Well, there was always that stereo or quadraphonic equipment. You could close your eyes and the digitally reproduced music would duplicate the sound of a live concert.

Sports went professional in the 20th century. Once an amateur endeavor undertaken by the monied elite in their spare time, it was now a business whose games were played by professional athletes. And sports became professional internationally.

- ☛ Football (soccer): All continents

- ☛ Baseball: Asia/Pacific, South America, Central America and North America

- ☛ American Football: United States and Canada

- ☛ Basketball: United States, Europe and Japan

- ☛ Volleyball: South America, Central America, North America, Europe, and the Asia/Pacific region

Sports became a trade function with exports and imports. In some sports only so many foreign players may be allowed on one team, the foreign players proving so much more skillful than the natives there was a tariff on their import. On top of that, there were nationalist sports that stayed home and prospered financially.

Fitness became more prevalent, but its popularity was mainly concentrated in certain locales, such as the urban areas of the Asia/Pacific region, Europe and especially the United States, where it was practiced even in the rural areas. Less developed countries had little need for it, their exercise usually occurring through job labor or in the search for food. Aerobic exercise was at the heart of the movement, with more and more people looking to live up to actuary chart standards.

Ironically, recreational drug use was up, too. Marijuana, cocaine, heroin, opium, hallucinogenics, methamphetamines, and all sorts of derivatives could be found in every country. In fact, it was a bigger business than that of fitness. Mimicking the operating standards of any industry or business, it often found itself working hand-in-hand with everybody from consumers to governments. The only major difference between the drug industry and legitimate industries came in an area thought to be essential to doing business: Marketing—it is all word-of-mouth in the illicit drug industry.

☛ ☛ ☛ ☛ ☛ ☛ ☛ ☛

"This earth of ours came a long way in the last 200 years," said the old man. "Business and competition was in its childhood in the 19th century. The Industrial Revolution and most of the original discoveries were born in Europe. Americans took their cue and made many discoveries of their own, especially in television, computers, advanced communications and entertainment. Americans then contributed the business concepts of ENTREPRENEURSHIP, MARKETS, MARKETING, and COMPETITION. Companies in the Asia/Pacific region then took their cue from the Americans. They took products, particularly electronic services and cars, and made them better. They took the American business concepts and applied them—in America and around the world. At the end of the 20th century, North America and Europe were taking their cue from Japan."

"The 20th century can be characterized as adolescence. The child companies had grown into their teenage years. These adolescent companies desired to be independent. Like typical teenagers, they were also obnoxious, desired to have their own way on everything, and often cheated in games. As a result, competition was fierce and bloody at times. Hostile takeovers were not uncommon. Using marketing muscle to force products to market was a daily occurrence. Squeezing suppliers into razor thin profit margins was commonly practiced. Competition came to be thought of as war. Companies believed they were fighting battles in the marketplace. They believed that winning was necessary, no matter what the cost. Many business decisions were being made, not on a logical and systematic review of information, but based on emotion. Did they get their own way? Yes. Did they win in the marketplace? Maybe."

"The business evolution and revolution will continue, and as we enter the 21st century, it appears that businesses will reach adulthood. Will this mean more competition? Or less? If you use the human analogy, younger people tend to be more competitive than older people. This might suggest less 'competition' and more 'cooperation.'"

"So, which companies REALLY made a difference in the 20th century, and what can we learn from them?" the old man wondered.

CHAPTER 6

COMPANIES THAT HAVE MADE A DIFFERENCE
IN THE 20TH CENTURY

The old man's brain hurt, jammed as it was with 200 years of information—and a light bulb that had gone on in his head. "That's it—that's why companies got big!" thought the old man. "Only big companies could reach all those people with what they needed—and wanted. They used to call them big, slow, and lumbering, and sure to die," grumped the old man. He said it with a snort that showed he thought otherwise now.

"Big, slow and lumbering. When compared to their quicksilver small cousins, it rings true. But it also rings hollow. A business world without large companies is akin to a group of suburbs without a big city nearby. And although the big players have faltered at times—some very recently—they will survive for the most part. Why? Because of economies of scale, in which large projects demand large resources. Add to that capitalization that can absorb failed endeavors and expensive write-offs. And even in downsizing times, the big companies still have large pools of employees where they can go fishing for new ideas."

"IBM. Big Blue. Now that was a 20th century company!" The old man reflected on the IBM stock he had purchased after World War II. He was indeed a comfortable retiree today as a result of that investment. But there were other companies equally, if not more, impressive. Let's look at the list.

Europe	ABB—Switzerland/Sweden
	Bayer—Germany
	Daimler-Benz—Germany
	Electrolux—Sweden
	Glaxo-Wellcome—UK
	Hoechst—Germany
	Inchcape—UK
	Nestlé—Switzerland
	Philips—The Netherlands
	Renault—France
	Roche—Switzerland
	Royal Dutch Shell—The Netherlands/UK
	Siemens—Germany
	Unilever—The Netherlands/UK
	Volkswagen—Germany
North America	AT&T
	Boeing
	Disney
	General Electric
	Hewlett-Packard
	IBM
	Intel
	Johnson & Johnson
	3M
	McDonald's
	Motorola
	Northern Telecom
	Procter & Gamble
	Sprint
	UPS
	Whirlpool
	Xerox
Asia/Pacific	Canon—Japan
	Daewoo—Korea
	Evergreen—Taiwan
	Fuji—Japan
	Hyundai—South Korea
	Matsushita—Japan
	Mitsubishi—Japan
	Singapore Airlines—Singapore
	Sony—Japan
	Toyota—Japan

Europe

ABB Asea Brown Boveri (Switzerland/Sweden)

ABB was born because two big competitors decided to cooperate and build an entrepreneurial giant. Their industry: heavy-electrical and power-generation markets. ABB was a 50-50 merger between ASEA of Sweden and Brown Boveri of Switzerland. Much of ABB's business success since the merger can be attributed to its CEO, Percy Barnevik, who has combined a command and control management philosophy with marketing, technology and entrepreneurial spirit. Operationally, the company uses the matrix form of management, a bureaucratic system that features a series of contortionist's reporting lines. In it, a manager reports to a geographical superior as well as a superior for function or product. In spite of its rigid and formal bureaucracy, Barnevik claims that innovation, creativity and initiative are alive and well. What sharpens an otherwise dull edge is the nimbleness of over 1,300 small independent entities. Each independent entity consists of a very controllable number of employees, usually under 200 each. ABB has almost 5,000 profit centers in all. While it is still too early to tell for sure, ABB does appear to be prepared for the long term. In acquisition mode, they have targeted the strongest competitors in each market. The company wants to expand globally, although the short-term growth focus seems to be on Eastern Europe. When the Iron Curtain finally came down, ABB jumped in with both feet, gobbling up over 50 companies in over a dozen Eastern European countries. And they are not finished. Look for ABB to be around at the end of the 21st century.

Bayer AG (Germany)

Bayer is a global player with muscle. Its institutional resilience in the face of four wars is similar to the properties of synthetic rubber (which Bayer was the first to make). One example is Bayer aspirin, invented in 1899, lost in the first world war, and then repurchased in the early 1990s for US$1 billion. Bayer is an example of a company that not only understands the concept of turning R&D advances into commercial entities, but also has the managerial skills and strategic insights to pull it off. That is very important. It has long been an international player with operating companies in dozens of countries and sales that are derived mainly from outside of Germany. The company's bottom line success, though, is R&D. Historically, it has been the lifeblood of the company. This resilient company will continue to be on the charts in the 21st century.

Daimler-Benz (Germany)

Here is a company that introduced a product that was nothing less than revolutionary. The use of the word "revolutionary" is common now, but it is used here with all the impact it originally held. Even in light of that, revolutionary was the minimum effect this product has had on the world. In fact, along with electricity, the introduction of telecommunications, the computer, and possibly the railroad engine, this product is evolutionary. The product is the automobile, the successful wedding of the combustion engine and a free-roaming land transportation vehicle. For 100 years, starting in 1886, almost all of the company's efforts were concentrated in automotive products. After that they embarked on an acquisition strategy and bought companies that made aircraft components, heavy-vehicle engines, aerospace products and diversified electronics. But it is the automobile for which they are best known and respected, because not only did the company patent the world's first auto (Carl Benz, 1886), but it has perfected it. The Mercedes-Benz automobile is a symbol of quality engineering the world over. Daimler engines, and later Daimler-Benz engines, were engineering marvels that found use in early autos, airplanes and boats. Many of the implements of war used by the German army in World War II were made by Daimler-Benz, and they were the wonder of the Allies who admired their design and power. While the company has experienced some ups and downs with their recent acquisitions, and there is still some question as to whether or not the corporate culture can move from a well-engineered, single-product company into a product-diversified conglomerate, it must be remembered that cars are still the engine that drives this company. The engine will still be running at the end of the 21st century.

Electrolux (Sweden)

Swedish entrepreneur Axel Wenner-Gren intended all along to have his vacuum cleaner company become globally successful. He accomplished his mission. Wenner-Gren's Electrolux (established just prior to World War I) was an early champion of many marketing and advertising innovations, trailblazing many business elements that today are essential pieces in any business. Wenner-Gren embraced door-to-door salesmanship, and while not a new idea—Hoover vacuums were sold the same way—Wenner-Gren did it with passion. He also established many modern sales management practices that seem to work amazingly well today as they did back then. On top of the exceedingly deft use of marketing, sales and advertising, the company has long used acquisitions and mergers to establish markets and, most importantly, create growth, but never more so than in the 1970s and 1980s. Electrolux has displayed shrewd skills in identifying appropriate business additions and acquiring them for advantageous prices. The company has consistently displayed excellent skills in the nontechnical side of the business, while still showing surprisingly sound aptitudes in their engineering. The company's well-rounded business skills are particularly remarkable. They have established a balance between the hard and soft side of business exceedingly well. And, like ABB, they successfully manage a highly diversified portfolio of approximately 500 entities. Many baby boomers grew up with the Electrolux vacuum cleaner. Their grandchildren will too.

Glaxo-Wellcome (UK)

Glaxo-Wellcome has mixed a potent elixir for success. Using a shrewd merger in the 1950s and excellent R&D over the years, the company has propelled itself to a top global spot. After Glaxo merged with Allen & Hanbury's, an old UK drug company, the R&D pipeline began to flow, although even before that the company had become the first in the UK to make penicillin by the deep culture fermentation process, a vast improvement over a more tedious and time-consuming method that stifled world supplies. After the merger, the combined companies isolated vitamin B12, came up with hormone synthesis for hypothyroidism, and contributed heavily to the treatment of anemia and to research that led to the synthesis of corticosteroids. They also marketed Ventolin, which revolutionized the treatment of asthma. Probably their biggest product, though, was Zantac. Released to the market, it quickly became the world's best selling drug by volume, and grabbed more than half of the market in ulcer medications. The company has now used the profits from the incredibly popular Zantac to leverage its global presence even more. You can bet they will have a prescription for success in the 21st century.

Hoechst (Germany)

What is remarkable about Hoechst is its commitment to R&D. By way of example, in 1980 an American scientist, Dr. Howard M. Goodman, approached the company with an offer to establish a large bio-tech research facility associated with a major university in the United States. This effort was to run for 10 years without interference from Hoechst, at which time the company would be allowed to be the first to *license* (not own) the results. The cost was to be US$70 million. Hoechst jumped at the chance. It fulfilled Hoechst's basic tenet that risks must be taken in order to succeed, and provided the means to gain a foot in the door of a field, bio-tech, in which they had had no presence. The company has always challenged the unknown. Hoechst funded the scientist who discovered the pharmaceutical cure (penicillin) for syphilis. This discovery was notable because it was the first time a man had concocted a drug effective in combating infectious disease. Assuming Hoechst maintains its corporate values and mission, the company will be successful well into the 21st century.

Inchcape (UK)

Although incorporated in 1958 as Inchcape & Company, Ltd. (and now Inchcape Plc), the company's origins date back to the late 1700s, the starting point for the collection of several companies that have become Inchcape. Now describing itself as a services and marketing concern, with strengths in distribution and resources, its formation in the late 1950s was as a global trading company. It still is, and apparently an extremely effective one at that. More than half the company's revenues are derived from the Asia/Pacific region, giving the company familiarity and leverage in the region. This is important now, but will be even more so when underdeveloped countries such as China and India throw their considerable weight into the global economy. Therein lies the historical strength of Inchcape. It possesses a corporate affinity to explore new regions and their economic possibilities, and has established the distribution infrastructure to leverage those possibilities into reality. It may not be flashy, but it has been effective. The company is now well positioned to take advantage of substantial growth opportunities in the 21st century.

Nestlé (Switzerland)

Nestlé started as the Anglo-Swiss Condensed Milk Company, in Switzerland in 1866. Anglo-Swiss later merged with the Nestlé Company, taking on its name. The company came to understand international marketing intimately. The relatively small consumer base of Switzerland almost compelled them to initiate trade across borders. With early global efforts, the company had plants and distribution secured in Europe, North and South America, and Australia by 1925. That globe-galloping mindset is firmly entrenched in the company's corporate memory, and it currently boasts plants in over 60 countries and distributes to even more. Its product development initiatives are just as impressive. The company introduced baby formula (Nestlé invention, 1866), malted milk (Nestlé invention, 1920s), Nescafé (the first palate pleasing instant coffee), and Nestea (the first instant tea). While not always the first to invent products, they were often the first to develop ways to perfect and mass produce them. That is because for most of its existence, and still to this day, Nestlé has been a production-oriented company. It prides itself on innovative products that are the result of meticulous production quality control and which contain superior ingredients. Add all of this up, and you have a successful global company that will be around at the end of the 21st century.

Philips Electronics (The Netherlands)

Philips' name recognition in Europe is ubiquitous. The company's products can easily be found in almost any room of a European home. In many markets it competes against the powerful Japanese consumer electronics companies. Philips puts up an impressive fight, unlike the US firms that seem to have almost given up. A company noted for giving its subsidiaries lots of autonomy, Philips centralized only its manufacturing operations. In recent years, though, an effort has been made to improve productivity and bring more control to the company's bureaucratic organization. This strategic measure might help in the future, where a concentrated focus will be needed to stop the Japanese from making further inroads into Philips' markets. Notable lapses in marketing have seen Philips lose the audio cassette market it opened after being the first to develop that technology. They have also seen market share taken away in the video cassette recorder sector, another product they were first to introduce. Unlike US companies, though, Philips has displayed a tenacious will to retain its tradition as a worldwide firm providing quality consumer electronics—a reputation somewhat tarnished, but still deserved. Philips has the kind of staying power that will keep them a world leader for decades to come.

Renault (France)

Renault's claim to fame does not rest on engineering feats, although it was an innovator roughly through the first half of its existence. Its reputation also does not derive from its manufacturing prowess, although here too it once had capabilities that mirrored, if not rivaled, the early Ford Motor Company with its vast operations. Renault's exalted position is that of a national symbol, a company intertwined not only with France's auto history, but with France's very fortunes and misfortunes as a nation. Renault saw its name praised in World War I when hundreds of Parisian taxi cabs, most of them Renaults, sped thousands of French troops to the Battle of the Marne in a successful attempt to thwart a German advance on Paris. In World War II, the company saw its name disgraced when its CEO, Louis Renault, was charged with war crimes for manufacturing products for the Nazi war effort. This black mark so tarnished the automaker that, after the war, the company was nationalized. It produced many a popular car for all of Europe, but it never successfully cracked the US market. In tribute to its engineering muscle, it should be noted that through the years the company had perfected or pioneered many features now found on today's cars, including the removable spark plug, the hydraulic shock absorber, four-wheel drive and the hatchback auto. Renault is now in the process of being privatized. If the French government can successfully conclude its transition to a less socialistic capitalism, then Renault should be successful into the 21st century.

Roche (Switzerland)

Roche is R&D driven, like most pharmaceutical firms. The difference is that they put their money where their mouth is, spending as much as 20 percent of sales on R&D. That pride is well founded, with the company boasting three Nobel prize winners in medicine. The company introduced several pharmaceuticals that are recognized globally, including Librium (1960) and Valium (1963). Valium, itself, was a major blockbuster, some say the first real blockbuster in the pharmaceutical industry. Roche scientists also developed certain patents on liquid crystal displays (LCDs), and the company now licenses its patents to all LCD manufacturers. While it had an R&D dry spell during the mid-1970s through to the 1980s, its commitment to R&D is truly far-ranging, with its bio tech efforts including a majority ownership in the US company Genentech. On a management level, Roche realized, as many Swiss companies have, that there was no alternative to global marketing. Switzerland's small population demanded that international marketing efforts were required if the company was to survive, much less thrive. Roche has done a superb job that should be rewarded in the 21st century.

Royal Dutch Shell (The Netherlands and UK)

Under the strategic vision of Henri Deterding, Royal Dutch Shell found the way paved to being the second largest corporation in the world. For most of its post-World War II corporate life, Royal Dutch Shell has been a loosely organized operation, its corporate matrix system the innovative management tool of the 1960s. This is also the company that brought scenario planning to the corporate forefront. With the advent of the flat organization and its emphasis on "lean and mean," Shell's matrix system was doomed. A loose confederation of managers with overlapping responsibilities, it sported too many layers of management duplicated elsewhere in the company, a deadly redundancy in today's super competitive world. The company is in the first phase of a corporate makeover that will leave it more centrally managed. It is clear, though, that Royal Dutch Shell will be a major world player for at least another 100 years.

Siemens (Germany)

George Williamson of *Fortune* magazine once wrote that "'second is best' might as well be its motto," referring to Siemens, which has a history of successful refinement of the inventions of other companies. Sounds a bit like a few Japanese companies in the latter part of the 20th century, doesn't it? Siemens can count a long list of achievements:

- ☞ Built Europe's first long-distance telegraph between Berlin and Frankfurt in 1848

☞ Commissioned in 1853 to build Russia's fledgling tele-graph system

☞ Discovered the dynamo-electric principle in 1866

☞ Contributed to the first deep-sea telegraphic cable

☞ Held patent on first X-ray tube

☞ Helped in the development and manufacture of the V-2 rocket, the beginning of the intercontinental ballistic missile

☞ Developed nuclear power; built South America's first nuclear plant

☞ Designed and built Germany's first bullet train in 1965

In addition, Siemens was often one of the first, if not the first, to develop, discover or design breakthrough innovations, from automatic telephone exchanges to traffic signals. In a way, it excels at being second best—but never less. Second best will still take the company well into the 21st century.

Unilever (The Netherlands and UK)

As a business, Unilever has been described as a big lumbering dinosaur. But that's OK. It does not have to be fast, it is already everywhere. Here are some of the products it markets in the United States, and remember these are just some. In fact, other countries are stocked with their own cache of Unilever products, tailored to their particular geographic needs and tastes:

☞ Wisk detergent

☞ Lux dish soap

☞ Close-Up toothpaste

☞ Wishbone salad dressing

- Dove facial soap

- Birdseye frozen foods

- Vaseline

- Pond's facial cream

- Q-Tips

- Ragu spaghetti sauce

It stumbles, it bumbles, but it has a global presence with many products. So how has it grown so large? Quite simply, by acquiring companies throughout the world. Unilever also sells lots of companies. In a way, the company practices corporate portfolio management. But the key is that it is not trading companies. It is trading the underlying brands. What marketing and advertising do not contribute to success, they hope heavy R&D commitment will. This has long been a Unilever tradition. Throw in a hardy marketing and advertising effort (Unilever once had its own in-house ad agency that ranked as one of the largest in the world), and you find a good-natured grocer to the world who may not get all the details right, but he knows how to sell the cans on the shelf. Unilever will still be a grocer to the world at the end of the 21st century.

Volkswagen (Germany)

At the heart of the Volkswagen story is the Beetle. Lore has it that Ferdinand Porsche developed the car for Adolph Hitler, a car nut, to realize Hitler's dream of a "People's Car." In reality, Porsche had longed to build an inexpensive auto for the masses and had designed such a vehicle a number of years before. The Beetle was that car. Hitler became aware of Porsche's car and ordered it to be developed and manufactured by Germany's auto industry. The war came, and military vehicles were built, rather than the People's Car. It wasn't until after the war, under British occupation and a British administration, that the Beetle began production again as a tool for reconstruction of the German economy. From that humble beginning, Volkswagen built a company that had an unbelievable impact. The company built close to 21 million Beetles over

40 years—the best selling car ever. It can be credited with opening American eyes to economical automobiles, establishing a foothold that was later exploited by the Japanese (who gained confidence from Volkswagen's success to enter the US market). Its advertising campaigns had a notable impact on the advertising industry, changing the rules of the game in which negatives became positives and drawbacks became selling features. For example, their slogan and advertising campaign, "This car is a lemon," demonstrated the company's stringent quality standards. Another example was their "Ugly is only skin-deep" campaign which demonstrated their commitment to engineering. In the end, the common car produced some uncommon results. The Beetle is still being manufactured in Mexico and Brazil. No doubt the demand for the Beetle, and other Volkswagen products, will continue well into the 21st century.

North America

AT&T

AT&T began with Alexander Graham Bell's invention of a service-able telephone in 1876. Created as the long-distance arm of Bell and his investors, AT&T gave continental telephone access to the fledgling local phone companies in the United States. Later, Bell's group consolidated the two operations, local and long-distance telephone service, into one company in 1899. AT&T was the parent company. Into this came Western Electric for manufacturing equipment and Bell Labs for the R&D arm, providing equipment uniformity and a pipeline of new products. It was a monopoly in the making, which is an important factor to remember. Most phone systems throughout the globe were nation-alized by their respective national governments. One noteworthy differ-ence between a monopoly and a nationalized concern is that a monopoly invites criticism and receives pressure from both the public and govern-ment. A nationalized company is subject most notably to criticism from the public, the government being much more reluctant to criticize itself or take action against itself. Remember, clout and patronage have always weighed heavily in any society.

Thus, AT&T remained more consumer friendly. This was due largely to Theodore J. Vail, an early AT&T general manager and a man who realized the early local phone companies were overcharging and under delivering on quality services, angering the customers and opening the locals to competition and regulatory problems. He changed that when the locals became part of AT&T. AT&T was considered more technologically advanced (Bell Labs and Western Electric) and more professionally managed. Unfortunately, AT&T became too good, and too big. The US government forced AT&T to break up its businesses in 1984. When finally broken up, AT&T and the Baby Bells (seven regional operating companies) performed admirably in establishing themselves as independent businesses. As for AT&T, the added experience of dealing with the competition introduced by the breakup, plus its other learned corporate talents, positioned it to compete successfully internationally against newly privatized telephone companies. AT&T was with us at the beginning of the 20th century. They will also be around at the beginning of the 22nd century.

Boeing

The company's early years saw it not only manufacture airplanes, including some for World War I, but it also got into the flight business by transporting US mail, an important business on which most fledgling airlines depended for revenues. In fact, Boeing created United Airlines in the late 1920s from its various holdings in several airlines. So, while attempting to build a business in what was then an emerging market, Mr. Boeing formed two *Fortune 500* corporations that are still on the scene today. If Mr. Boeing and his company can hang their managerial hat on anything, it is the company's knack for capitalizing on opportunities and displaying adroit handling of business and economic crisis throughout the company's history.

Boeing was on the ground floor both of the mail-hauling business, the first real commercial use of the airplane, and of military application in World War I, the airplane's other important use. It entered the helicopter industry early on and developed a series of workhorse bombers during World War II (the B17, the B29 and, after the war, the B52). It survived the commercial jet age boom by changing its image (both externally to potential customers and internally as part of its corporate culture). The company changed its image as a military/air freight transportation plane manufacturer into a passenger plane maker that energized the industry with the 707, 727 and the first jumbo jet, the 747. Boeing weathered a bankruptcy crisis in the early 1970s that saw the company lay off over 60 percent of its workforce, later to rehire them when that drastic measure proved successful and the company returned to prosperity.

Boeing is in a difficult industry which requires excellent contingency plans as well as long-range strategic plans. However, the Airbus consortium in Europe is their only strong competitor, and the US government would probably never let them die. Boeing will be with us in the 21st century.

Disney

Disney's creation of animation was sheer genius. *Mickey Mouse* was the first film animation with sound. Add to that the marketing of those animated creations—with such tactics as the introduction and then periodic re-release of their acclaimed hits to movie theaters and video stores, the use of television and the creation of theme parks that not only produce revenues but extend the marketing message—and you have the hallmarks of the Disney Company's genius. Creative marketing, marketing creatively. The company did see some very lean times in the 1970s, and Euro Disney outside Paris was a revenue and profit failure its first few years. But Michael Eisner became CEO and helped turn the company's fortune around. Eisner continued many of the practices mentioned above, while also initiating his own profit-generating ideas. Just recently, Eisner pulled off the acquisition of Cap Cities/ABC, which positions the company well for the 21st century if managed correctly.

General Electric

If General Electric can be cited for one thing, it is its ability to juggle two almost diametrically opposed concepts: that of always focusing on its core competencies while also adapting to change. GE adopted both concepts long before it became fodder for the consulting mills. Essentially GE has fused the two together, enhancing its core competency of producing big-ticket items, whether they be consumer goods or industrial goods, with the skill to change those operations rather quickly when the need arises. Even in World War II, when most companies, including GE, switched to war production, GE developed and made war products that eventually would find their way into the commercial world. It is a clever trick of adapting to the times and then using those adaptations to the company's advantage. Acquisitions were made to shore up and fill in markets in which GE found itself weak or did not have a presence in— quite a feat for a so-called lumbering giant. GE has long been admired for its cost-cutting methods and the ability to produce innovative new products while improving mature products. They also get high marks for a strong commitment to R&D. All of this takes extraordinary organizational skills, which appear ingrained in the company's corporate culture. The company has endured defeats over the years, most recently with its financial arm, specifically Kidder Peabody and the bond scandal, and its ill-managed governance over NBC, but all companies should expect a certain amount of failure, because that is where true managerial ability shows itself. General Electric will have more wins than losses when the tally is made at the end of the 21st century.

Hewlett-Packard

Innovation and decentralization—these are the two basic premises of Hewlett-Packard's management which have served them well, very well. HP encouraged entrepreneurial engineers. On top of that, the company's divisions were intentionally kept small (no more than 1,500 workers). The result was usually swift, action-oriented decisions—which is precisely what is needed in the computer hardware industry. HP's start in the desktop printer business is an example. A number of years back, an HP engineer saw plans by Canon to produce the desktop printer. Canon was not really pushing the idea, but the HP engineer thought it was terrific. He convinced management to import the idea, buy parts from Canon, and push the machine out into the market. What made it even more remarkable was the fact that HP was at that time only in the printer business to supplement the main business of producing computers. And it was not even invented at HP! Over the years, HP also became one of the leading proponents of "cannibalizing" its own products—that is, introducing a new and improved version of its products even if the current ones were selling well. Did we mention product quality? When was the last time you had to have your HP Laserjet printer serviced? You probably never have. Hewlett-Packard has done very well on all fronts, considering that the business started in a garage. Unlike the other notable garage starter, Apple, HP is one garage business sure to survive in the 21st century.

IBM

Lou Gerstner has his work cut out for him at IBM, but do not count this heavyweight company down and out, yet. Sure the company looks monolithic, plodding and very confused, but it looked that way back in the late 1940s and 1950s when it was still a tabulating company that produced electrical-mechanical equipment as Remington Rand was trotting out the UNIVAC computer. UNIVAC was the first electronic computing system that had commercial uses. Well, IBM saw the writing on the wall and hit the brakes before hitting the wall. Using their corporate intuition and knowledge, the company foresaw opportunity and, better yet, the way to pull it off. Capitalizing on Rand's ill-conceived notion that only a handful of these computers would ever find use in the business world, IBM swung their considerable expertise in R&D, sales and marketing into action. A few years went by before the IBM 360 rollout, but when it came, it was a hit with units selling in the thousands. It is interesting to note that IBM had stopped cold what was already then a corporate bureaucracy to embrace a new technology and successfully advance it into the marketplace. The company relied on its superior R&D, sales and marketing, and a belief that it is never too late to act, to pull themselves out of an industry that was dying (tabulating machines) and into one that was flying. The same circumstances exist today. Wait and see. IBM in the future might stand for "In Business for the next Millennium."

Intel

Intel is lightning fast in taking a new chip design from the idea stage to the production stage. They have to always be looking over their shoulder as they move forward, because the competition is on their heels. The company operates in the microprocessor industry, an arena that demands incredible quickness in R&D, manufacturing and distribution. Intel should know. They invented this frenzied pace. And therein lies the answer to the company's strength—an intimate knowledge and understanding of the business they are in. Realizing early on that the computer industry operated at a high rate of speed and taking their cue from the software side of the business and its rapid development pace, Intel demanded that the company meet the industry's rule of thumb—processing power doubles every 18 months. Once again, Intel should know, because the company identified that phenomenon originally.

Marshaling their resources (R&D and manufacturing/distribution), marketing their products, and competing relentlessly against Japanese inroads into their customer base are the hallmarks of this company. If they continue to be nimble and quick, they will be around for a long time in the 21st century.

Johnson & Johnson

J&J is another blockbuster company that wholeheartedly believes in decentralized management, a practice started in the early 1930s by Robert Johnson and extremely relevant today. The company also recognized very early that globalization was important when the Johnson clan took a trip overseas in the early 1920s. They saw market opportunities and the faces of their future competitors. Another corporate cultural manifestation is that while there is a bottom line to watch, the company's focus is this: the customer is king—respond to them. This thinking led J&J to quick action in the Tylenol poisonings, which led to positive customer relations, which led to rebounding sales. Neat trick. Product development is also paramount to success at J&J. The company's R&D function is well-funded and productive. In recent years J&J found that the company had grown so large and global that a restructuring was in order, with the surprising result that operations were somewhat centralized. While running counter to their "decentralize and diversify" strategy, it appears to have been a response to an organizational structure that had grown too large and unwieldy. If anything, it points back to some of the company's strengths—great internal perceptions of itself and a willingness to act on its perceptions. J&J will prove again that a Band-Aid from time to time will keep you healthy for a long time.

3M

Prodigious and creative R&D coupled with an excellent management practice that not only understands R&D but, better yet, understands how to efficiently and profitably benefit from R&D has been the hallmark of this company since the beginning of the 20th century. Management wants original ideas. The company fosters intrapreneurialism. Management expects their scientists to devote at least 15 percent of their time to projects of the scientists' own choosing. The real magic, though, comes when a project holds promise. It is swiftly guided through an analysis process and, if the project survives, it is just as quickly turned into a product. Out of this approach have come products such as Scotch Tape, Masking Tape, Post-it Notes and notable improvements in products they had not invented, such as improved sandpaper for the fledgling auto industry. If no one tinkers with the corporate culture, there is no doubt that this midwestern US company will be around at the end of the 21st century.

McDonald's

McDonald's Ray Kroc saw a market that no one else saw—fast food, the family car and fun. None of these things would seem to point to superior organizational management, but they do. To move his dream to reality the company required extreme corporate focus on maintaining uniform standards and procedures. They had no choice. With what amounts to tens of thousands of branch offices (the stores themselves), lax or insufficient organizational controls would cause the system to fall apart. That is because customers demand a company's operations be the same wherever they use the company's services or products. If not, what is to stop customers from trying the competition, even if the competitors are an unknown? While customers may recognize the McDonald's name, uneven standards and quality would mean that going to an unfamiliar McDonald's is just as much of a risk as trying Greasy Jack's Burger Barn. And that leads to another McDonald's strength—marketing. They didn't invent it, they just perfected it. The golden arches. Ronald McDonald. Ray Kroc. Big Mac. It's all as American as McDonald's. And if you did not take exception to the statement "as American as McDonald's," then you accept it, too. Now THAT is marketing—the kind of marketing that will ensure our grandchildren's children will eat under the golden arches.

Motorola

Motorola is a supercharged company that is full of contradictions. They push relentlessly for a team-based organization and have largely achieved it, yet competitiveness is not just directed externally toward the competition. Individual business units are strongly encouraged to compete against each other. This translates into developing new products not only at the expense of old products—known as "cannibalism," and widely practiced within the electronics/computer industry—but also against products of other divisions. The end result is excellent products that are the result of commitment, not committee. Another apparent paradox is that while Motorola pushes teamwork, it is very devoted to decentralized management, in the belief that superior products and systems are engineered in environments far from the reaches of upper management. And the watchword for all of this? Quality. The zealots at Motorola aim for zero-defects, or Six Sigma as it is known at the company, and they, out of all the US companies, are closest to achieving it. What holds it all together? It is the extraordinary management talent that resides within the company. From the battery eliminator to the car radio to satellite communications, Motorola is able to adapt to change. It will not just survive in the 21st century. It will prosper.

Northern Telecom (Canada)

Canada's Northern Telecom, a telecommunications equipment supplier, has never been shy about competing. They have even taken on AT&T in its own backyard, back when that American company had nothing to do all day but squash smaller competitors. Northern Telecom uses a one-two combination punch of savvy economic tactics and aggressive R&D to maintain that competitive streak. When World War II ended, Northern Telecom immediately increased their work force to 12,000 employees from the original 9,000, most of whom were devoted to war production. At the same time they began making products for civilian telecommunications needs, while still changing over from war production. They quickly capitalized on their perception that there was an explosive need in the market for telecommunications. Beefing up R&D, the company made a long-range commitment to develop a new switch system. The risk paid off, and by 1975 Northern Telecom had sewn up not only the Canadian market, but also 25 percent of the US market. The company ventured a later wager (and big money) that "digital" switching would eventually triumph over analog. AT&T thought otherwise. By 1990 Northern Telecom had, by some estimates, one-third of the now-standard digital market in the United States. The competition in the telecommunications world is getting red-hot, but Northern Telecom won't get burned in the 21st century. In fact, they will turn the heat up a notch.

Procter & Gamble

Two words sum up P&G's contributing difference to business in the 20th century: brand management. In effect, each brand operated as a separate business, competing with the products of other firms as well as with those of Procter & Gamble. Marketing—and advertising—have always been crucial to the company's strategy. Often P&G has been a pioneer in introducing new precepts to the two disciplines. Remember, this is the company that created the concept of "soap operas." Starting in 1933 the company saturated radio shows with their commercial advertising messages. In 1939 they advertised Ivory soap on a televised baseball game. Even mistakes were turned into advantages in the company's marketing efforts: Ivory soap's ability to float was a manufacturing mistake that was turned into a marketing coup. Even without those "happy" mistakes, the company has always had innovative products in the pipeline, and well they should. P&G is a big believer in R&D and well known for it. Some very recognizable products have come from their labs: Tide, Cheer, Camay, Crest, Pampers, etc. Recent changes have seen the company adopt "low, everyday prices" and a reconfigured brand management system (called category management) which reduced the amount of internal competition between the different company brands. Assuming the marketing innovation never stops, P&G will be around at the beginning of the 22nd century.

Sprint

Sprint is the fiber optics champion that beat AT&T and MCI in this technological upgrade. Using it to good advantage, the company marketed the clarity of its long-distance fiber optics service versus AT&T's land-line phone system and the microwave system of MCI. While only third in the US telecommunications race, following behind MCI, with AT&T at the top, it has grabbed almost nine percent of the US$90 billion communications market, in contrast to MCI's 14 or so percent and AT&T's 64 percent. This should not be discounted, not when you consider that this is a mature industry with well-established players who are extremely competitive. While relatively young, the company has made its mark by pushing the communications industry into the next frontier through fiber optics. It is an ideal medium not only for telecommunications, but also for enhanced computer capabilities, improved commercial cable opportunities, and a host of other new technologies on the horizon. They capitalized on it with shrewd marketing, hyping only the elements that benefited their immediate concern, long-distance telecommunications. The next step is expanding their global capabilities. Sprint is committed to this business for the next 100 years.

UPS

UPS parlayed a vastly superior distribution operation over its earlier rivals, such as the US Postal System and now defunct REA Express, into a strong competitive position. UPS is well positioned to compete against its current spirited rivals of today: DHL, Federal Express and Roadway. Using a management style that has been referred to as militaristic, the company built a grassroots organization early on. Management positions as low as the supervisor level were motivated to perform with high salaries and, better still, with generous bonuses of stock. In essence, all layers of management owned the company; its success was their success. By adhering to a rapid delivery service that hums, UPS gained a reputation for reliability and customer satisfaction. That became its primary marketing message. Interestingly enough, UPS historically did not spend any money on advertising. However, the company was forced to advertise when it entered the highly competitive air freight business. Incidentally, their ground delivery service consistently handles more packages annually than the US Postal Service. Look for those brown trucks and uniforms in the late 21st century.

Whirlpool

Whirlpool's chief contribution to the 20th century's business annals is that of developing good- to high-quality durable consumer goods and then forging close relationships with retailers and distributors. Sears has traditionally been a close partner with Whirlpool, a relationship that harks back to 1916. Currently, Whirlpool is aggressively seeking international outlets and has acquired the appliance business of Philips. Whirlpool plans to be a fierce global competitor. In the mid-1990s, Whirlpool entered the market in Sweden with an advertising blitz that was reminiscent of Kruschev ("We will bury you"). To build its impressive array of goods, the company has never been shy about acquiring consumer lines to enter emerging markets as they unfold, or to gain entry to markets where they were under-represented. In addition, the company has always made every attempt to produce a stream of new products by its own initiative, and to support those efforts with en-hanced customer services—all designed to keep the customer a Whirl-pool customer. If they can maintain the brand loyalty, Whirlpool will continue to be a tough competitor well into the 21st century.

Xerox

Xerox rates a place among corporations that made a difference in the 20th century by virtue of its development of the plain paper copier. The creation of this now indispensable office machine rocketed the company from a small-time operation (originally called Haloid Corpo-ration, 1906) into a *Fortune 500* company in just a few years! It is a noteworthy predecessor to the Apple and Microsoft stories with remark-able similarities, except for the fact that Xerox could have become Xerox, Apple, Microsoft, and Hewlett-Packard combined. Xerox in-vented the first PC, the first graphical user interface, the first mouse, the first laser printer, and the first local area network. As the story goes, management wanted to concentrate on the company's areas of core competence (i.e., copiers). Ah, hindsight is always 20-20, isn't it? The good news is that Xerox is still a strong competitor in the global marketplace, even holding its own against Asia/Pacific competition. Odds are it will continue to be strong into the 21st century.

Asia/Pacific

Canon (Japan)

Big, bold marketing, double-speed technological development and fearless venturing into the competitor's home turf—that is a snapshot of Canon. Just ask Xerox or Nikon (cameras). Xerox never saw the Canon aimed right at them until the company shot down Xerox's copier with a technologically superior machine that cost less. Customers ate it up, and Canon ate Xerox's lunch, at least in the short term. Nikon insists it makes a better quality 35mm camera, and maybe they do, but Canon began out-marketing and outselling Nikon starting in the 1980s. That's not to say Canon has not made mistakes. It had a few strategic pitfalls in the late 1960s and early 1970s. But the company learned from those experiences and began a campaign that would redouble its marketing efforts. When Canon rolls out new products in the 21st century, watch out!

Daewoo (Korea)

Daewoo is a chaebol, a Korean conglomerate consisting of many companies tied to a central entity that is similar to a holding company in the United States. Maybe that is why Daewoo is so comfortable forming alliances and partnerships with companies outside Korea, a successful maneuver that has served the company well. It is one of the company's historical strengths. What makes a company like Daewoo, and its long-time leader, Kim Woo Choong, so intriguing is that the Korean government can order chaebols, such as Daewoo, to take on failing or stumbling companies in order to save them, even those outside that particular chaebol's expertise. It is very often a drain on the chaebol's management, strategic planning and resources to have to do so. It very often is a drain on profits, too. Yet Daewoo, led by Kim, has exhibited extraordinary skill in doing just that. Renowned for its large-scale, worldwide construction business (it has many other diversified operations including automaking, heavy machinery and wearing apparel), it was ordered by the government to assume the building, and then management, of what would be the largest and most efficient shipbuilding facility in the world, a project that was near bankruptcy at the time. While that is a highly-visible example, it is just one testimony to Kim and Daewoo—the ability to take on extremely difficult circumstances and situations, turn them around, and profit from them. Although Kim will face charges of bribes to government officials, he will continue his aggressive strategy to dominate Third World auto markets It is not difficult to see that Daewoo will be successful in the 21st century.

Evergreen (Taiwan)

Evergreen has become the largest container-shipping firm in the world. In terms of competitive strategy, the company competes on the basis of price. They have been very price competitive, particularly on the Pacific routes. Led by Y.F. Chang, the company is among the few in the world to use information for strategic advantage. The company developed a global service so that they could provide customers with single-source shipping all the way to their final destination. This required much coordination of its own fleet, as well as use of competing ships, to make sure the cargo would reach its final destination on time.

This kind of service was considered unique in the industry. Evergreen has also turned scheduling and expediting into a science—through satellite communications and fax, linking operations (the ships) with its offices. Competitors are amazed this company is profitable. But Chang's response is leveraging machines so that fewer laborers are required. As a result, they usually employ half the number of crew as a competitor. Chang, who worked his way up through the ranks of ocean shipping before founding Evergreen, is now handing over the reins of the operation to his son, K.H. Chang. The company, though diversified into many other transportation-related fields, is first and foremost an ocean shipping business. Look for Evergreen to continue to make waves in the 21st century.

Fuji (Japan)

The Fuji Photo Film Company is a plodder, but one that continues the pace, slow as it may be, onward and forward, year after year. It started out in Japan selling inferior film. Then slowly but surely, it improved its product, first in the professional photographic market, where quality is the only selling point. When the professional market in Japan eventually warmed up to the company's film and bought it to the point that Fuji owned the market, the company attacked the consumer market and won that too. Then, Fuji went overseas, building plants to both establish a presence and to soften the currency problems associated with silver buying. Silver, of course, is a critical photographic film material. In international markets, Fuji used the same strategy as in its home market and, again, the company took healthy market shares. Its hardiest competitor, Kodak, still owns its own home market (the United States), but Fuji has steadily increased its original US share from 2 percent to its current 12 percent. It has now diversified into electronic imaging systems in order to lessen the burden a financial hit would place on its traditional film business. Its market share is small and that should worry competitors, because it means the plodder will be on the move again. Slow, sure, steady, and successful. The bottom line is that Fuji has a quality product that they have been successful at marketing and selling. It is easy to picture them as a leader in the competitive race of the 21st century.

Hyundai (Korea)

The company is the largest of the top four chaebols in Korea, and it is the product of one man's will, Chung Ju Yung. Nothing is impossible for Chung. The company, which is comprised of 30 or so subsidiaries in such industries as construction, ship building, cars, microchips, furniture and athletic footwear, is extremely aggressive. Chung's brash ways have rubbed his own government the wrong way—he has stridently challenged government officials to do things his way. This is not well received by the government, and he has recently paid for those transgressions in rigorously conducted company audits. Later, Chung saw himself accused of misusing company funds. On top of that, he is selling a controlling interest in Hyundai Heavy Industries and Hyundai Merchant Marine, and disengaging himself from Hyundai's insurance and hotel holdings, a move thought to be prompted by government pressure. It appears that he could become a victim of the old saying, "He who lives by the sword, dies by the sword." It is ironic that one of the most influential chaebol leaders in Korea—a man who literally helped build the country back up and then used those skills to promote Korean expertise as a global construction expert—is now considered suspect. Odds are that the government will come to realize that, in the global marketplace, its anti-Chung efforts are perceived as negative marketing for Korea. Expect both Chung and the government to mellow a bit in the 21st century and direct their energies at global competitors.

Matsushita (Japan)

This is a well-managed company. How well managed? In a country world-renowned for its consumer electronics companies, Matsushita is the brand found in all Japanese homes, and usually in more than one room. It beats Sony, Hitachi, and Toshiba. And it owns Panasonic, Technics and Quasar. In addition, Matsushita has made products for others to sell under their own brand names, including IBM, GE, J.C. Penney, Magnavox and Kodak. On top of that, Matsushita gave up a one-year lead to powerhouse Sony in the emerging VCR market. Then they perfected what would later be the eventual winner of the "format" war. VHS won out over Sony's Beta and Philips' V-2000 systems and took over the market from Sony, the early front runner. Konosuke Matsushita, the founder and creator of the company's managerial system, created a corporate culture which mixed a type of spiritual humanism with hard-nosed business practices (Matsushita devised his own version of GM's Alfred Sloan's divisional management organization at roughly the same time). The company is willing to partner with others, or go it alone, whichever scenario plays best. And while it may lose battles, it never loses the war. Matsushita will continue to stay one step ahead in the 21st century.

Mitsubishi (Japan)

Japan's economic might is tied to the centuries-old zaibatsu, which has been described as a trading company. Mitsubishi is probably Japan's largest and most powerful zaibatsu, a business concern that started out in shipping over a hundred years ago. While many of its component companies—giants in their own industries—are legally separate entities, they do work in intimate concert. To give an idea of their power and impact, note their company roster, the different industries represented, and their rank in *Business Week's Global 1000*:

	Rank
☛ Mitsubishi Bank	(8)
☛ Mitsubishi Heavy Industries	(73)
☛ Mitsubishi Trust and Banking	(82)
☛ Mitsubishi Corp.	(108)
☛ Tokio Marine & Fire	(110)
☛ Mitsubishi Electric	(149)
☛ Mitsubishi Estate	(156)
☛ Kirin Brewery	(206)
☛ Mitsubishi Chemical	(244)
☛ Mitsubishi Motors	(343)
☛ Mitsubishi Materials	(494)

☞ Mitsubishi Oil   (615)

☞ Nikon   (790)

☞ Mitsubishi Rayon   (988)

☞ Mitsubishi Warehouse & Transportation   (999)

Is there any doubt that Mitsubishi will be a 21st century zaibatsu?

Singapore Airlines (Singapore)

Singapore Airlines is known the world over for its exceptional service. They had this mission from the beginning because they wanted to be one of the best in international air travel. Their service to a customer begins on the ground and ends on the ground. Providing for passenger welfare is their first concern and the focus of their overall marketing strategy. The airline secured landing slots at some of the world's largest hubs, and then forged an alliance with British Airways to fly the Concorde between Singapore and London. Although the Concorde venture lasted but a short time, the resulting media attention garnered more press and free marketing for the growth airline. By building a new airport in Singapore that catered to passengers, the company's customer service reputation grew even more. Revenue passenger miles and profits are up, and the projection is a continued upward trend. They will continue to be strongest in the Asia/Pacific region, and they will continue to be the benchmark company for other airlines as we move into the 21st century.

Sony (Japan)

Their secret to success? Be a leader rather than a follower. This is the philosophy on which Masaru Ibuka founded Sony. Former co-founder Akio Morita agrees. He was instrumental in developing the Sony Walkman, an invention not offered by anyone else, and one that took the audio industry by storm. The company is always looking for ways to give consumers more convenience and more benefits. And the company has done just that, either being the first or one of the earliest to offer products such as:

☞ Pocket-size transistor radios

☞ Trinitron TVs

☞ Walkman radio/recorders

☞ Camcorders

☞ CD players

More than 1,000 new or updated products are rolled out each year. The company spends an extraordinary amount of money and effort on its R&D, and then rushes its discoveries out to market as fast as possible, where it pumps production up to warp-speed levels to flood the market before competitors can react. When the competition finally gears up its own production, well, Sony moves on to the next design and production. To sum it up: Sony miniaturizes, mass-produces, and moves on. It is an unbeatable formula which will keep them around until at least the end of the 21st century.

Toyota (Japan)

Innovation, R&D, and advanced management techniques—these are the elements that have propelled Toyota into the auto-making stratosphere and made it a world-class business. The company is praised by many car owners, and damned by competitors for their excellent cars, the result of constant tinkering. Tinker they do, and not just in car design. Toyota is firmly committed to continuous improvement, just-in-time inventory, robotics, and employee team concepts. The company's management is very perceptive and forward thinking. When the oil embargo of 1973 caused auto production to plummet worldwide, Toyota made capital expenditures to build more plants, while increasing R&D to improve car mileage. Their reasoning was that cars are a must for everyone, rich or poor. When sales would again rise, and they definitely would, surmised Toyota, the company would be ready. Well, sales did rise, and Toyota was ready. Very few other manufacturers were, and the company made a bundle. Enlightened management and innovation constitute Toyota's global legacy. Toyota will be making cars at the end of the 21st century when others have abandoned the market.

🐦 🐦 🐦 🐦 🐦 🐦

The old man mused, "Those were SOME companies. Wish I had owned stock in all of them. I would be a rich man today! I at least wish I could have met some of the men behind those organizations. If only walls could talk, I bet we would hear some pretty interesting stories."

CHAPTER 7

THE 20TH CENTURY HALL OF FAME—
THE LEADERS THAT REDEFINED BUSINESS
AND CHANGED OUR LIVES

"Those successful companies of the 20th century really HAD to grow as big as they did," said the old man to himself. He was rather amazed by the concept. "I mean, how could you conceive of something THAT involved, THAT complex, if you did not know for sure what the future was going to be like?" Saying it out loud made the old man even more incredulous.

He thought to himself that probably some of the founders or the CEOs could not even have imagined their companies could or would get that large. "But you know that some of them must have been dreaming all along of a business reaching all over the globe," he mused. "Yeah, that is the way to go." Something so big that what you make in a New York plant is sold off the shelf in a New Zealand store. Or maybe it consists of drilling deep down into the ground, pulling out oil and shipping it all the way from the Philippines to Paris. Now, the old man was excited. "Hey, at some point those guys must have figured, 'why not go for it?' *Why not!*" But then the old man's face screwed up. You could see that his thinking had just hit a wall. "But what if it didn't work out? I mean, what if you plow everything into it—money, time, hard work—and it turns out you were wrong?"

He thought about some of the early companies, like Daimler-Benz. What was it like when the company first started? And what were they thinking about when they built their first car? The first car ever built! "Here it is, 1885, and this guy Benz thinks he will just sit down and build himself a car. A CAR! For what? What did he ever see in it? What was the value? What could he use it for? Jeez, what the heck was he even thinking of?" The old man was actually agitated by the thought that anyone could think to build the first car, by the thought that there were not any real roads to begin with. "Come on," said the old man with skepticism. "What are you going to do? Drive it around some dirt roads—maybe cobblestone, if you are lucky. But what's next? Oh, yeah. Sure. I get it. Someone is just going to come around and build you a road just because you built a car. Sure...SURE! Build it and they will come!" he snorted. By this time the old man was almost spent. He slumped back against the kitchen counter. He slipped another pill under his tongue.

Slowly the old man's face began to relax. The agitation began to subside. And then a look—no, more of a glimmer—came to his eyes. Then came the look, a look of things coming into place. A look of recognition. Then acknowledgment. "That's right," said the old man. "That is what those leaders saw. They said, 'If I do it...just do it, I will be successful.' That is because those leaders had vision. And they were *real* leaders." The old man was really putting it together, now. "Those guys saw what existed out there, and they saw what *would* or *could* exist out there, the possibilities. Then they decided they would just have to lead everybody to it."

The old man was building up steam, now. "Nobody pampered them; nobody coddled them. They went out and pushed the darn thing forward by themselves. Sure, maybe if you were the CEO of something already going it might be a little easier, but even those guys, the ones who succeeded, had to keep the vision going for everybody else. Someone should honor people like that. Someone should let people know what those guys did, what they accomplished!"

The old man thought they should have a Business Hall of Fame. "You know, honor those guys who put a heck of a lot more time into their profession than sports celebrities. Every sport has a Hall of Fame. Why not a Business Hall of Fame? Here is who I would include," said the old man.

Europe	ABB—Percy Barnevik
	Bayer—Friedrich Bayer
	Danone—Antoine Riboud
	Marks & Spencer—Michael and Simon Marks
	Nestlé—Henri Nestlé
	Roche—Fritz Hoffman-LaRoche
	Royal Dutch Shell—Henri Deterding
	Siemens—Werner von Siemens
North America	AT&T—Theodore Vail
	Black & Decker—S. Duncan Black and Alonzo G. Decker
	Boeing—William Allen
	The Carlson Companies—Curtis Carlson
	Chrysler—Lee Iacocca
	Ford Motor Company—Henry Ford
	General Electric—Jack Welch
	General Motors—Alfred Sloan
	IBM—Thomas Watson
	Kellogg's—W. K. Kellogg
	Mary Kay Cosmetics—Mary Kay Ash
	McDonald's—Ray Kroc
	Merck—Roy Vagelos
	Microsoft—William Gates
	Nike—Phil Knight
	Wal-Mart—Sam Walton
Asia/Pacific	Cheung Kong—Li Ka-shing
	Daiei—Isao Nakauchi
	Honda—Soichiro Honda
	Honda—Takeo Fujisawa
	Hyundai—Chung Ju Yung
	Matsushita—Konosuke Matsushita
	Sony—Akio Morita
	Tata Group—Tata
	Toyota—Eiji Toyoda

Europe

Percy Barnevik—ABB (Switzerland/Sweden)

Percy Barnevik believes that strategy development should be a continuous activity. He has often been called the management superstar of Europe. His thoughts and actions propose that every business will eventually be global. The charismatic CEO of ABB has developed corporate strategies which position ABB as lean, responsive and global. For example, in 1988, following the merger of ASEA and Brown-Boveri, Barnevik reduced the headquarters staff from 2,000 to 176. The measure was reflective of Barnevik's desire to maintain a lean operation. Regarding the need to be responsive, Barnevik has stated, "the costs of delay exceed the costs of mistakes." His T-50 (time minus 50 percent) program, in part, proposed cutting 50 percent from ABB lead times. ABB's responsiveness was one reason the company, along with Marks & Spencer, was voted the most admired company in a recent poll of European managers. Barnevik's global policy suggests ABB managers should seek expansion in their own markets. Barnevik's geographic focus of the 1990s is Eastern Europe and China. The focus is reflected in ABB's US$2 billion in investments into those markets over the first half of the 1990s.

Friedrich Bayer—Bayer (Germany)

Friedrich Bayer started his company in 1863 as a vendor of aniline dyes. At the same time, many companies were making an effort to enter the German chemical industry, but Bayer was one of the few to flourish. One of Bayer's primary strengths was his ability to surround himself with talented and dedicated individuals. For example, Bayer hired Karl Duisberg, who at the age of 22 became Bayer's research director. Bayer and Duisberg built the company's research operations to the point that the company became the recognized leader of the German chemical industry. Bayer hired the best, motivated them to achieve beyond their capabilities, and rewarded them well.

Antoine Riboud—Danone (France)

In 1958, Antoine Riboud inherited a glassmaking company founded by his great uncle. At the time, the company was generating US$10 million in sales. Throughout the next decade, Riboud focused his attention exclusively on the glassmaking industry. In 1969, Riboud attempted the first hostile takeover in French history. Although his effort to take over Saint-Gobain failed, Riboud became renowned in many circles for his aggressiveness. Thereafter, Danone began to attract young, aggressive managers with keen marketing skills. Following the takeover attempt, Riboud decided to diversify through acquisitions into a number of markets including dairy products, baby food and beer. His acquisitions were based on his plan to charge premium prices for brand name food and beverage products. Riboud has continued his success by purchasing top notch organizations and through distinctive advertising. Using that formula and a continuous series of acquisitions, Riboud has proven to be a businessman of considerable prowess.

Fritz Hoffman-LaRoche—Roche (Switzerland)

Hoffman-LaRoche launched his company in 1894 on a bedrock of international expansion and aggressive marketing. Hoffman-LaRoche was one of the first to realize the potential for proprietary products in the medical field. He quickly became recognized as a pioneer of marketing to doctors and pharmacists, a genuine innovation at that time. Additionally, Hoffman-LaRoche was an early proponent of scientists publishing findings in medical journals. By his direction, the company became the first in Europe to publish its own journal. Hoffman moved quickly on the global front, too, starting six subsidiaries throughout the world by 1911. The company had a presence in Paris, New York, London, St. Petersburg, Vienna and Yokohama, all prior to World War I.

Michael and Simon Marks—Marks & Spencer (UK)

The success of Marks & Spencer lies in the wishes of Simon Marks to create a business where everyone from employees to outside suppliers felt as if they were an integral part of the effort. To that end, Simon introduced an eclectic array of advances that included everything from a revolutionary innovation of buying directly from manufacturers to a welfare department that attended to the needs of the company's employees. By directly purchasing the store's goods from the vendors, Michael Marks began his campaign to develop closer ties. He felt that such a relationship would benefit both his stores and the manufacturer. Communication between the maker and the seller was needed to sell the product. That would result in better and more accurate distribution, improved stock inventory practices, and elimination of supply deficiencies. The relationships worked, which led other manufacturers to enter into ventures with Marks. In fact, the strategy worked to such an extent that even today Marks & Spencer retains many supplier relationships started in the first half of the 20th century. Simon catered to the customer by making sure that the product was well made. To that end, he initiated a testing lab to make sure products met his standards and started a private label, St. Michael, to market that point. It all led up to strong consumer loyalty and continued success.

Henri Nestlé—Nestlé (Switzerland)

Henri Nestlé founded his company in 1866 with the idea of offering nutritional products to consumers. His first product was a milk-food for infants, and he went to great lengths to make the product known to doctors as well as consumers. The biggest contribution that Henri Nestlé made to his company was a relentless pursuit of approval for his new product. Nestlé was not a huckster selling his product. He passionately believed his product was revolutionary, and that it represented much more than milk laced with nutritional ingredients. Henri sought to prove that its unique composition provided undernourished infants with the correct balance of nutrients required for good health and growth. In an age of high infant mortality, this was no idle endeavor. A successful formula could save many lives, and it is here that Henri succeeded in making a global impact.

Henri Deterding—Royal Dutch Shell (The Netherlands/UK)

Henri Deterding paved the way for Royal Dutch Shell to become the second largest corporation in the world today. His entrepreneurial philosophy combined financial ingenuity with visionary strategic initiatives. Unlike John D. Rockefeller, Deterding built his organization through alliances and partnerships, rather than through head-to-head competition that saw losers merged into the Standard Oil fold. In fact, the company today is a partnership between corporate parties in The Netherlands and the UK, thereby representing one of the few corporations owned by interests of more than one country. Not surprisingly, Deterding exhibited the same degree of tenacity as Rockefeller. He and Shell often bested Rockefeller and Standard Oil. While Rockefeller might have been the oil king in the United States, Deterding bloodied

Standard Oil many times in the global market. So, while it might not be said that Shell won, it can be said they definitely did not lose, and that did not happen very often to John D. Rockefeller.

Werner von Siemens—Siemens (Germany)

Werner von Siemens, inventor and engineer, began what was to become one of the largest and most respected electrical engineering firms in the world. The company was driven by the desire to invent new products, but also kept an eye on the innovations of competitors. Siemens stressed the need to quickly identify competitor developments and convert such ideas into practical products. Today there is a saying at the company that "second is best," a motto that supports the idea that improving on others' inventions is not without its own pride. Werner's achievements included being awarded the contracts to build the first European and Russian telegraph lines. What may be more significant is Werner's discovery of the dynamo-electric principle. The discovery that mechanical power can be converted into electric current without using permanent magnets was a key to developing electric power transmission.

North America

Theodore Vail—AT&T

AT&T, the Baby Bells and Bell Labs owe their existence to Vail. When J.P. Morgan took control of the company in 1907, the company was in serious debt and viewed poorly by both the public and employees. In addition AT&T had poor service and technological problems that made solving service issues difficult. Vail was able to save AT&T from ruin in less than 10 years. He accomplished this by addressing each one of the company's problems. He worked to eliminate the company's debt by selling millions of dollars in bonds at a discount to shareholders. This also rebuilt confidence in the company. He made R&D a primary focus in order to address technological issues. This R&D move eventually became Bell Labs. Lastly, he divided personnel into groups of future forward thinkers and daily operations people in order to address service problems. Vail was the one who deliberately set AT&T on a monopolistic course, snapping up ailing and failing telephone companies and then reorganizing them into state and regional entities. There were several government interventions, but eventually the telephone system was recognized as a service requiring regulatory monopoly.

S. Duncan Black and Alonzo G. Decker—Black & Decker

Black & Decker was one of the pioneers of the power tool consumer market, but that was not the original goal of the company. At first, Black & Decker was a workman's power tool company, the do-it-yourself market at the time being neither sophisticated nor large. Instead, Duncan Black and Alonzo Decker attacked and won the tradesman niche, then dominated by heavy, cumbersome German power tools. Black & Decker opened its first service centers in 1918 in Boston and New York City. The company's sales approach was aggressive, and advertising became a key focus beginning in 1921. But all of these efforts were directed at the working tradesmen, not the home consumer market. During World War II, Black and Decker decided that at the war's end they would apply their marketing and promotional expertise to enter the consumer market. Modifying their products for home use (using such things as plastic housings), the company burst onto the scene in 1946 and quickly came to dominate this newly emerging market. Incidentally, Black & Decker found that in the 1980s the professional tradesman had come to disdain their tools as strictly for the home do-it-yourselfers. Tradesmen considered the tools of a Japanese firm, Makita, to be superior. The company took note of the complaints and introduced a new line of power tools geared to the professional. The brand name given to this new line was DeWalt, a company that Black & Decker had acquired some number of years before. Using their trademark salesmanship and aggressive marketing, Black & Decker once again was competitive in the professional tool market.

William Allen—Boeing

World War II was over, and William Allen knew it was a watershed mark in Boeing's corporate history. With warplane orders drastically cut, Boeing was pondering its fate as a company. Traditionally, 80 percent of Boeing's sales had been to the US Air Force, but management determined the company had to enter the commercial aircraft market and compete against Douglas, the industry leader. The cost would be prohibitive. Allen, Boeing's CEO, shrewdly decided to pursue a different course of action. Boeing would design an aircraft capable of serving the commercial and military markets, but would first sell it to the Air Force as a tanker. Following that strategy, the military would invest in the development of the aircraft, and significant funds would transfer over to commercial production. Several setbacks came to face Boeing, however. This included competition from the de Havilland Comet, the first commercial jetliner, weaker jet engines in the projected 707 than in the Douglas DC-8 jetliner, roomier cabins in the Douglas DC-8, and a perception that the 707 was a warmed-over military plane. Allen then did something that had never been done before at Boeing. He listened to prospective customers and incorporated their changes into the design. To accommodate those changes, Allen essentially began to offer custom-made jets. It added tremendously to development and production costs, and it infuriated the company's engineers, something not done at Boeing, where the engineers were considered gods. Allen subsequently told the engineers, "We are all salesmen now." With that momentous change, the commercial airlines began to flock to Boeing, knowing they could order planes that specifically matched their cost factors and profitability needs. Boeing won the race with Douglas, a race so crucial to each company's fortunes that its outcome forced a wounded Douglas to merge with McDonnell Aircraft in order to survive.

Curtis Carlson—The Carlson Companies

Carlson started his entrepreneurial ways by launching the Gold Bond and Top Value trading stamp company. In the image of its founder, the company made aggressive salesmanship the keystone of its corporate culture. Carlson once stated, "My operating principle was to travel by night and work during the day, and I spent so many crazy hours going in and out of airports that I would occasionally be hard-pressed to tell someone exactly where I was." Carlson always saw opportunities. When he bought the original Radisson Hotel in Minneapolis, Carlson realized that a regional sales association held several major trade shows in the city. Carlson built an exhibit complex across the street from his hotel connected to the hotel by way of a skyway. With that start, and trading on the Radisson's excellent reputation in the region, Carlson expanded the hotel operation. At first, Carlson bought older hotels with long traditions, but he came to realize that "no matter what you did with an old hotel, it was still an old hotel." There were exceptions to the rule, but Carlson understood that to make a profit, hotels had to become physically attractive and efficient. Carlson then built new hotels, but as part of a chain, one where standards could be implemented. This gave the company operational efficiency and economies of scale. Carlson fueled the company's growth by acquisitions and expansion of existing operations. Branching out into other arenas, Carlson established or acquired restaurant chains (TGI Friday's), travel agencies (Ask Mr. Foster, P. Lawson and Cartan Tours) and other hospitality or promotion companies.

Lee Iacocca—Chrysler

The public thinks of him as a "car" man. Detroit insiders know his forté is marketing. Many think he built the Mustang by hand, himself. Actually, others were the real builders of that car. What Iacocca saw was a great product to market, and he knew how to market. Even his greatest triumph, the saving of Chrysler from utter failure, was never a one-man effort. Iacocca, a former marketing and public relations manager for Ford, explained to the public the dire condition of the company and the ramifications the company's failure would have on the economy. Eventually, the US government agreed to bail out Chrysler. What must not be discounted was Iacocca's energizing commitment. His will to succeed was a personal goal, but in order to bask in that glory, the company had to succeed. The two goals, Iacocca's personal triumph and the company's financial well-being, were intertwined. Iacocca's relentless push achieved them both. The accomplishment was an extraordinary feat. Under Iacocca's watch, the company did create or popularize two markets. The minivan was a Chrysler original and the Jeep Cherokee 4-wheel-drive took the market by storm. Iacocca also put US$1 billion into a research center during some financially shaky times. The investment paid handsome dividends.

Henry Ford—Ford Motor Company

He did not invent the automobile, but he did revolutionize its use and the way it was manufactured. With that he unleashed both a business and social maelstrom. He built the first mass-produced car for the general public, and in the process pioneered mass manufacturing, the result of his ingenious invention of the assembly line. He invoked the eight-hour day at his plants and paid his workers the ungodly sum of US$5 a day, very comfortable wages for the times. Neither was meant as a charitable expression. Eight-hour shifts best suited his around-the-clock assembly lines, and the US$5 was a wage inducement to stay on the job in an industry that often saw employee turnover reach as high as 380 percent a year. In fact, Henry Ford lamented, "Why is it that I always get a whole person when what I really want is a pair of hands?" Ford was, however, sensitive to business opportunities. His decision to be among the first to seek overseas business development has translated into Ford Motor Company being recognized as a company successful at pursuing cross-border opportunities.

Jack Welch—General Electric

GE's fortunes had been in decline when Welch was named CEO in 1981, but with his appointment came radical change. He decentralized management in order to give control back to the divisions. However, he retained predecessor Reginald Jones's system of classifying divisions according to their performance. His stated goal was to make GE number one or two in every market. GE has been able to operate profitably while competing almost entirely in traditional established industries which have many worldwide competitors to reckon with. GE's traditional businesses include electricity generation, appliances, lighting, medical systems, plastics, locomotives and aircraft engines. Jack Welch decided GE should focus on manufacturing "big ticket" capital goods. That has historically been what the company has done best. Achieving his goal required accomplishing two objectives: expanding into international markets and getting rid of "the fat." Welch knew if foreign competitors were allowed to compete in markets where there was no competition, the competition would eventually be strong enough to challenge GE's market in the United States. Neutron Jack (his nickname because of his tactics in wiping out products and employee jobs) also knew that in order to stay focused on "big ticket" items, he needed to get rid of waste. Waste was defined as products in which GE could not compete, needless jobs, whole manufacturing locations, or whatever it took. That is not to say Welch did not have any problems. Two—the Kidder Peabody trading scandal and the relative weakness of NBC compared to its competitors—have been vexing Welch lately, but Neutron Jack will probably find a way to level those mountains into molehills.

Alfred Sloan—General Motors

Sloan picked up where William Durant left off, adding a strong measure of managerial command and financial control to the company's impressive array of auto products. He structured GM into divisions. Each division was run by an executive who was solely responsible for its performance. Division executives all reported directly to GM's central management. Such a sharply defined and narrowly focused system had never before been attempted. Sloan had championed the first glimpse of modern American management. Sloan and his newly created management team then organized GM's divisions by price point, most expensive to least expensive. The same GM divisions are still in operation today. Sloan described the divisions as "Cadillac for the thriving, Buick for the striving, Oldsmobile for the arriving, and Chevrolet for the surviving." Under his watch, the General Motors Acceptance Corporation came into existence because bankers were extremely reluctant to offer loans for autos. It was an immediate success, and a feather in the cap of Sloan, who recognized its significance. In the end, Sloan not only set GM on its course to becoming an industry giant, but he innovated managerial concepts that survive and thrive even today.

Thomas Watson, Jr.—IBM

Remington Rand was the computer age's front-runner in bringing computers into the business world. Thomas Watson, Sr. did not see Rand as a threat and was not interested in entering the computer business. His son, Thomas Watson, Jr., on the other hand, was strongly in favor of entering the computer industry. Thomas Watson, Jr. became president of IBM in 1952 and dedicated almost all of IBM's R&D program to developing a computer as quickly as possible. By 1955 IBM had developed a successful product, the IBM 705 general purpose business computer. By 1956 IBM had already surpassed Rand in the marketplace. IBM accomplished this through its superior sales force, which already had 85 percent of the target market for computers as existing IBM customers. IBM induced their existing customer base to switch from IBM's electro-mechanical tabulating machines to the company's new computers. Watson Jr.'s perceptive vision, coupled with a driving urgency, not only pushed IBM's fortunes higher, but it saved the company from certain death. The products the company sold prior to the computers, tabulating machines, were shortly slated for obsolescence. Watson believed the old saying, "change or die." They changed, and became one of the largest companies in the world.

W.K. Kellogg—Kellogg's

When W.K. Kellogg started his company in 1906 he was not one of the first entrants into the breakfast food industry. But because of his marketing and advertising skills, in addition to his perseverance, Kellogg survived where many did not. During the last 90 years or so, Kellogg's has sold nearly 800 billion bowls of cereal. Although the company has been immensely profitable, it has not been without a struggle. A devastating plant fire, corn shortages caused by World War II, and legal problems with his brother were some of the early obstacles that plagued the company. Through it all, Kellogg persevered, always returning to the strategy he knew best. Kellogg knew he had to market his products in such a way that they would stand out from the rest. This strategy is so ingrained in the culture of the Kellogg company that it is still a bedrock tenet held by the company today.

Mary Kay Ash—Mary Kay Cosmetics

Mary Kay Ash built her company from virtually nothing. Over 30 years ago, she began Mary Kay Cosmetics with the vision that it would present to women opportunities that were not available elsewhere. Presently, the company has 2,100 employees and over 300,000 beauty consultants. Over the past two years alone, Mary Kay Cosmetics has generated over US$1 billion in revenue. Ash built the company with the focus always on the consumer and the beauty consultant. The company acts not only as a distributor for the company's products, but also as a cheerleader for the consultants, lavishing them with attention and dangling prizes for top sellers. The consultants respond enthusiastically, and in turn not only sell products, but also recruit new consultants.

Ray Kroc—McDonald's

Ray Kroc in 1955 changed the way America ate. Each year, 96 percent of Americans, and an increasing number in other parts of the world, will eat in a McDonald's restaurant. McDonald's is a cornerstone of American culture. The man who started it all was Ray Kroc, a milkshake machine salesman. He spotted the McDonald's brothers' California restaurant, with its extremely efficient food processing and serving system, and bought the rights to franchise the operation. While Kroc did not conceive the original idea, he did refine and expand the concept.

McDonald's global franchise system, with all its intricacies, was his creation and a driving force in making the company successful. The emphasis on marketing and advertising was also the result of Kroc's vision. An indication of how influential McDonald's has become is that it is one of the 30 companies that make up the Dow Jones Industrial Index.

P. Roy Vagelos—Merck

Vagelos is responsible for making Merck one of the industry leaders in the pharmaceuticals business. Vagelos saw a different way to produce effective pharmaceuticals. He ordered researchers to focus on developing agents to stop the biochemical reactions that a disease causes. Research became so important that Vagelos pared the company down to concentrate almost solely on its pharmaceuticals. Merck continued to get rid of businesses which did not center on the company's core competency. Today 90 percent of Merck's revenues are generated from pharmaceuticals. Once Merck had the products developed, Vagelos was also an expert at marketing the products. Merck had a vast experienced salesforce with a tremendous physicians' network. Vagelos used sales representatives to the fullest, having them constantly market the pharmaceuticals to physicians. He felt that a strong relationship with those physicians was paramount, the result being brand loyalty to Merck products.

William Gates—Microsoft

The man who many consider to be the ultimate propeller-head just might be the world's best marketer, too. In this day and age of MS-DOS and MTV, that combination can be considered the Midas touch. Gates, like Jobs and Wozniak of Apple, got in on the ground floor of the personal computer ascent. A computer geek who started his own computing business while still in elementary school, Gates displayed an acute business acumen and a very insightful vision of the industry's potential. He understood early on the significance of retaining the rights to his company's software, even as he made attempts to buy all rights to programs developed outside of Microsoft. His earliest triumph was buying the operating system that has become almost a global standard, MS-DOS, and then turning around and licensing it to IBM as the operating system for their PCs. Gates grabbed IBM's coattails and let them muscle their way into the market, something that could be achieved by IBM, whose industry-leader reputation allowed access denied to upstart computer companies. And therein lies a Gates' strength: the ability to understand that it is not just the products you produce, but how you maneuver and manipulate the market to accept your products. Gates has an innate feel for the market and what it wants.

Phil Knight—Nike

Nike, named for the Greek goddess of victory, is Phil Knight through and through. Knight, the company's founder, has built the organization around the corporate culture which he envisioned. He demanded loyalty from his employees and, in turn, returned that loyalty. *Sports Illustrated* has called Knight "the most powerful man in sports," ranking higher than any other individual, not to mention ranking higher than even the professional sports leagues themselves. Ironically, Knight never intended to manufacture athletic shoes. He left that to contracted manufacturers. What Knight desired was to design and market "performance." Rather than worrying about plant problems, such as equipment and production snafus, he wanted to concentrate all his efforts on shaping the market, much like commodities traders who buy and sell carloads of wheat on paper, but never see or touch the actual commodity. Knight moved the market by muscling competitors with marketing, by wielding information-age influence. Nike Town, Michael Jordan, Bo Knows, "Just Do It," etc. exist not just to move people into sports shoes, but to move Nike into sports. By equating sports with Nike, and Nike with sports, Knight wants to integrate sports with his product, making them one.

Sam Walton—Wal-Mart

Walton did not conceptualize the discount retail business. E.J. Korvette's is usually attributed with that honor. But he did perfect a version of it that is a category killer: Wal-Mart. "We discovered people would drive to a good concept," he said many times. Walton wanted very large stores offering very "small" prices on a huge array of brand-name products. Initially, he placed them in rural towns, making them destination points for the local region. The everyday low prices meant there was little to advertise since there were no temporary price reductions, or sales prices, to announce. That lowered marketing and advertising costs. And since that normally constituted a healthy portion of any retailer's expenditures, it further reduced costs. He built warehouses to hold huge inventories, which meant he could restock his stores quickly, control the price, and lower his transportation costs from regional warehouses. Much like Ray Kroc, Walton's concept is an intricate business ballet, bringing more detail and control to the retail world than it had known before. Maybe Walton's true genius is that of an expert weaver of systems and processes, rather than as a sharp retailer.

Asia/Pacific

Li Ka-shing—Cheung Kong Holdings (Hong Kong)

The future of Hong Kong is shrouded in mystery. With the planned takeover by China in 1997, the UK's long reign and influence will abruptly come to an end—a paradoxical turn of events for this city-state. In that year a Communist country will assume control of a die-hard capitalist enclave. And while China has taken to some capitalist enterprises, it must be noted it has not embraced capitalism; it is just dabbling. That is what makes Li Ka-shing and his attempts to build an empire so interesting. Cheung Kong was the first entity in the property-to-telecommunications industry in Hong Kong. Li Ka-shing is responsible for the industry's success. Li Ka-shing, who now controls over 14 percent of the stock on the Hong Kong stock exchange, began his career in 1960 by making plastic flowers. In addition to residential real estate developments, Li controls 6.9 million square meters (76.7 million square feet) of land. Very perceptive in his take on Hong Kong commerce and finance, Li has called some excellent shots, venturing opinions on the Hong Kong business market that have been uncanny in their accuracy. Take a look at some of his maneuvering. In 1973, recognizing the static nature of the Hong Kong property market, Li Ka-shing increased rental income from his company's properties to ensure shareholders' interests. A year later the maneuver proved to be a good one when Hong Kong's property market hit a depression. Cheung Kong's development plans continued to be successful. Li sees long range, both in time and in distance. In 1977, Li foresaw how the then European Common Market, with its various restrictions on imports, would have a negative impact on Hong Kong's industry and, by extension, his company. Hong Kong's industry sector was influenced by the local property market. So, the property market depression was sure to have a negative effect on industry.

Would high global interest rates affect the local Hong Kong property market? He responded by hedging with mortgages and property development. Feeling the shadow of future Communist rule? He responds by hedging with overseas property investments. Property and development looking questionable? His response is to buy up interest in electricity, communications, wholesaling, distribution, manufacturing, quarrying and concrete markets. Not only diversify, but use them to support the property development. Everything is temporarily working against you? That happens, says Li, so ride it out. Of course, against this backdrop is the looming problem of future control by China. However, Li Ka-shing has influence with Chinese leaders in Beijing. His influence was born out of the large volume of business his company conducted with China. He has also done things like working with China's investment arm to construct a US$10 billion electric plant. For the future, Li Ka-shing's future should continue to increase based upon his increasing influence in Hong Kong, and his diversification internationally.

Isao Nakauchi—Daiei (Japan)

Nakauchi is referred to as the Sam Walton of Japan. Nakauchi and Sam Walton started their respective retailing giants within 10 years of each other. Daiei was a high-volume, low-price retailer in a country which saw many companies work together to ensure higher prices and larger profit margins. In an effort to keep overhead low, stores were opened in suburban areas rather than expensive urban "high rent" districts. Daiei was an admirer of Mao Tse-tung's strategic wisdom, and modeled himself after Mao in order to gain support from consumers. Nakauchi's "icon-like" presence caused him to be both admired and hated, not to mention shunned by the business community. This treatment only fueled his desire to revolutionize the retail industry. Well, the masses loved it, and Nakauchi laughed all the way to the bank. And he did not stop there. Nakauchi eagerly formed alliances with Western retailers such as J.C. Penney, Marks & Spencer, Wendy's, and Au Printemps. Nakauchi's strength was not just the very perceptive vision he had. It was the incredible determination he exhibited in pulling it off.

Soichiro Honda—Honda (Japan)

It has been said that Soichiro Honda was the greatest grease monkey since Henry Ford. On top of that, he had Ford's vision and drive to boot.

Soichiro Honda was a true entrepreneur. He identified a consumer need and created a product to fill the void. He did it with both motorcycles and automobiles. In both cases he developed superior technology which made previous products almost obsolete to some degree. Additionally, these products were not developed solely for the Japanese market, but were intended to have global appeal—so like Henry Ford. In 1958, along with Honda's complementary half—Takeo Fujisawa, a marketing and distribution wiz in his own right—Honda developed the lightweight and inexpensive 50cc Supercub motorcycle for the small business delivery market. It not only won that market, but also the average Japanese person who needed economical transport. By 1959 Honda was the largest manufacturer of motorcycles in the world. As of the mid-1980s Honda had sold 15 million, and the Supercub was exported to the United States.

Next came Soichiro Honda's car. At first a dismal failure—he pushed for an air-cooled vehicle before colleagues convinced him to switch to liquid-cooled—Soichiro came up with the Honda Civic, a terse, little statement of a car that was surprisingly peppy. The timing was perfect. The oil crisis created a worldwide market for the energy-efficient Japanese compacts. It was at this point that Soichiro stepped down from day-to-day operation of the company, but the plans were set for the next triumph, the Honda Accord. It was considered a "milestone automobile" by many, with the quality of the distinguished German luxury cars. Not bad for a guy with grease under his fingernails.

Takeo Fujisawa—Honda (Japan)

Honda Motors should almost be named Honda-Fujisawa Motors. That is how instrumental Takeo Fujisawa was in bringing Soichiro Honda's dream to life. Whereas Soichiro was the engineering genius, Fujisawa was the marketing muscle, as well as the administrative, financial and distribution powerhouse. It was Fujisawa who convinced Soichiro Honda to use his engineering and racing skills to produce a particular type of motorcycle. Fujisawa challenged Honda to design an inexpensive motorcycle that Japan's small business owners would view as a wise investment because of its safety and ease of use for delivering packages. In 1958, Honda produced the 50cc Supercub, a lightweight, zippy motorcycle that was easy to handle and cost little to operate. It was a smash hit. By 1959 Honda had become the top Japanese motorcycle manufacturer. Fujisawa decided to attack the United States. Using an ad campaign devised by an advertising student at the University of California, Los Angeles—"You meet the nicest people on a Honda"—Fujisawa took the existing images of cycling from one of bad boy bikers to mainstream American riders. And America took to Honda's motorcycle. But Americans had to do so by regions, because Fujisawa realized the company could not raise the capital or develop the distribution system overnight. Starting with the West Coast, which Fujisawa recognized as a trend-setting locale, he moved toward the East Coast, accumulating market share and capital as leverage for entering the next region. It was a brilliant strategy that not only achieved Fujisawa's initial goal, but set him up for his next move. With banks now lending money for middle-class consumers to buy Honda's motorcycles, the dealers began losing the financial power they had obtained by extending that credit themselves. Honda stepped in and demanded that dealers pay cash on delivery for its motorcycles, rather than on a consignment basis. The dealers relinquished their remaining financing authority (why tangle with the people providing your main source of income?) and effectively removed themselves from being creditors by giving up the cash float they had used to extend credit. That allowed Honda to set up its own credit arm. Shrewd maneuvering such as this gave Honda tons of cash and market share, just the things you need for new-product start-ups. In 1967, the company began its production of autos and trucks, a push that resulted in the Honda Civic, Honda Accord, and later, the Acura. So, if not for wily Takeo Fujisawa, Honda might be the best vehicle you have never heard of.

Chung Ju Yung—Hyundai (South Korea)

Hyundai's success is the vision of one man. Chung Ju Yung was the first-born son of a poor rice farmer. After World War II, Chung started a construction company which snowballed into a myriad of industrial businesses. In fact, Chung tried to get his hands in everything. Just look at the number of companies he started or industry markets he entered:

- ☛ 1940s: Started national construction company.

- ☛ 1950s: Started national construction supply company.

- ☛ 1960s: Started national cement company.

- Entered international construction industry; does big business in the Middle East and has significant business in the United States.

- Entered international construction supply business.

- Started auto assembly company to produce cars for Ford.

- 1970s: Started international shipbuilding company.

- Started international electrical-engineering company.

- Started manufacturing cars under its own name and began export soon after.

- Started an international trading company to facilitate export and import of the company's and other companies' products and services.

- Started lumber and furniture-making concern.

- Started international marine concern for cargo transport, brokering and related services.

- Started metal concern by buying national steel and aluminum companies.

- 1980s: Started electronics company to capitalize on high technology.

- Entered national politics with a presidential campaign.

- 1990s: Entered US and European car markets.

He lives to work. He is known for starting work at the crack of dawn. He is also known for cheering on the troops under him at any given time or place. Cheering on the troops might be stretching the core truth of his management techniques. He had an autocratic and unconventional style of management. He will not take "no" from subordinates, and he loves an opportunity to make the impossible possible. His company built the Seoul-Pusan expressway on a ridiculously low budget even though the World Bank had advised the then Korean president, General Park Chung Hee, that such a feat was not feasible. Korea never manufactured ships until Chung built the first shipyard in Ulsan. When completed, it was the world's largest such facility, sprawling across 5 million square meters (55.5 million square feet). Then he packed off 60 employees to the UK to learn how to build ships from their naval experts. In the Middle East, competitors viewed Hyundai as a company that would bid on projects even though it was unsure how it would complete them. This strategy propelled Hyundai to become one of the largest construction companies in that region. That is the interesting thing about Chung. He was off and running even when he had no right to be in the race. Using sheer determination, cunning thinking and a willingness that almost bordered on recklessness in taking risks, Chung built a national powerhouse with unbeatable aspirations.

Konosuke Matsushita—Matsushita (Japan)

How respected is this guy, or at least how respected is his legacy, now that he is dead? Well, in Japanese management, he is considered a "god" of business management. He even rated a *Time* magazine cover. His management style was highlighted by Richard T. Pascale and Anthony G. Athos in their 1981 bestselling book, *The Art of Japanese Management*. In their book, they said, "Perhaps it would not be too great an overstatement to suggest that in the person of Konosuke Matsushita the Japanese have a managerial genius of world caliber." Never heard of him? Well, how about Panasonic, Technics, National and Quasar? That's his company, Matsushita Electric. The philosophy that drove Konosuke Matsushita and the company is a paradoxical mix of the spiritual and the bottom line. And that's often the key to a great manager, the ability to envision seemingly contradictory ideas as workable actions or solutions, and then convince others of the validity of your vision. You must see what others cannot, and then see it through. Matsushita was 20/20 on both counts.

Akio Morita—Sony (Japan)

Masaru Ibuka and Akio Morita wanted to make innovative products from the beginning. Thus Sony was born. In 1950 the company brought out the first Japanese tape recorder, a machine so unfamiliar to Japanese that they did not understand its potential uses. Morita had to demonstrate the benefits of the tape recorder to the public. Like Ray Kroc, who was building his McDonald's empire at about the same time, and preceding Steve Jobs and Bill Gates' efforts, Morita understood the incredible power of marketing done right. While Ibuka created wonderful new products with high technology, especially in the niche of consumer miniaturization, Morita pushed all the right marketing buttons. Morita's salesmen sold the first pocket radios by demonstrating how they fit in a shirt pocket (actually the radios were a little larger than a shirt pocket—so Morita made custom shirts with pockets large enough to accommodate the radios). Morita also pushed the company to go global, truly global. He didn't just sell products in the United States, he established a US headquarters, a new concept for Japanese managers, and one that kept Morita's company finely tuned to its biggest market.

Jamsetji Tata and his sons Dorabji and Ratanji—Tata Group; Central India Spinning, Weaving and Manufacturing Company (India)

Tata is a conglomeration of companies in India and the name of the family that controls this loose federation of businesses. But it is Jamsetji Tata, and later his two sons, Dorabji and Ratanji, that figure most prominently in the Tata epic. Jamsetji was a member of a tiny religious minority who brought to India, through sheer determination and with incredible drive, the Industrial Revolution. Through his experiences in visiting industrialized nations, he had come to identify three essential elements for a modern industrial economy: steel production, hydroelectric power, and technical education. In steel, he scoured the country for mineral deposits, imported American steel experts to help establish the plant, and made plans for hydroelectricity to power the operation. He donated land and buildings in an effort to start a science and technical school. In addition, he made revolutionary strides in the plant. He installed the first humidifier to improve cotton quality through climate control. Plants were also equipped with overhead sprinklers to prevent fire. Tata also provided employees with a pension plan in 1886 and workman's compensation in 1895. All would be fulfilled after his death in 1904 by his sons, but not before he built the Taj Mahal Hotel in 1903, the first structure in India to be illuminated by electric lights.

Four years after his sons, Dorabji Tata and Ratanji Tata, took over the business, they began developing the steel operation. By the 1930s not only had they established the steel operation, but it was the largest steel plant anywhere in the British Empire. On top of that, a Tata power company began supplying hydroelectric power to the city of Bombay in 1910. This power company was the first of three the Tatas would develop. In dealing with the corporation's employees, Dorabji and Ratanji were no less advanced, taking their cue from their father, who had shown an almost parental concern toward employees. In 1912 the Tatas instituted the eight-hour day, which was in place for 36 years before the Indian government made the eight-hour work day law in 1948. The Tatas consulted Sydney and Beatrice Webb, British pioneers of social reform, to determine which social, medical and cooperative services should be implemented for the newly established Jamshedpur. As a result, schools, recreational facilities, creches and other amenities were established on site. The sons even created a profit-sharing plan in 1934. By all accounts, Jamsetji Tata and his sons, Dorabji and Rataji, were astute businessmen who created something extraordinary in a place where everyone said they could not. Now THAT is being entrepreneurial.

Eiji Toyoda—Toyota (Japan)

You do not think of employee strikes when you think of Japan, and you especially do not think of strikes when it comes to Japanese automakers, but that is what eventually brought Eiji Toyoda, cousin of the founder of Toyota, to head the company. Even though his cousin had founded the company, Kiichiro Toyoda was ousted as part of a compromise in settling a union strike. Eiji took his place, a fortunate result of such an unfortunate event. Eiji was a very insightful man, and it served him well. In the early 1950s Eiji visited the United States and toured the auto industry, specifically, while also mentally cataloging American business methods generally. What a payoff. He returned to implement some of what he saw. Toyota workers were encouraged to suggest any improvements they thought of, a practice that served Toyota so well that Japanese business as a whole adopted the practice. From that practice came the concept where an assembly-line worker could flip a switch and stop the line in order to correct a problem. Eiji Toyoda also made a commitment to use only the most modern production facilities. He was viewed as the primary proponent of advances in productivity and quality. Throughout the 1950s Toyota aggressively made capital investments in new equipment for all its production facilities. As Toyoda predicted, the company increased in efficiency almost immediately after each investment. Here too was an early example of the now popular concept of continuous improvement, in which processes and methods are re-engineered constantly. Having seen the most advanced and modern technology put to use in the United States, Eiji instinctively knew that such a competitive edge was key. In 1954, Eiji Toyoda introduced the synchronized delivery system, Kanban. He got the idea from supermarkets that replenished store stock on shelves as customers shopped and depleted the stock. The Kanban system, which is better known as just-in-time delivery, became the foundation of the company's entire production system. Toyoda's commitment to cutting edge manufacturing plants is one that remains today.

☞   ☞   ☞   ☞   ☞   ☞   ☞

The old man said, "These leaders were awfully inspiring. Each had a vision—a strategy. But they could also translate the strategy into an organization structure and systems that worked. They practiced what they preached. And what they preached turned out to be the best thing going—what everybody is calling 'best practices' now."

CHAPTER 8

Best Business Practices of the 20th Century

"That is what it takes," said the old man "Opening your eyes to the possibilities—having vision. And the gumption to go after it. That is what all those successful business leaders showed everybody. They had a vision that no one else could see until they built it. But having the vision was just the beginning. To accomplish their vision they had to create something that did not exist before. Or perhaps it existed, but nobody had tried it in that kind of business." The old man was picking up steam again. "So they innovated, tinkered and invented what they needed. Those people knew how to innovate back then."

The old man was on a roll. "Let me tell you about the innovators in my time," he said. "There were a lot of them, and most of them did not even need consultants to figure out what to do. Did you notice the new vocabulary of the 1990s—benchmarking, reengineering, downsizing, rightsizing, etc. Of course, the consultants would like you to believe that all of this was designed to make companies more competitive, to give them additional advantage over their competitors. They were probably right on this one. The search was on for 'best practices' or 'best in class' companies. Companies seemed to especially pounce on the 'new' concept called 'benchmarking'."

"The idea was to compare a small portion of your own company with those companies that performed the same operation best. The objective was to learn something so that process improvements could be implemented. Xerox popularized the benchmarking concept in the late 1970s and early 1980s. I know that many companies, including Xerox and AT&T, now use benchmarking on a continuous basis," said the old man. "Interestingly enough, I first read about benchmarking in 1913. Yes, that's right. I told you about it earlier. Henry Ford benchmarked the meat-packing industry and used his findings to develop the assembly-line concept. See, you can learn a lot from an old man. Many business concepts are not new—they are simply updated and repackaged. With benchmarking, that's great. I think it is great when a company understands that the learning process is continuous. But let me tell you about some of the other 20th century 'best practices' companies. Here is my list."

Europe	Daimler-Benz—engineering excellence
	Electrolux—business development
	L'Oreal—research
	Nestlé—global expansion
	Philips—R&D and business development
	SAP—partnership development
	Unilever—brand marketing
North America	Federal Express—distribution technology
	General Motors—organization structure
	Johnson & Johnson—decentralization
	3M—product development & intrapreneurship
	Merck—R&D
	Microsoft—business development
	Motorola—quality improvement
	Procter & Gamble—brand management
	Wal-Mart—customer satisfaction
	Xerox—innovation and benchmarking
Asia	Canon—business development strategy
	Casio—marketing strategy
	Honda—international market penetration
	Matsushita—business development
	Sony—international marketing
	Toyota—continuous improvement

Don't rely on conventional wisdom.

This is where you might find people saying, "Well, we've always done it this way," or "That competitor has always had inventory turns of 14 times, you can count on it." It is all those rules of thumb that have been developed over the years where an automatic answer is provided even before the intelligence is gathered. This should be avoided at all cost.

Don't always believe that two heads are better than one.

Many times a task force becomes a default cure for studying the problem and coming up with a solution. This is not necessarily the right answer, because two heads are not necessarily better than one. A committee or task force will work wonderfully if it has a strong facilitator who understands structured decision-making techniques. If the task force does not have a strong facilitator, it can produce some bloody awful decisions.

Don't forget those who influence the decision maker.

The biggest problem is basically this. A report is prepared for the decision maker. It gets passed around to others who influence the decision maker. Let's say four people receive the report. It is possible to have four very different reactions to the report. One is very happy. One is very angry. And then there are a couple of people who are in between in their reactions.

So, when linking intelligence with the decision-making process, the BI professional must take into account not only the decision-maker's point of view, but also the points of view of everyone influencing the decision maker. This includes internal and external points of view.

One of the reasons that people have different points of view on the same topic is because everyone has their own definition of accuracy.

And there really is no such thing as accuracy in business. It doesn't exist—never has, never will.

Perpetual Strategy Process

The BI process should tie directly to the decision-making process, in theory. In practice, however, they act as two stand-alone processes that do not interface on a continuous basis. The perpetual strategy process, which is continually fed by the BI process, can help to solve this problem.

You will recognize many elements of this perpetual strategy process. They are not particularly new or revolutionary. What is different is the way they fit together.

Provide for continuous monitoring of the external environment.

This is traditional BI. Competitors, customers, suppliers, other market forces, potential new competitors, new products, etc. must be actively monitored on an ongoing basis.

Continuously monitor company plans and the process.

This is a traditional strategic planning activity done by virtually everyone involved in the planning process. It involves a constant reassessment of the company's position in each of its markets. It also involves continuous strategy development in response to market conditions.

Monitor stakeholder actions and options.

This is where tradition ends. This is where the BI professional should continuously monitor the internal stakeholders, the management people within his or her organization. The BI professional must also continuously monitor external stakeholders that exist, whether they are investors, customers, regulatory bodies, or leaders in the marketplace.

The BI professional as a perpetual strategist has to understand management's thinking process. How do they come to decisions? Keep an eye on both their current and their past decision-making processes. This becomes very important on the back end of the intelligence process. The perpetual strategist will be preparing not just one report, but several different reports. Each report is tailored not only to management but also the stakeholders, in an effort to facilitate the decision-making process.

Make frequent recommendations for changes in strategies.

The BI professional as a perpetual strategist should be working in partnership with management. The perpetual strategist must get management to work as a team. The perpetual strategist needs more than the perfunctory top management support and involvement. To accomplish this, the BI professional must learn to think more like a senior manager. Likewise, the senior manager must learn to appreciate the role and value of the BI professional. Over time, the relationship can be built, one decision at a time.

Provide for continuous reengineering of the process.

Things are always changing in the internal and external environment, and the process needs to change as conditions change. Internally, managers and departments are changing to flatten the organization, cut costs and thereby help the company become more cost competitive. Externally, markets are continually changing to meet the changing needs of customers. The perpetual strategy process is a decision support process that needs to be implemented as a prototype and continually fine-tuned over time.

Build in maximum conflict for best decisions.

Most decision makers tend to lean too strongly toward a historical point of view, both as it regards the intelligence and the decisions they will make. Conversely, the perpetual strategist tends to be more future oriented. Immediately, there is a conflict to resolve. Even more conflict will come from the results of internal and external lobbyists, those people who also have a stake in the decision.

The perpetual strategy process should encourage maximum conflict. It is through a high degree of conflict that the best decisions are made. The conflict resolution should come in the report writing and the communication process at the end of the intelligence gathering effort.

Design the perpetual strategy process.

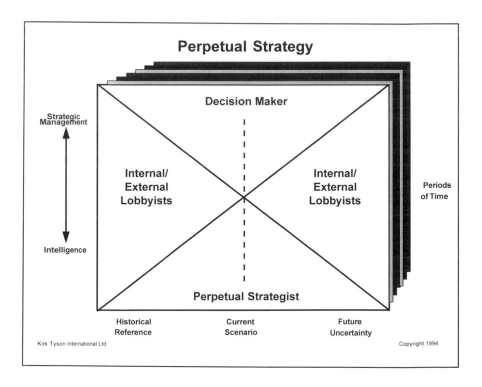

As you can see in the illustration, the perpetual strategy process is simple, yet complex. On the left axis are the BI and strategic management functions. The arrow implies that continuous streams of intelligence flow to strategic management. The arrow also suggests that continuous streams of feedback flow from the strategic decision maker to the BI professional.

On the bottom you can see that the intelligence should be a balance of historical performance information, current information, and future scenarios. As you are developing your intelligence you usually like, for example, three to five years of historical information on competition. You also want to understand what the current scenario is—what is their present position in the marketplace, what are their strengths and vulnerabilities. Finally, probably the most important intelligence will discuss the probable future intentions of competitors.

On the right you see periods of time. The proper time context is also important. In reality, when you gather intelligence, you are taking a snapshot at one point in time. That snapshot changes often, perhaps even daily. Short of using a Cray supercomputer, however, you may be content to establish this as a weekly or monthly snapshot.

Inside the box, you see the decision maker that will make the decision, and at the bottom, the perpetual strategist. Coming in from the side are the people that have tended to be ignored over the years, the internal and external lobbyists. These people, too, have thoughts and opinions on what strategic and tactical decisions should be made.

Initially, the perpetual strategy process can be done on a manual basis, although at some point in time you will want to think about computerization.

Is it complex? Yes, but that is actually good. In the past, many companies have tried to find a simplistic way of accomplishing BI and strategic management on a routine and ongoing basis. It can be done simply, but the linkage between the two is essential for success of the overall process. The way to truly facilitate linkage is to understand the total problem—past, present and future. You must also understand the people who are involved in the decision-making process, and provide training in how to analyze information and how to make structured decisions.

Under this scenario, the roles of the perpetual strategist (i.e., BI Coordinator, Change Agent) become:

- Facilitator of the intelligence gathering and analysis process,

- Facilitator of the strategy process,

- Network coordinator, coordinating information coming and going amongst the internal and external networks,

- Process engineer, and

- Trainer.

You will notice that some of these roles have traditionally been held by BI professionals, some have been held by planning people, some held by the decision maker. The perpetual strategist actually wears all of these hats simultaneously, becoming a true partner with the decision maker.

🖝 🖝 🖝 🖝 🖝 🖝

The old man summarized aloud. "There is a need for more partnership between BI professionals and decision makers. Executives need more value-added input for decision making. Intelligence professionals can provide that input if they work as perpetual strategists, shoulder-to-shoulder with management in an interactive manner. Management needs to be challenged on the front end of the process to better define how the intelligence will be used. BI professionals need to do a better job on the back end of the process in relating the analysis to the decision to be made. Quick fixes along the way are fine for the natural evolution of the perpetual strategy process because the process must be continuously reengineered."

"The benefits of perpetual strategy? The perpetual strategy process will allow you to avoid surprises in the marketplace. It will allow you to capitalize on opportunities in the marketplace. It will help minimize threats. It will help you to focus on key success factors, on those things that are truly important because you have more of a partnership with your key decision makers. Lastly, you will have much more timely decision making."

"Sound familiar? Yes, these are the same benefits that you've heard related to BI. Perhaps with a perpetual strategy process providing the needed linkage with strategic management, you will finally realize some of those benefits."

The old man paused a moment. "I hope that company managers and executives can see the value of this kind of approach. They have been slow to recognize information as a corporate asset, as intellectual property. We need companies to become learning organizations, knowledge-oriented, and more systematic in their processes. Continuous change in a company's market environment will force it. This is the only way they will make it in the Intelligence Age."

The old man got up from his chair and proceeded to his bedroom. It had been a long day.

CHAPTER 10

TOWARD THE 22ND CENTURY

...and the competition monster got bigger and BIGGER, AND BIG-GER AND BIGGER, gobbling companies throughout the world until there were only two—the Global Business Store and the Global Consumer Store.

The old man awoke with a start. As soon as he got his bearings, he jumped out of bed. He had done enough dreaming. Going downstairs, he picked up his morning paper. His dream of the competition monster had bothered him greatly. "This is not right," he said. "Surely there must be some checks and balances in the capitalist system that would prevent a future which looks like that."

He began to look at the newspaper. He glanced at the date—July 14, 1996. He smiled. It was his birthday.

With all of the downsizing, reengineering, rightsizing and thousands of people out of work, his birthday wish was that business and competition could be somewhat less intense. What is the business world coming to? What will it look like in 100 years? Will the year 2096 represent business utopia or anti-utopia? Will the 21st century bring the rise of China and the fall of Japan? Will the countries of Europe ever really unite? Can American business managers become less short-sighted before their companies self-destruct? Will the countries of the former Soviet Union be a factor in global business of the 21st century? "We all have the opportunity to shape the future of competition," mused the old man as he struggled with deep thoughts.

Although he had slept quite a bit lately, he was tired. He had dreamt a lot. And in a way, it had been quite a chore, but it had been illuminating. Very illuminating. And what he had dreamt had made quite an impact on him.

"The bottom line is simple: PEOPLE, COMMUNICATIONS, COOPERATION, KNOWLEDGE DEVELOPMENT, KNOWLEDGE SHARING, INTELLIGENCE AND PERPETUAL STRATEGY," said the old man. "Companies must rediscover that their greatest asset is their people. They must work toward better communications, better partnering, better teams, and better networks. People are social animals and need a sense of belonging. People need to share information and ideas. People need a common mission that doesn't ignore their personal mission. Employers must find ways to integrate employee personal time with business time through creative programs such as on-premises child care facilities, company-organized home maintenance, errand running, grocery shopping, etc. Business executives need to CARE, to care about the future of their industry, their company, and their employees. Many executives tell me they don't have time to care anymore. Too many things to do. Too many priorities."

"Well, if they want more time, I suggest they pick just one priority, which will provide the foundation. One that works! I would pick the 'perpetual strategy process.' This is the overriding solution that guides all other activities in the company," said the old man. "That's the glue to hold the whole thing together. It was in the past. And it will be in the future."

"It was my visit to the 21st century that taught me that a perpetual strategy process comes first, followed by a systematic business intelligence process. That will give them time. Time to strategize, time to think, and time to get people back into the equation. I also learned that many of the old sayings of the 20th century no longer hold true. In my 96 years of life, including over 45 years as CEO of a major multinational corporation, I have concluded that these will be the new rules of the 21st century:

1. **Nice guys finish FIRST.** The nice guys build strong companies—companies that care about the future of their industry, their company, and their employees. Strong companies become strong competitors.

2. **You CAN teach an old dog new tricks.** Company employees love to learn and enjoy continuous learning. They don't mind change if they can participate in the change process. With continuous training and participation, they become even more committed to the mission of the company. Committed employees become committed to beating the competition.

3. **Two birds in the bush are worth MORE than one in the hand.** The 20th century version of this saying said that your family would eat if you had one bird in the hand. But in the 21st century, the company will be fed only if it goes after the two birds in the bush. A company must be constantly alert to new opportunities—new products, new markets, new technologies, and new global partnerships. A business intelligence process to continuously monitor the business environment is essential. Continuous monitoring equals higher profits than competitors.

4. **The grass is NOT always greener on the other side.** In the last half of the 20th century, the rush was on to expand internationally. Companies throughout the world were looking for countries and niches where they could stake their claim. Many of these early efforts failed because they tried to do it alone without developing local partners. The grass was not greener on the other side for these companies. In the 21st century, the lesson will be slightly different. Companies will learn that their biggest competitive strength, and their greenest grass, will continue to be in their own domestic market. The greenest grass discourages competitive weeds and pests.

5. **It is NOT imperative to stick to your knitting.** The 20th century saw companies see-sawing back and forth between diversification and sticking to areas of core competence. In the 21st century, the dilemma will finally be resolved. Diversification, like alcohol, is healthy in moderation. Diversification can stimulate the company, add to its knowledge base, and motivate employees. Expanding your knitting activity will also improve your overall company health and competitiveness.

6. **Businesses started in the garage CAN become global leaders**. Just look at companies like Coca-Cola and Hewlett-Packard. Many of the world's leading multinational companies started in a garage, or a backyard, or on a kitchen table. Some of the most successful companies in the 21st century will emerge in exactly this way—companies in high tech, biology, artificial intelligence, etc. Respect these entrepreneurs, for the "G" in garage will soon stand for "Global." Global "garagers" will be the fiercest competitors.

7. **Strategic planning is NOT a dirty word**. Although the watchwords will change to 'intelligence,' 'knowledge,' and 'perpetual strategy,' the roots will always be 'strategic planning.' Long gone will be the 'once-a-year scramble.' Perpetual strategy will be exactly as its name suggests— ongoing, daily, weekly, monthly, continuous. Strategic planning, when practiced 'perpetually,' will allow weak competitors to become strong, and strong competitors to become even stronger.

8. **Competitors can cooperate as well as compete.** In the 20th century, most companies thought of competition as war. They fought battles in the marketplace. Win the battle at any cost. Take no prisoners. In the 21st century, competition will be more of a game. Just as the governments of the industrialized world have graduated from military battles to economic games, the same will be true of business. This is healthy because it allows companies to relate to competitors as people. It will allow them to share knowledge and develop stronger relationships. The strongest competitors will also be the strongest cooperators.

9. **The old people should not be ignored or retired too early.** One of the biggest mistakes of the 20th century was throwing away knowledge. Massive quantities of competitive intelligence and knowledge were lost as a result of all of the downsizing. No system was in place to capture the knowledge of the most experienced employees before they left the company. This will change dramatically in the 21st

century as we move from the Information Age to the Intelligence Age. The knowledge of the old people will be captured in a 'knowledge base' to be used by future generations. Expert systems and artificial intelligence applications will be built that will create a synergism never before seen. The next time your computer spits out an answer, think of the old people behind the computer."

"Yes, the secrets of competing successfully in the 21st century absolutely shatter the time-worn myths of the 20th century," said the old man. "The keys to unlocking the future are based on these provocative lessons."

"Maybe I should go back to my old company and teach them a thing or two," said the old man. "They could really benefit from what I've learned." He thought about this for a moment and changed his mind. "The learning experience will be much more valuable if they do it themselves."

The old man fell asleep—AGAIN!

APPENDIX 1

INDUSTRIAL REVOLUTION TIME LINE

1765 Steam Engine   James Watt of Scotland invents the first practical steam engine, decreasing the consumption of steam and fuel. His invention was an improvement over the Newcomen steam engine of 1712.

1814 Chemistry   Jons Jacob Berzelius, Swedish scientist, discoverer of several chemical elements, suggests that chemical bonds are due to electrical charges. Berzelius is considered one of the founders of modern chemistry.

1816 Photography   Nicéphore Niepce of France invents "heliography" and makes the first photographic image.

1816 Stainless Steel   Brearley of England develops stainless steel.

1818 Bicycles   Baron Karl de Drais de Sauerbronn of France constructs a running machine, the predecessor of today's two-wheel bicycle.

1819 Atom   Rutherford of England is the first to split the atom.

1820 Electricity/Oersted   Hans Christian Oersted of Denmark discovers magnetic effect of electric currents which inspires the development of electromagnetic theory. This was actually discovered by Italian Gian Domenico Romagnosi in 1802, but his announcement was ignored. Gauss of Germany was also a pioneer in this field in 1799. The Oersted (centimeter-gram-second system of physical units) was previously called the Gauss.

1820 Electricity/Amp   André-Marie Ampère, French physicist, investigates electrodynamics and formulates Ampère's Law which describes mathematically the magnetic force between two electric currents. Ampère also was the first to develop an instrument to measure electricity, now known as the galvanometer.

1822 Heat   Jean-Baptiste-Joseph Fourier, French mathematician, proposes his analytical theory of heat.

1823	Computer	Charles Babbage, English mathematician and inventor, designs the difference engine to calculate mathematical functions to eight decimal places.
1824	Thermodynamics	Nicolas-Léonard-Sadi Carnot, French engineer, publishes his fundamental ideas on thermodynamics (Carnot cycle). His ideas are used as a standard of performance for all heat engines operating between a high and a low temperature.
1825	Electromagnet	William Sturgeon, English electrical engineer, constructs the first electromagnet capable of supporting more than its own weight, and exhibits it to the public.
1826	Electricity/Ohm	Georg S. Ohm, German physicist, develops his theory of electrical conductivity, Ohm's law. The physical unit measuring electrical resistance was given his name.
1828	Chemicals	Friedrich Wöhler, German chemist, succeeds in synthesizing an organic compound (urea) from an inorganic one (ammonium cyanate). About the same time, he developed a process for preparing metallic aluminum.
1829	Propeller	J. Ressel of Austria invents a screw propeller in 1827 and carries out experimental trials with a propeller-driven steamship.
1829	Photography	Louise-Jacques Daguerre, French painter, convinces Nicéphore Niepce to develop a partnership for developing and exploiting heliography. Daguerre reduces exposure time and takes out a patent on the photographic technique developed jointly with Mr. Niepce. Niepce had created the first photographic image in 1816 and the first photographs on metal (pewter) plates in 1827. Others were also involved in the beginnings of photography, including two Englishmen, Thomas Wedgewood and William Henry Fox Talbot.
1830	Steam Railway	First steam railway line between Liverpool and Manchester in England.
1833	Telegraph	Wilhelm Weber, German physicist, along with Carl Friedrich Gauss of Germany and Carl Friedrich, German mathematician, build and operate an electromagnetic needle telegraph. The magnetic unit, termed a Weber, formerly the Coulomb, is named after Wilhelm Weber.
1833	Computer	Charles Babbage, British mathematician, develops plans for a program-controlled calculating machine, the forerunner of today's computer. He designs a punched card system, a memory unit, sequential control, etc. as part of his "Analytical Engine No. 2." His design of the mid-1830s was forgotten until his unpublished notebooks were discovered in 1937. In 1991, British scientists built the computer to his specifications. It was accurate to 31 digits.

1834	Reaper	Cyrus Hall McCormick of United States patents his reaping machine.
1837	Telegraph	Samuel F.B. Morse, US painter and inventor, constructs an electromagnetic telegraph. C.A. Steinheil of Germany and Charles Wheatstone and William Fothergill Cooke of England independently have the same invention at the same time. Wheatsone and Cooke hold the English patent. Morse endured many legal claims from partners and rival inventors until 1854, when the US Supreme Court upheld his US patent rights.
1841	Bunsen	Robert W. Bunsen, German chemist, develops a carbon-zinc electric cell, the Bunsen element, that finds wide application. The famous Bunsen burner was designed by others.
1842	Thermodynamics	J.R. Mayer of Germany formulates the principle of conservation of energy.
1843	Thermodynamics	James P. Joule, English physicist, formulates the basis of the law of conservation of energy, the first law of thermodynamics.
1843	Electricity	Charles Wheatstone, English physicist, constructs a bridge designed by Samuel Christie. The bridge measures electrical resistances, and it is called the Wheatstone bridge.
1844	Telegraph	Samuel Morse of the United States installs electric telegraph line from Washington to Baltimore. First message, "What hath God wrought?"
1845	Electricity	Gustav R. Kirchhoff, German physicist, formulates the laws of current branching in systems of electrical conductors. Discusses calculation of the currents, voltages and resistances of electrical networks.
1847	Electricity	H. Helmholtz of Germany extends the law of conservation of energy to electricity.
1851	Telegraph	First submarine telegraph message is sent from Dover, England to Calais, France.
1851	Energy/Kelvin	William Thomson (Lord Kelvin), Scottish engineer, mathematician and physicist, introduces the term "energy." He also develops an absolute temperature scale (cited in Kelvins).
1852	Telegram	The word "telegram" is proposed in the United States for telegraphically transmitted messages.
1854	Electric Lamp	H. Goebel of the United States constructs and operates a carbon filament lamp in New York.
1854	Steel	Henry Bessemer of England invents an economical method of steel manufacture, called the Bessemer process. However, he doesn't apply for a US patent until 1856 and, as a result, he is beaten by William Kelly, an American.

1859	Chemistry	G.R. Kirchhoff of Germany and R. Bunsen of Germany develop chemical spectrum analysis.
1859	Oil	The first successful oil well is erected by Edwin Drake in Pennsylvania.
1860	Electric Light	Joseph W. Swan, English physicist and chemist, invents a primitive electric light, one that uses a filament of carbonized paper in an evacuated glass bulb. His design was different than Goebel's of 1854, but it was substantially the same as the one used by Thomas Edison almost 20 years later.
1860	Gasoline Engine	J.J.E. Lenoir of Belgium designs a practical, though as yet uneconomical, gasoline engine.
1861	Telephone	Johann P. Reis, German physicist, constructs the first electrical telephone. It was capable of transmitting musical tones.
1863	Subway	Construction of first underground steam railway starts in London. Its operation starts in 1884.
1867	Dynamite	A. Nobel of Sweden invents dynamite.
1869	Brakes	G. Westinghouse of the United States develops a compressed air brake for railways, perfecting it three years later.
1870	Chemistry	D. Mendeleyev of Russia and J.L. Meyer of Germany establish the periodic system of the elements, independently of each other.
1870	Microscope	E. Abbe of Germany defines the resolution of a microscope.
1873	Electricity	J.C. Maxwell publishes his treatise on electricity and magnetism developed in the early 1860s, which culminates in Maxwell's equations.
1873	Electric Motor	Zènobe-Théophile Gramme builds the first truly commercial electric motor. It was a practical, efficient machine that could be used either as a motor or as a generator. It provided the basis for early DC electric supply. Others had experimented with electric motors over the years, including Jacobi as early as 1834.
1876	Telephone	Alexander Graham Bell of the United States designs a serviceable telephone capable of transmitting speech.
1876	Gasoline Engine	N.A. Otto of Germany constructs four-stroke internal combustion engine.
1877	Phonograph	Thomas A. Edison of the United States builds a cylinder phonograph.
1878	Microphone	D.E. Hughes of England designs carbon microphone.
1879	Electric Light	T.A. Edison of the United States builds a carbon filament light bulb and subsequently creates the basis for the power supply system required for electrical household lighting.
1881	Electrical Engineers	First international electrical engineering exhibition is held in Paris, with the incandescent lamp as a main attraction.

1882	Power Plants	First public electricity generating plants start operation in London and New York.
1883	Electron Telescope	P. Nipkow invents the TV aperture disk, the "electrical telescope," registered as a patent in 1884.
1883	Suspension Bridge	First suspension bridge is completed over the East River in New York, now called the Brooklyn Bridge.
1884	Aluminum	Aluminum is first extracted by electrolysis.
1884	Industrial Revolution	A. Toynbee introduces the concept of the "industrial revolution" in a posthumous work on this subject.
1885	Skyscrapers	The first skyscraper making use of steel girder construction is built in Chicago. It is 10 stories tall.
1886	Automobile	C.F. Benz builds the first gasoline engine motor car.
1887	Phonograph Records	E. Berliner, German emigrant to the United States, replaces phonograph cylinders with a circular disk, the "record," and calls the player a "grammophone."
1889	Punched Cards	H. Hollerith of the United States registers for a patent on his automatic punched card counting machine.
1890	Electric Subway	London operates first electrical underground railway.
1892	Telephone Exchange	First automatic telephone exchange is installed in LaPorte, Indiana, using selectors designed by the system of American inventor A.B. Strowger.
1892	Diesel Engine	R. Diesel of Germany develops heavy-oil "diesel" engine.
1895	Cinematography	L. Lumière of France invents the first cinematograph.
1895	X-rays	W.C. Röntgen of Germany discovers X-rays.
1896	Wireless Telegraphy	Guglielmo Marconi of Italy performs successful pioneering wireless telegraphy trials in the Bristol Channel. He obtains a British patent in 1897.
1897	Cathode Ray Tube	Karl Ferdinand Braun of Germany develops the cathode-ray tube (CRT), the forerunner of the television tube and radarscope. He demonstrates the first oscilloscope (Braun Tube) in 1897. Later, in 1909, he and Marconi receive the Nobel Prize for physics for the further development of wireless telegraphy.
1898	Radium	Marie and Pierre Curie of France discover radium and polonium.
1899	Radio	J. Zenneck, assistant of Ferdinand Braun, both of Germany, broadcasts radio messages over more than 30 kilometers (18.6 miles) with Braun's inductively coupled transmitter at Cuxhaven, Germany.

APPENDIX 2

20ᵀᴴ CENTURY BUSINESS AND WORLD EVENTS TIME LINE

1900   Population

Great Britain	38 million
Germany	30
France	39
United States	75
Japan	44
Russia	126

1900   China   China's Boxer Rebellion (the systematic extermination of foreigners) is quashed by Great Britain, Germany, France, United States, Japan and Russia.

1900   Zeppelin   The Zeppelin takes its first trial flights.

1900   AT&T   AT&T begins first year as parent company of the Bell System. Professor Alexander Graham Bell, and his assistant Thomas A. Watson, experimented with the telephone in 1875. "Mr. Watson, come here, I want you" were the first words spoken on Bell's experimental phone. The first telephone line was installed in 1877, and the box telephone was introduced commercially in that same year. AT&T was incorporated 3 March 1885 in New York as a wholly owned subsidiary of American Bell Telephone Company. Its original purpose was to manage and expand long-distance telephone service of American Bell and its licensees. On 3 December 1899, AT&T assumed the business and property of American Bell and became the parent company of the Bell System.

1900   Cable & Wireless   The UK's Cable & Wireless, known then as the Eastern and Associated Telegraph Companies, operates the largest global telecommunications system in the world. Most of it consists of submerged cables.

1900	Auto Show	The first automobile show in the United States is held in Madison Square Garden. There were almost 14,000 vehicles registered in the United States in that year.
1900	General Electric	GE Research Laboratory is established by Dr. Willis Whitney, and the GE trademark is registered. The Edison Electric Light Company was founded in 1878, and the first "practical" incandescent lamp was invented by Edison in 1879.
1900	Otis Elevator	Otis introduces the escalator at the Paris World's Fair. Otis Elevator was founded in 1853 by Elisha Graves Otis in Yonkers, New York, after he invented a safety mechanism for a lifting platform. Otis elevators were installed in many countries prior to 1900.
1900	Philips	Philips of The Netherlands is founded and begins manufacturing incandescent lamps.
1900	Siemens	The Braun-Siemens-Gesellschaft für drahtlose Telegraphie (Braun-Siemens company for wireless telegraphy) is founded. The Siemens & Halske Telegraph Construction Co. was founded in Berlin in 1847, and the first electric telegraph link between Berlin and Frankfurt was installed in 1849. Siemens later installed the first successful deep sea cable in 1857, discovered the dynamo-electric principle and constructed the first dynamo machine in 1866, developed the universal galvanometer for measuring current, voltage and resistance in 1868, completed development of the electric blocking system for railways in 1872, completed the laying of the first transatlantic cable from Ireland to the United States in 1875, invented the differential arc lamp in 1878, introduced the first electric elevator in 1880, introduced the first electric tramway at Lichterfelde near Berlin in 1881, and obtained the first X-ray tube patent in 1896.
1900	Kohler	Kohler Co. moves its entire plumbing manufacturing operation four miles away from Sheboygan, Wisconsin, to the junction of two Indian trails. The newspaper of the day headlined it "Kohler's folly." A century later, Kohler would be the largest manufacturer of plumbing products in the United States.
1900	Hoechst	Hoechst, a German chemical company, celebrates the 37th anniversary of its founding.
1900	Bayer	Bayer celebrates the first anniversary of the invention of aspirin. Aspirin was registered 1 February 1899 at the Imperial Patent Office in Berlin. The general partnership Friedr. Bayer et Comp. was formally registered in 1863 for the manufacture of aniline dyestuffs. The company was incorporated in 1881 as Farbenfabriken vorm. Friedr. Bayer & Co.
1900	Tata Group	Tata celebrates its 26th anniversary in business in India.

1900	NEC	Nippon Electric Co. celebrates first anniversary as a joint stock company with Western Electric Company of Illinois. Western Electric owns 54% after treaty revisions with Western nations encourage the influx of foreign capital.
1900	Renault	Renault celebrates the second anniversary of its founding in France.
1900	Glaxo	Glaxo celebrates its first anniversary as a UK company. The company was founded in New Zealand by Joseph Nathan, son of a London tailor who emigrated first to Australia and then to New Zealand. The company started out as an import-export business dealing in general merchandise. From there they started selling patent medicines with names like Dew of the Alps and Lediard's Knickerbocker Schnapps.
1900	Procter & Gamble	P&G celebrates the 10th anniversary of its founding in the United States.
1900	Kodak	George Eastman's Kodak Co. celebrates 12th anniversary of its first practical consumer camera. Customers were required to send the camera (loaded with the exposed film) to Kodak for developing.
1901	US Steel	US Steel is formed in 1901 when J.P. Morgan organizes a consortium to purchase not only Andrew Carnegie's then huge organization, but additional steel makers, suppliers, shippers and other peripheral businesses. In valuation it is the world's largest merger or buyout (inflation-adjusted) of the century.
1901	Boer War	The Boer War begins in South Africa.
1901	Marconi	Marconi transmits his first transatlantic radio messages from Cornwall, England to Newfoundland.
1901	Daimler-Benz	Wilhelm Maybach constructs the first Mercedes auto at the Daimler works in 1901. C.F. Benz invented the first car in 1886, and Daimler-Benz was founded in the same year.
1901	McKinley	US President William McKinley is assassinated by an anarchist. Theodore Roosevelt is sworn into office.
1901	Japan/GE	The entire Tokyo tramway system is equipped by GE. Called "the largest electric plant in Asia."
1901	Anheuser-Busch	Anheuser-Busch sells one millionth barrel of beer. George Schneider opened the brewery for business in 1852 in St. Louis, Missouri, and sold it five years later to a group largely financed by Eberhard Anheuser. Eberhard's daughter, Lilly, married a young brewery supplier named Adolphus Busch. In 1864, Busch joined the Anheuser brewery as a salesman, later becoming a partner and finally president. As the driving force that took a floundering local brewery and transformed it into an industry giant, he is considered the founder of the Anheuser-Busch Company.

1901	British Petroleum	William Knox D'Arcy obtains a concession from the Shah of Persia (Iran) to explore for oil.
1901	Motorbikes	The first motor-driven bicycles are seen on the roads.
1901	Nordstrom	John W. Nordstrom and Carl F. Wallin form a partnership and open their first store, Wallin & Nordstrom, in Seattle, Washington. Nordstrom believed that success would come only by offering customers the very best service, selection, quality and value.
1902	Panama	The United States strikes a deal with Panama concerning the Canal. This treaty grants the United States perpetual control over the Canal.
1902	Antitrust	President Teddy Roosevelt directs the Attorney General to file a trust-busting suit against Northern Securities, a railroad holding company, and the Chicago Beef Trust. Under the Sherman Antitrust Act both suits were upheld.
1902	Merck	George Merck becomes a citizen of the United States and starts manufacturing fine chemicals in Rahway, New Jersey and St. Louis, Missouri. The parent company was E. Merck of Germany, originating in the 17th century. By the late 19th century, E. Merck was exporting many of its 4,000 products to the United States, where the pharmaceutical industry was relatively backward. The US company gradually expanded its product line of American-made morphine, cocaine, bismuths and iodides.
1902	Bosch	G. Honold at Bosch in Germany invents high-voltage magnet ignition for motor vehicle engines.
1902	3M	Minnesota Mining and Manufacturing Co. is founded in Two Harbors, Minnesota.
1902	Philip Morris	Philip Morris & Co., Ltd. is incorporated in New York. Philip Morris made his first cigarettes in 1854.
1903	Wright Bros.	The Wright brothers of the United States fly their first successful powered flight in a heavier-than-air vehicle.
1903	J.P. Morgan	The International Mercantile Marine Company is founded by J.P. Morgan. The company will eventually build and operate, for a very short time, a passenger ship named the Titanic.
1903	Harley-Davidson	Harley-Davidson of Milwaukee, Wisconsin, builds its first motorcycle.
1903	London Taxis	London sees its first taxicabs.
1903	Packard	The first transcontinental auto trip in the United States is completed by a Packard in a journey from San Francisco to New York City. Records differ on the time it took—some say 52 days, some report 65 days.
1903	Ford Motor Co.	Henry Ford starts the Ford Motor Co. with US$100,000 in capital.
1903	Philip Morris	Dr. Ludwig Roselius, head of a large European coffee

business, discovers a method for removing 97% of the caffeine in coffee without harming its flavor and aroma. Roselius introduces the product in France under the brand name Sanka.

1903 FMC
The hand-held "Magic Pump," designed by John Bean, spurs the Bean Spray Pump Company to incorporate after John Crummery, president, receives orders for the new higher-pressure device from fruit growers throughout California. The company is incorporated in 1904.

1903 Marks & Spencer
Marks & Spencer is registered as a private limited company in England. Michael Marks arrived in England in 1882 and began selling hats. He could not read or write English, so his slogan in 1884 was "Don't ask the price—it's a penny." Spencer joined him in 1894.

1904 Russo-Japanese War
The Russo-Japanese War starts with the Russians on the defensive from the beginning.

1904 Rolls-Royce
Rolls-Royce motor works is established in Britain.

1904 Telegraph
The first telegraphic transmission of photographs, from Munich to Nuremberg, is accomplished by Arthur Korn.

1904 France
The 10-hour work day comes to France.

1904 3M
3M makes the first sandpaper.

1904 Roche
Roche of Basel, Switzerland introduces Digalen from the plant *Digitalis purpurea* (foxglove) to treat heart disease. At this time, a preparation which offered consistent efficacy represented a great step forward. Digalen maintained its position in the market for over 50 years. Roche was founded in 1882.

1905 Railroads
The Pennsylvania Railroad and the New York Central Railroad, with its Twentieth Century Limited, inaugurate 18-hour train service within a week of each other. These two runs are considered the fastest in the world. Within a week both trains are involved in wrecks, killing 19 people.

1905 Russo-Japanese War
Russia loses the war with Japan. The Czar is forced to cede some power. The Duma, Russia's Parliament, is formed. The first workers' soviet is formed in St. Petersburg.

1905 Einstein
Einstein develops the Theory of Relativity.

1905 Rayon
Using the viscose process, rayon yarn is produced commercially for the first time.

1905 Neon
Neon lights are used for the first time.

1905 Siemens
Siemens develops first metal filament incandescent lamp, W. Bolton's tantalum lamp, to the marketing stage.

1905 Nestlé
Nestlé merges with the Anglo-Swiss Condensed Milk Company. Nestlé was founded in Switzerland by Henri Nestlé in 1867. The first product in 1867 was infant cereal (baby formula), invented by Mr. Nestlé. The product was a major breakthrough of the time because

		one in five babies was dying before their first birthday due to nutritional deficiency. During the period 1905 to 1929, Nestlé became a full-fledged chocolate manufacturer.
1906	CIGNA	San Francisco earthquake; five square miles of the city is in ruins; 400–700 dead according to various accounts, US$400–US$500 million in damages estimated. Insurance Company of North America (the oldest US stockholder-owned insurance company) and Aetna, unlike other companies, promise to pay losses in full to their customers. Connecticut General becomes part of CIGNA at a later date.
1906	Amplifiers	R. von Lieben of Austria and L. deForest of United States independently invent cathode-ray tubes suitable as amplifiers.
1906	General Electric	Alexanderson of GE produces first practical high-frequency alternator used in pioneering voice and music broadcasts.
1906	Kellogg Corn Flakes	The Battle Creek Toasted Corn Flake Company starts production in 1906. Soon after it was renamed after its founder, W.K. Kellogg.
1907	Shell	The Netherlands' Royal Dutch Oil and the UK's Shell Transport merge to become the Royal Dutch Shell Co., strengthening the company's competition against the Standard Oil Co. of the United States. Shell's original founding date was 1890.
1907	J.P. Morgan	J.P. Morgan forges a coalition to stem the 1907 financial panic. In gratitude, President Teddy Roosevelt grants Morgan's US Steel immunity from Sherman Antitrust Act prosecution.
1907	Scott	Scott Paper Company introduces the first paper towel.
1907	UPS	United Parcel Service is founded in the United States.
1908	General Electric	Dr. William Coolidge renders tungsten ductile, paving the way for modern lighting.
1908	Kohler	Kohler invents the one-piece lavatory with integral back. It was now time for everyone to install indoor plumbing.
1909	Model T	Henry Ford introduces the Model T. It lists for US$850, although by 1924 the price is a mere US$290. An inexpensive yet hardy automobile for the masses is now available.
1909	Xerox	Xerox is founded as The Haloid Co., Rochester, New York, to manufacture and sell photographic paper. Chester F. Carlson, inventor of xerography, is born in Seattle on 8 February the same year.
1909	Plastics	Leo H. Baekeland of the United States, a German immigrant, patents a production method for Bakelite in 1908, and it is commercially produced for the first time in 1909. It is the dawn of the Age of Plastic.

1909	Siemens	Siemens installs the first automatic telephone exchange in a major European city, initially for 2,500 subscribers, in Munich-Schwabing.
1909	British Petroleum	The Anglo-Persian Oil Company, as BP was first known, is formed. The company was the first to strike oil in the Middle East, in Persia (Iran) in 1908.
1909	Safety Glass	Laminated safety glass invented by Benedictus of France.
1910	Black & Decker	S. Duncan Black and Alonzo G. Decker start a small machine shop in Baltimore, Maryland. They call it The Black & Decker Manufacturing Co.
1910	Aluminum	A process for manufacturing "duraluminium" is developed to the point where it can be used for mass production.
1910	Diesel Engines	Diesel engines are used for the first time in German submarines.
1910	Bayer	Bayer receives first patent for a process for the manufacture of synthetic rubber.
1910	Electrolux	Electrolux is founded, and vacuum cleaners are sold door-to-door.
1911	Traffic Lanes	The automobile and the country's infrastructure converge: Edward Hines hand-paints white lines on River Road near Trenton, Michigan, in 1911 to mark traffic lanes.
1911	Airlines	World's first commercial air service is initiated in Britain by the Grahame-White Aviation Co. The air service consists of a series of mail flights between Hendon and Windsor.
1911	Semiconductors	J.G. Koenigsberger and J. Weiss introduce the term "semiconductor."
1911	IBM	Computing-Tabulating-Recording Co. (C-T-R) is established as a business combination of the Tabulating Machine Co. (1896), the Computing Scale Co. (1891), and the International Time Recording Co. Dr. Herman Hollerith, an engineer who served briefly as a statistician in the US Census Office, devised a series of electrical machines that processed data stored on punched cards. The value of these tabulating machines was first recognized during the 1890 US Census, when tabulation time was reduced from seven to three years.
1911	Kohler	Kohler introduces the integral apron bathtub.
1911	Standard Oil	The US Supreme Court decrees that the Standard Oil combination be split up into 34 independent operations. The Standard Oil Co. was founded in Cleveland, Ohio, in 1870 by John D. Rockefeller. In the subsequent development of his oil interests, Rockefeller amassed one of the world's largest private fortunes. After the split-up in 1911, Rockefeller was left with just Standard Oil of Ohio (Sohio).

1912	Vitamins	Professor Elmer McCollum of Yale announces that two recently discovered organic compounds affecting body health, vitamins A and B, are required to prevent dietary deficiencies.
1912	Titanic	The Titanic sinks in the North Atlantic; 1,500 men, women and children go down with the ship.
1913	Federal Reserve	The Federal Reserve Board is established in the United States through the Federal Reserve Act of 1913. It effectively loosens the grip that the big US banks had on the country's currency and credit system.
1913	Benchmarking	Henry Ford finishes his benchmarking of the meat-packing industry and lifts one of their innovations. After reengineering, 1,000 Model Ts each day roll off Ford's new conveyer-belt system for continuous production.
1913	Atomic Energy	N. Bohr of Denmark succeeds in applying the quantum hypothesis to the atomic model of E. Rutherford of England, thus deriving the Bohr atomic model.
1914	Mexico	US President Wilson orders American troops to seize Vera Cruz, Mexico after Mexican President Huerta had a number of US sailors arrested in Tampico. The action was successful, with the results leading to a chain reaction of events and the eventual fleeing of Huerta from his own country.
1914	Ludlow War	Labor-management relations display a tragic rough-spot in the so-called Ludlow War in the United States. Coal miners striking—and some say sabotaging—John D. Rockefeller's Colorado Fuel and Iron Co. in Ludlow, Colorado, were attacked by company guards and National Guardsmen, with a number of deaths ensuing. Before the strike, or war, was over, 74 people, including women and children, were counted among the dead.
1914	Traffic Lights	The first traffic light in the United States is installed in Cleveland, Ohio. It uses only green and red signals.
1914	Northern Telecom	Northern Electric is founded in Canada.
1914	Panama/GE	Panama Canal opens, using GE Selsyn system of interconnecting locks. The canal had been under construction since 1881.
1914	World War I	World War I breaks out on 28 June.
1915	AT&T	Speaking into a replica of his original phone, Alexander Graham Bell, along with his longtime assistant, Mr. Watson, initiates the first transcontinental telephone service between San Francisco and New York City. Also in this year, AT&T engineers first experimentally transmit the human voice across the Atlantic Ocean via radio. Mr. Bell first patented the telephone in 1876. This accomplishment can be gauged by noting other phone firsts: The first telephone line connecting two American cities was between Boston and Lowell,

		Massachusetts, 1879; the first telephone line connecting New York City and Chicago was installed in 1883.
1915	World War I	The Lusitania is torpedoed by a German U-boat on 7 May, and the war in Europe is threatening to pull the United States into its destructive vortex.
1916	Boeing	The Pacific Aero Products Co. is incorporated in the state of Washington. A year later, the name was changed to the Boeing Airplane Co.
1916	Artificial Limbs	F. Sauerbruch of Germany devises artificial limbs.
1916	Black & Decker	Black & Decker develops and markets the first portable electric drill with pistol grip, trigger switch and universal motor. The drill is sold to manufacturing-related businesses.
1916	General Motors	General Motors Corp. is founded in the United States.
1917	World War I	On 4 April 1917, the United States enters the Great War by declaring war on Germany. The United States is the 13th country to enter into conflict against the Central Powers. In keeping with the lingering effects of anti-war isolationist sentiment, 6 senators and 50 congressmen oppose the declaration.
1917	October Revolution	The October Revolution in Russia takes place under the leadership of V.I. Lenin. The USSR is founded a few years later in 1922.
1917	Merck	The US government seizes the Merck & Co. stock owned by the parent company, E. Merck of Germany. George Merck, with help from investors, is able to purchase the stock from the government.
1918	Aisne-Marne	The Aisne-Marne Offensive takes place between June 6 through the 25th. The four-week attack is the turning point in the First World War. Later that year, on November 11th, the war comes to an end.
1918	Influenza	By October 1st, the worst US influenza epidemic is producing a little over 200 deaths a day. Before it subsides in early 1919 nearly 500,000 die. Influenza, while still considered serious to this day, is no longer the medical scourge it once was, thanks to advances in prevention and treatment.
1918	General Electric	GE builds record capacity water-wheel generator for Niagara Falls.
1918	General Electric	Armistice message transmitted via transatlantic radio systems designed by Alexanderson of GE.
1918	Bayer	The US Alien Property Custodian sells the confiscated Bayer subsidiaries in the United States to Sterling Drug, Inc. for US$5.31 million.
1918	Mitsubishi	Mitsubishi is founded in Japan.
1918	World War I	World War I Armistice on 11 November.
1919	Prohibition	The Volstead Act becomes law in the United States, enacting the 18th amendment and its prohibition against alcohol. With that, an entire industry becomes

		illegal. Anheuser-Busch, Schlitz, and numerous other breweries and saloon keepers are sent scurrying to find new sources of income, legal or otherwise.
1919	Electrolux	This global maker of vacuum cleaners and other household convenience products is formed.
1919	Rockwell	Willard Rockwell buys a small axle plant called Wisconsin Parts Co. to produce a new improved axle based on his own designs.
1919	Airlines	The first passenger air service comes to Britain, when A.V. Roe & Company run an operation linking Manchester with Southport and Blackpool. In the same year, Alcock and Brown flew nonstop over the Atlantic, and Ross and Keith Smith flew the first air journey from Britain to Australia.
1919	KLM Airlines	KLM is founded, but it has to wait until 1920 before launching its inaugural flight due to adverse conditions—winter had set in.
1920	Women's Rights	The Woman's Suffrage Amendment is ratified in the United States when Tennessee becomes the 36th state to vote for its passage.
1920	Airports	United States establishes the first municipal airport in Tucson, Arizona. The American infrastructure begins to accept air transportation of mail and passengers as a reality.
1920	Roche	Founder Fritz Hoffman dies. Founded in 1894 as F. Hoffman, Traub & Co., the company established a factory in Grenzach, Switzerland, subsequently founding subsidiaries in Paris (1903), New York (1905), Vienna (1907), London (1909), St. Petersburg (1910) and Yokohama (1911). The company's first big product was Sirolin, a drug said to have antibacterial properties.
1920	League of Nations	League of Nations established on 10 January.
1920	FINA	The Compagnie Financière Belge des Pétroles, PETROFINA, is founded by a group of investors from Antwerp. Their first venture was to search for, extract and refine petroleum products in Romania.
1921	TB Vaccine	First tuberculosis vaccine, the B-C-G tuberculosis vaccine, is developed by Albert Calmette and Camille Guerin.
1921	Warren Harding	Warren Gamaliel Harding is elected US president. He takes office in 1921 and dies there, only two-and-a-half years later.
1921	Einstein	Albert Einstein proposes time as the fourth dimension.
1921	Johnson & Johnson	J&J introduces Band-Aid brand adhesive bandages and Johnson's Baby Cream. J&J was incorporated in 1887 and produced the first sterile and antiseptic cotton and gauze dressings in 1891.
1921	FMC	The Anderson-Barngrover continuous pressure cooker and cooler is introduced and hailed by the American

		Society of Engineers as a landmark in American technology.
1921	Siemens	Siemens completes Rhineland telephone cable between Berlin and Cologne, which sets the pattern for a European long distance cable network.
1922	Refrigerators	Baltzar von Platen and Carl Munters, students at the Royal Institute of Technology in Stockholm, build a machine that creates cold temperatures from heat by a unique use of the absorption process. It can run on electricity, gas or kerosene. Shortly, refrigerators are built using this machine.
1922	Fiat	Fiat of Italy presents the first automobile with a stress-bearing body versus the body-on-chassis construction.
1922	Teapot Dome Scandal	The Teapot Dome oil scandal in the United States begins to brew up. The Navy's in-ground oil reserves, being administered by the Department of Interior, were secretly leased to the Mammoth Oil Co., headed by Harry F. Sinclair.
1922	Sound Films	H. Vogt, J. Engl and J. Massolle of Germany demonstrate sound movies according to their Triergon sound-on-film system in Berlin.
1922	BBC	British Broadcasting Corp. is formed in the UK.
1923	Television	John Logie Baird of Scotland invents television.
1923	*Time* Magazine	Henry Luce and Briton Hadden publish *Time* magazine for the first time in the United States.
1923	General Motors	Alfred P. Sloan becomes president of the hapless General Motors Corp. He institutes the famous divisional system of management, which not only brought GM into the forefront of American companies, but served as a managerial example for countless other companies.
1923	Japan Earthquake	Great Kanto Earthquake on 1 September. Tokyo suffers tremendous destruction and loss of life.
1923	Electric Shavers	Colonel Jacob Schick files a patent for the first electric shaver.
1923	Herman Miller	Herman Miller, Inc. is founded when the Star Furniture Co. is purchased by D.J. DePree and his father-in-law, Herman Miller.
1923	Siemens	Siemens installs a telephone exchange with automatic charge accounting according to time and zone in the Weilheim district network, Upper Bavaria. It is a precursor of the German nationwide dialing system introduced in 1952.
1924	Kleenex	Kimberly-Clark introduces the world's first facial tissue.
1924	Zenith	Zenith introduces the world's first portable radio, a suitcase-like affair with built-in loop antenna and horn-type loudspeaker that sells for US$200.
1924	Philip Morris	Unfiltered Marlboro cigarette is introduced, initially marketed as a woman's cigarette. Thirty years later in 1954, it is marketed as a full flavored man's cigarette.

1924	Glaxo	Infant milks were the company's principal interest until 1923. In 1924, they licensed a process to extract vitamin D from fish oil. The original purpose was to enrich the milk, but they also developed vitamin D as a separate product called Ostelin.
1925	Caterpillar	Daniel Best and Benjamin Holt start Caterpillar to build tractors for farming. They will become the world's largest manufacturer of construction and earthmoving equipment.
1925	Chrysler	Chrysler Corp. is founded in the United States.
1925	Model T Colors	Henry Ford once said, "You can have any color car as long as it's black." This year, 1925, finds Mr. Ford offering two more colors for the first time: "deep channel green" and "rich Windsor maroon."
1925	General Electric	First hermetically-sealed domestic refrigerator announced by GE. It is called the "Monitor Top."
1925	Sears	First Sears retail store opens in catalog center on Chicago's west side. The original Sears catalog was published in 1888, featuring the watches of Alvah Roebuck as well as jewelry. The corporate name Sears, Roebuck and Co. was established in 1893.
1925	3M	Dick Drew, a young researcher, acting on his own initiative, develops Scotch Masking Tape.
1925	Otis Elevator	Otis installs first elevator permitting automatic operation without an operator.
1925	Pratt & Whitney	Frederick Brant Rentschler founds Pratt & Whitney on the assumption that the best aircraft can only be built around the best engine. The company's first engine, the Wasp, became the standard for US Navy and Air Force planes.
1925	AT&T	AT&T sells International Western Electric Co. to the newly formed International Telephone and Telegraph Co. (ITT) for US$33 million, retaining only AT&T's interests in Canada.
1925	Nomura	The Nomura Securities Co. Ltd. is registered in Japan by Tokushichi Nomura II.
1926	40-Hour Week	A US auto industry sales depression moves Henry Ford to initiate the 8-hour work day and the 5-day week. Even though the workers have thinner paychecks, they avoid unemployment. In addition, Ford retains his skilled workforce, avoiding a major industry problem—chronic turnover due to workers' aversion to the numbing repetitiveness of assembly-line work.
1926	FCC	US Congress passes a law establishing the Federal Radio Commission (subsequently renamed the Federal Communications Commission).
1926	Radio	The National Broadcasting Co. establishes itself as the first nationwide radio broadcasting network in the United States.

1926	Admiral Byrd	Rear Admiral Richard Byrd is the first to fly over the North Pole.
1926	Zenith	Zenith develops and puts on the market the first home radio receiver that operates directly from regular AC electric current. Push-button tuning is introduced the following year.
1926	McKinsey & Co.	McKinsey begins a management consulting practice that eventually goes international.
1926	Nomura	Nomura Securities begins operations in Osaka as a bond house.
1926	Lufthansa	Lufthansa Airlines is founded in Germany.
1927	Talkies	The first talkie movie in the United States, *The Jazz Singer*, makes it debut.
1927	BMW	BMW engines set 29 of the 87 world records—in aviation.
1927	TV Transmission	AT&T develops the first successful television transmission, beaming a pictorial image of company vice president J.J. Carty from Washington, DC to Manhattan, New York.
1927	Boeing	Lindbergh and the "Spirit of St. Louis" reach Paris. This 33-hour-and-29-minute flight opens the air, and numerous minds, to the possibilities of air travel. Also in this year, Boeing Air Transport, Inc., predecessor to United Air Lines, is founded to operate a mail route between Chicago and San Francisco.
1927	Iron Lung	New York City's Bellevue Hospital installs the first electric respirator, popularly called the iron lung.
1927	AT&T	AT&T inaugurates commercial transatlantic telephone service to London using two-way radio. Initially, these calls cost an exorbitant US$75 each for just five minutes of talk time.
1927	Nomura	Nomura Securities opens New York office.
1927	Kohler	Kohler introduces "matching colors" in plumbing fixtures.
1928	Color Motion Pictures	George Eastman shows the first color motion pictures in 1928.
1928	IBM	C-T-R is renamed International Business Machines. Data capacity of a punched card increases from 45 to 80 columns of information, paving the way for a new series of machines that can do more than add and subtract.
1928	Rockwell/Fokker	North American Aviation is started as an American holding company to produce Fokker aircraft.
1928	Penicillin	British scientist Alexander Fleming discovers penicillin, the first therapeutically effective antibiotic.
1929	Incomes	A study indicates that 60% of Americans earn US$2,000 a year, thought to be the minimum to sustain life.
1929	Great Depression	On October 24, the stock market takes a plunge. It's grim enough to prompt J.P. Morgan to once again

		organize a group of financiers to take action. It works, and the market temporarily props up, but a few days later, on Black Tuesday, the 29th, the bottom drops out and so does the American dream. The economic repercussions are felt the world over and for many years to come. The US stock market will not see such a devastating downturn again until October of 1987.
1929	Unilever	Unilever is founded.
1929	FMC	John Bean Manufacturing Company holds a contest to choose a more appropriate name. The winning entry is Food Machinery Corporation (FMC).
1929	Whirlpool	Whirlpool is founded as Nineteen Hundred Corp. in the United States.
1929	Nestlé	Nestlé merges with chocolate makers Peter, Cailler, and Kohler. Daniel Peter was the inventor of milk chocolate.
1930	3M	Minnesota Mining and Manufacturing introduces "Scotch Tape," an invention of Dick Drew. The company was founded in 1929.
1930	Disney	Mickey Mouse makes his first appearance in a cartoon titled *Steamboat Willie*.
1930	Motorola	Galvin Manufacturing introduces the first practical and affordable auto radio. Paul Galvin coins the name Motorola for the company's new products, linking the ideas of motion and radio. The company was founded in 1928.
1930	Siemens	Siemens completes two remarkable industrial buildings designed by H. Hertlein for Siemensstadt, the Switchgear and Werner Works high-rise factories. They are the first of their kind in Europe. Also, Siemens introduces first expansion-type circuit breaker in Hamburg.
1930	Jet Engine	Frank Whittle of England invents the jet engine.
1931	Empire State Bldg.	The Empire State Building in New York is completed. At 381 meters (1,250 feet), it is the world's highest building for many years.
1931	Procter & Gamble	Neil McElroy introduces the concept of brand management via a company memo. It not only becomes a keystone of Procter & Gamble's operations, but is imitated by many other marketing-based companies.
1931	Brazil/GE	Monument of Christ the Redeemer on Corkovado Mountain in Rio de Janeiro is lit by GE lights, which Marconi turned on for the inaugural display by radio from his yacht anchored in the Bay of Naples, Italy.
1931	AT&T	AT&T introduces radio telephone service to Hawaii.
1931	Miles	Dr. Miles introduces Alka-Seltzer to the American market.
1932	Great Depression	The US Depression is raging, wages are 60% less than

in 1929, and unemployment has hit 13 million people (approximately 11% to 12% of the US population).

1932	Procter & Gamble	Procter & Gamble sponsors a radio drama called "The Puddle Family" and soap operas begin their reign.
1932	Polaroid	Edwin H. Land invents the first Polaroid glass.
1932	Frito-Lay	First Fritos® corn chips made at Elmer's Confectionery in San Antonio, Texas, in the garage adjoining his family home. First sales were handled out of the back of his Model T Ford and averaged US$8 to US$10 a day, yielding a profit of about US$2.
1932	Siemens	Siemens introduces diesel and turbo-electric drives for express trains and ocean-going vessels.
1932	Bayer	Bayer introduces drugs to successfully fight malaria.
1933	Adolf Hitler	Adolf Hitler is appointed Chancellor of Germany.
1933	Japan	Japan withdraws from the League of Nations 27 March.
1933	US Prohibition	Prohibition on alcohol is repealed.
1933	TVA	The Tennessee Valley Authority is established as a federal US corporation to provide electricity to the rural southern United States.
1933	Siemens	First public telex networks start operation.
1933	Roche	T. Reichstein succeeds, in his laboratory in Zurich, in synthesizing ascorbic acid (vitamin C).
1934	SEC	The Securities and Exchange Commission is established by the US Congress.
1934	AT&T	AT&T introduces radio telephone service to Tokyo.
1934	Siemens	Siemens develops autopilot flight control system for aircraft.
1934	Canon	Canon introduces Japan's first 35mm camera in prototype form, the Kwanon.
1934	Fuji	Fuji Photo Film Co. is founded in Japan.
1935	AEG	E. Schüller, of AEG in Germany, invents "Magnetophone" tape recorder.
1935	IBM	IBM introduces its first electric typewriter.
1935	Siemens	Siemens introduces coaxial cables for carrier-frequency telephone calls and television transmissions.
1935	Boeing	Boeing introduces the B-17, nicknamed the "Flying Fortress."
1935	Matsushita	Matsushita is founded in Japan and manufactures light sockets.
1936	Franco	General Francisco Franco leads Fascist forces as they force the start of the Spanish civil war in mid-1936. Franco is reinforced with German air support and Italian troops.
1936	Motorola	Motorola introduces the Police Cruiser, an AM auto radio that is pre-set to a single frequency to receive police broadcasts.
1936	British Airways	British Airways is formed as a combination of Hillman Airways, Spartan Air Lines, United Airways, and British

		Continental Airways. The organization was called Allied British Airways, but it was quickly shortened to British Airways.
1936	DC-3 airplane	At the behest of American Airlines, which needed a more economical airplane in order to turn a profit on passenger traffic, Douglas Aircraft designs the DC-3, one of aviation's most memorable airplanes.
1937	Golden Gate Bridge	Golden Gate Bridge is completed in San Francisco.
1937	Motorola	Motorola introduces push-button tuning, fine tuning and tone controls on its auto radios.
1937	Bayer	Chemist Otto Bayer, no relation to the company's founders, invents polyurethane chemistry.
1937	Toyota	Toyota is founded in Japan.
1938	Snow White	*Snow White and the Seven Dwarfs* is the top moneymaking movie.
1938	Munich Pact	The Munich Pact is signed by Great Britain, France, Germany and Italy. It effectively gives Czechoslovakia over to Nazi Germany. A Gallup poll of Americans shows most approve of this act.
1938	General Electric	GE announces development of the fluorescent lamp.
1938	Frito-Lay	Frito-Lay introduces the first point-of-sale materials for display racks.
1938	Xerox	Chester Carlson of Xerox makes the first xerographic image in Astoria, in the New York City borough of Queens.
1938	Carlson Companies	Curtis Carlson, a Procter & Gamble salesman, introduces Gold Bond trading stamps to grocers. The trading stamp had been used for the first time in 1895, at Schuster's Department Store in Milwaukee, but that program and others, including S&H Green Stamps and Eagle Stamps, were redeemable only for cash and were available primarily in department stores.
1938	Ballpoint Pen	Bird of Hungary invents the ballpoint pen.
1938	Hewlett-Packard	Dave Packard moves into a new house in Palo Alto, California, and rents a cottage behind the house to Bill Hewlett. Dave and Bill begin part-time work in the garage with US$538. First product is the resistance capacity audio oscillator, an electronic instrument used to test sound equipment. It represents a breakthrough in technology from existing oscillators in size, price and performance. Walt Disney orders eight oscillators for the production of the movie *Fantasia*.
1938	Walt Disney	Walt Disney Co. is incorporated.
1938	Roche	P. Karrer is successful in synthesizing tocopherol (vitamin E), the production of which begins in 1939.
1938	Nestlé	Nestlé introduces the first practical instant coffee product, Nescafé, in Switzerland.
1938	Volkswagen	Volkswagen GmbH entered in commercial register in Berlin.

1939	World War II	Germany invades Poland on 1 September. Two days later Great Britain and France declare war on Hitler.
1939	TV, Nylon, Plastic	Television, nylon and plastic are first displayed at the International Exposition in New York in October. Nylon and Perlon were invented in 1937.
1939	General Electric	GE research lab isolates a tiny quantity of Uranium 235.
1939	Zenith	Zenith goes on the air with W9XZV, the first all-electronic US television station built to then-current standards. For nearly three years this was the only television station operating in Chicago.
1939	Herman Miller	Herman Miller gambles on "contemporary office furniture" and wins.
1939	L'Oreal	L'Oreal is founded in France.
1939	Turbojet Aircraft	The first turbojet-powered aircraft, a Heinkel He 178, is flown in Germany. Sir Frank Whittle developed a turbojet earlier but did not see it fly until 1941.
1940	World War II	The United States approves Britain's receipt of 50 decrepit destroyers, and the United States is granted long-term leases on several key military bases in exchange. The year is 1940, and the war is fast ending the days of American neutrality.
1940	Nylon	DuPont's initial production of women's nylon stockings is a stunning success. In New York City alone, the 72,000-pair allotment is sold out in 8 hours. Dr. Wallace Carothers' 1937 nylon patent will be used to make many other products.
1940	Helicopters	Igor Ivan Sikorsky completes the first successful American helicopter flight. He flies for 15 minutes.
1940	Motorola	Motorola develops the first hand-held two-way radio for the US Army Signal Corps. The portable "Handie-Talkie" becomes a World War II symbol.
1940	FMC	Donald Roebling lands a contract for FMC to provide 200 "alligators" to the US Navy. The alligator was a 1932 Roebling invention for an amphibious landing craft. James Hait refined the craft, subsequently called the "water buffalo," which was used to transport Marines from ship to shore during World War II battles.
1940	Radar	Radar is introduced by Watson Watt of Scotland, and used by both Axis and Allied powers during World War II.
1941	World War II	The Japanese attack the United States at Pearl Harbor on 7 December. The Pacific War begins.
1941	Boeing	Boeing B-17 "Flying Fortress" is first flown in combat in World War II by the British Royal Air Force.
1941	Volkswagen	The first VW Beetles are produced for testing and publicity purposes. It isn't until after WW II that production models for public use are manufactured.

1941	Motorola	Motorola introduces the first commercial line of two-way FM radio communications products.
1941	Computer	K. Zuse of Germany presents a program-controlled electromechanical digital computer, the Z 3.
1942	World War II	The interment of 110,000 Japanese-Americans, Bataan Death March, Doolittle's Tokyo raid, gas rationing, the Battle of Midway, the fight for Guadalcanal.
1942	Nuclear Reaction	Enrico Fermi succeeds in producing the first controlled uranium nuclear chain reaction in Chicago.
1942	Boeing	The first production model of the B-29 "Superfortress" takes to the air.
1943	Motorola	Motorola introduces the "Walkie-Talkie" backpack radio, designed by Motorola's Dan Noble.
1944	IBM	IBM, in a joint venture with Harvard University, completes its first operating machine that can execute long computations automatically, the ASCC (Automatic Sequence Controlled Calculator).
1944	Process Controls	K. Zuse of Germany operates first digital computer for process control. The application was automatic bearing surface measurement.
1944	Civil Aviation	Fifty-two nations participate in the "Chicago Conference" which spawned modern air transport. The conference was a success in laying the foundation for standardization in the operating procedures and navigation practices of international air transport. It created the International Civil Aviation Organization, now an agency of the United Nations.
1945	General Electric	GE jet engines power the P-80, the world's fastest plane.
1945	3M	3M introduces first electrical tape with vinyl plastic backing.
1945	WW II/Boeing	The B-29 "Enola Gay" drops the world's first atomic bomb on Hiroshima, Japan. Three days later, the B-29 "Bock's Car" drops another atomic bomb on Nagasaki. Shortly thereafter, on 15 August, the Pacific War ends.
1945	United Nations	United Nations established on 24 October.
1946	Computers	The ENIAC (Electronic Numerical Integrator and Computer), designed for the Remington Rand Corporation by J. Presper Eckert, Jr. and John Mauchly at the University of Pennsylvania, goes on-line. It incorporates 18,000 vacuum tubes and occupies a 45.7-square-meter (492-square-foot) room. The project was initiated in 1943 and was largely completed in 1945.
1946	United Nations	The United Nations meets for the first time in London in January. The following session takes place in Lake Success, New York, and then in its permanent residence in New York City. It was John D. Rockefeller, Jr. who donated the land.
1946	"Iron Curtain"	Winston Churchill coins the expression "iron curtain."
1946	Nuclear Power	The Atomic Energy Commission is established in the

United States to promote the peaceful application of atomic power.

1946	Bank Drive-Thru	The automobile continues to challenge US culture: The Exchange National Bank of Chicago introduces the Autobank— the country's first drive-through teller. Sitting behind bullet-resistant glass, up to ten tellers could handle transactions using slide-out drawers.
1946	General Electric	GE demonstrates nuclear operation of steam turbine using sodium-cooled reactor.
1946	IBM	IBM introduces the IBM 603 Multiplier, the first small commercial electronic calculator.
1946	Black & Decker	Black & Decker introduces the first portable electric drill for consumers.
1946	Sony	Tokyo Tsuskin Kogyo is founded in Japan and later renamed Sony.
1947	Cold War	US financier Bernard Baruch tags the East-West political confrontation, the "Cold War."
1947	Tubeless Tires	B.F. Goodrich rolls out the tubeless tire.
1947	Sound Barrier	In 1947, Charles Yeager, a US Air Force captain, breaks the sound barrier in a Bell X-1 aircraft.
1947	Zenith	Zenith introduces world's first subscription television system.
1947	Hyundai	Hyundai is founded in South Korea.
1948	Church vs. State	The US Supreme Court declares religion in the public schoolroom to be a violation of the First Amendment.
1948	Marshall Plan	The United States passes the Marshall Plan to provide foreign assistance. Eventually it will be funded with over US$100 billion.
1948	Columbia Records	Columbia Records introduces the 33 1/3 "long-playing" record.
1948	Berlin Airlift	Stalin tries to squeeze the West by putting a stranglehold on Berlin. United States and British forces organize the "Berlin Airlift."
1948	Solar Heating	Dr. Maria Telkes designs a solar heating system and has a Dover, Massachusetts home equipped with it.
1948	Bell Labs	The transistor is invented by William Bradford Shockley, J. Bardeen and W.H. Brattain at Bell Telephone Laboratories in the United States on 1 July.
1948	Xerox	The Haloid Co. and Battelle Development Corp. jointly announce development of xerography. Battelle held Chester Carlson's basic xerographic patents until 1947.
1948	3M	3M develops nonwoven fabric, a technology leading in later years to Scotch-Brite cleaning and finishing products, Thinsulate insulating materials, surgical masks, disposable baby diapers, absorbent materials for oil, etc.
1948	IBM	IBM introduces the SSEC (Selective Sequence Electronic Calculator), the first operating computer to combine electronic computation with stored instructions.

1948	Xylocaine	Sweden's Astra Pharmaceutical Company launches production of Xylocaine, a local anesthetic that finds worldwide acceptance and use.
1948	Velcro	Velcro is produced by de Mestral of Switzerland.
1948	Honda	Honda is founded in Japan.
1949	Bikinis	The French introduce the bikini.
1949	Gene Photography	Doctors Daniel Pease and Richard Baker successfully photograph the gene.
1949	Information	K. Küpfmüller writes his fundamental paper on system theory of electrical information transmission.
1949	NATO	The NATO pact is established.
1949	Cortisone	Cortisone is discovered. Initially, it is used for rheumatoid arthritis.
1949	Xerox	Xerox introduces the Model A copier, the first commercial xerographic product.
1949	Volkswagen	Volkswagen begins shipments of the VW Beetle.
1950	McCarthyism	US Senator Joseph McCarthy begins his attacks on communism.
1950	Korean War	The Korean War begins on 25 June.
1951	Color TV	First color television introduced in United States.
1951	Hewlett-Packard	H-P invents the high-speed frequency counter, used by radio stations to accurately set frequencies to comply with FCC regulations.
1952	Japan	Japan joins the International Monetary Fund on 14 August.
1952	NEC	The Deming Prize for Quality (first in the communications industry) is awarded to NEC.
1952	General Electric	GE develops autopilot for navy jet aircraft.
1952	IBM	IBM introduces its first large vacuum tube computer, the IBM 701, which executes 17,000 instructions a second. Nineteen are produced and used primarily for government and research work.
1952	Daiei	Mr. Isao Nakauchi (called the Sam Walton of Japan) starts a small store in Osaka with 13 employees.
1952	British Airways	British Airways fits Rolls-Royce jet engines to its Comet 1 Aircraft and initiates inaugural service from London to Johannesburg.
1952	Bayer	Bayer introduces another drug to fight tuberculosis, called Neoteben. Finally, all forms of tuberculosis are curable.
1952	SAS	SAS Airlines is the first commercial passenger airline to schedule flights over the polar ice cap. The route is a shortcut between Copenhagen and Los Angeles
1953	Stalin	Joseph Stalin dies.
1953	Korean War	27 July finds an armistice ending the Korean War.
1953	Anti-infectives	Cephalosporin C is isolated by a research group at Oxford University. Over 8,000 antibiotics are subsequently identified before the 21st century.

1954	McCarthyism	The Army-McCarthy hearing take place. It results in McCarthy being completely discredited.
1954	Segregation	The US Supreme Court rules that segregated education is illegal in its Brown versus The Board of Education of Topeka decision.
1954	Sony	Sony introduces the transistor radio. Although not the first to produce a transistor radio (a US company named Regency Electronics rolled one out a few months earlier), Sony is the first to make it pocket-sized. It was a big seller in both Japan and the United States.
1954	General Electric	GE designs the J-79, the world's first jet engine to move aircraft at twice the speed of sound. Also, GE installs first industrial numerical control for machine tools.
1954	3M	3M introduces Scotch magnetic video tape used in the first recording of television pictures.
1954	Texas Instruments	TI produces first commercial silicon transistor. Also designs first commercial transistor radio, called Regency, built and marketed by IDEA Corp.
1954	Zenith	Zenith introduces the first 21-inch, three-gun rectangular color picture tube.
1954	Siemens	Siemens develops zone refining process for preparation of ultra-pure silicon.
1955	Japan	Japan joins GATT on 10 September.
1955	General Electric	GE creates man-made industrial-grade diamonds. Also, USS Seawolf is launched, powered by KAPL's first nuclear reactor for naval use.
1955	Xerox	Xerox introduces first semi-automatic xerographic printer which makes continuous copies on ordinary paper.
1955	McDonald's	McDonald's Corp. is incorporated in the United States.
1955	Philip Morris	Marlboro cowboy appears for the first time as a part of the cigarette's rugged new masculine image.
1956	Polio Vaccine	Dr. Jonas Salk's polio vaccine is produced in mass quantities.
1956	Sea-Land	The first containerized shipping system is pioneered.
1956	Nuclear Power	First nuclear power station of the Western world starts operation in Calder Hall in Cumberland, UK
1956	Rank Xerox/UK	Rank Xerox Limited formed as joint venture of The Haloid Co. and The Rank Organisation PLC.
1956	3M	Scotchgard fabric and upholstery protector is introduced.
1956	Motorola	Motorola introduces pagers and begins to sell semiconductors to other manufacturers.
1956	AT&T	AT&T provides telephone service to Europe via the first transatlantic submarine telephone cable. The cable was operational in 1955.
1956	Siemens	Siemens begins trial operation of the first fully-transistorized data processing system, the 2002.
1956	Canon	Canon introduces its 8mm cinecamera, the Canon 8T.
1957	Space	Sputnik I is launched by the USSR.

1957	Wankel Engine	F. Wankel develops the rotary piston engine to production stage.
1957	Common Market	Western European nations form The Common Market under the Treaty of Rome.
1957	EEC	Signing of Rome Treaties founds European Economic Community (EEC) and European Atomic Energy Community (Euratom).
1957	General Electric	GE receives first US atomic reactor license from the Atomic Energy Commission for operation of the 5-megawatt Vallecitos atomic power plant.
1957	IBM	IBM offers FORTRAN programming language to its customers.
1957	Boeing	Boeing delivers its first Boeing 707 passenger jet to Pan American. Said Juan Trippe, Pan Am president, "People thought we were crazy." However, in the first two years of jetliner service, air travel almost doubles. The 707 helped create an entire industry in international air travel.
1957	Casio	Casio is founded in Japan.
1958	Xerox	Changes name from The Haloid Co. to Haloid Xerox, Inc.
1958	Texas Instruments	TI invents first integrated circuit, demonstrated by inventor Jack Kilby.
1958	Inchcape	Inchcape is incorporated. Inchcape's origins date back to the British Empire in the 1700s.
1959	Alaska	Alaska becomes the 49th US state.
1959	Astronauts	The first seven US astronauts are selected.
1959	Stereo Records	Stereo records are generally introduced.
1959	Xerox	Xerox introduces the 914 copier, the first automatic office copier to make copies on ordinary paper at the rate of 7.5 copies a minute. Xerox purchases from Battelle all remaining worldwide patents on xerography.
1959	Mattel	Mattel introduces the first Barbie™ doll.
1959	Motorola	Motorola introduces the "Motrac," the first two-way mobile radio to have a fully transistorized power supply and receiver.
1959	SABRE	American Airlines introduces the SABRE system. It is the largest computerized reservation system in the world.
1960	Laser	T. Amaiman of the United States invents a laser as a light amplifier of maximum intensity.
1960	NEC	World's first telephone electronic switching central office becomes operational in Chicago on 11 November.
1960	General Electric	GE designs re-entry system, recovery system, and space capsule for space shuttle Discovery.
1960	IBM	IBM introduces solid-state 7000 series computers, replacing the 700 series of vacuum tube machines.
1960	Herman Miller	Robert Propst invents the open-plan office furniture system.
1960	Carlson Companies	Carlson purchases first hotel in Minneapolis and establishes Radisson Hotel chain.

1960	Rockwell	North American Aircraft has now built 42,700 military aircraft, including the P-51 Mustang fighter, the B-25 Mitchell bomber, the T-6 Texan trainer, the F-86, F-100, A5A, B-70, X-15 rocket plane and B-1B bomber.
1960	Roche	Roche introduces Librium for the treatment of psychological or psychosomatic diseases.
1960	FINA	Inflatable rings, dolphins and air beds from FINA's "Bonnes Vacances" publicity campaign invade the beaches of Europe.
1960	OPEC	Organization of Petroleum Exporting Countries (OPEC) formed.
1961	Executive Crime	In 1961, 29 major electrical companies, including General Electric and Westinghouse, and 44 of their executives, are convicted of bid rigging and price fixing. Seven of the executives receive jail terms of 30 days.
1961	Space	Yuri Gagarin, of the USSR, is the first man into space, orbiting the earth in Soviet spaceship Vostok 1.
1961	Berlin Wall	GDR builds Berlin Wall to prevent East German citizens from fleeing to the West.
1961	Vietnam	The first US troops arrive in Vietnam. Their role, as it stood in 1961, is advisory in nature.
1961	Germany/GE	GE produces nuclear power station in Kahl, Germany, which is the first privately financed nuclear power in Europe.
1961	Xerox	Changes name from Haloid Xerox, Inc. to Xerox Corp.
1961	FCC/Zenith	FCC approves stereo FM radio broadcast system, invented by Zenith, and still in use worldwide.
1961	Black & Decker	Black & Decker introduces the first cordless electric drill, powered by nickel cadmium cells.
1962	Cuban Blockade	The United States blockades Cuba. It is in response to that island's missile threat, created by the USSR.
1962	Xerox/Japan	Xerox launches Fuji Xerox Co., Ltd. as joint venture of Rank Xerox and Fuji Photo Film Co., Ltd.
1962	Wal-Mart	First Wal-Mart store is opened in Bentonville, Arkansas, by Sam Walton.
1962	Motorola	Mariner II, on its flight to Venus, carries a Motorola transponder which provides a radio link spanning 54 million miles. Also, Motorola introduces the fully transistorized Handie-Talkie.
1962	IBM	IBM guidance systems are designed to be used for Saturn launch vehicles and the Gemini Space Program.
1962	Texas Instruments	Introduces digital seismic technology.
1962	AT&T	AT&T places the first commercial communications satellite, Telstar I, in orbit.
1962	IBM	Business finds that the emptiness of space is full of possibilities. Using Telstar, IBM engineers send computer information between Endicott, New Jersey, and LaGaude, France.

1963	US/Russian Hotline	The "hotline" is installed at the White House and the Kremlin in 1963. Its presence is meant to foster communications and prevent nuclear war.
1963	NEC	First successful experimental satellite TV relay from the United States to Japan on 23 November.
1963	John F. Kennedy	US President Kennedy is assassinated on 22 November. Lyndon Baines Johnson is quickly sworn in as President.
1963	General Electric	GE introduces self-cleaning oven.
1963	Japan/GE	GE builds first nuclear power plant in Far East.
1963	McDonald's	Ronald McDonald makes his debut in Washington, DC, played by Willard Scott, who later became the weatherman on NBC's "Today Show."
1963	Roche	Roche introduces Valium, a "blockbuster" tranquilizer.
1963	Boeing	The three-engine Boeing 727 flies for the first time. The company expected to make only 250 of them, but subsequently made over 1,800.
1963	Philips	In its 72nd year, Philips of The Netherlands invents the compact cassette which becomes a world standard. The company began electric incandescent lamp manufacturing in Eindhoven, The Netherlands, in 1891.
1963	Mary Kay Cosmetics	Mary Kay Cosmetics is founded in the United States.
1963	Nuclear Test Ban	USSR, United States and the UK sign a nuclear test ban treaty.
1964	Salad Oil Scandal	Antonio De Angelis perpetuates the infamous "Salad Oil Scandal" in 1964. This scam caught Mr. De Angelis substituting sea water for salad oil in the bulk containers that were supposed to hold the dressing oil. He did so to fool potential investors, and was successful to the tune of US$175 million.
1964	Alaska Quake	On March 27, one of the more lethal earthquakes in history shakes Alaska. It measures 8.4 on the Richter scale and kills 117 people, while leaving US$750 million in damage.
1964	Narrows Bridge	Verrazano Narrows Bridge is completed in New York between Brooklyn and Staten Island. It is the longest suspension bridge in the world, spanning 1,278 meters.
1964	Japan	Japan admitted to OECD on 28 April.
1964	Xerox LDX	Long Distance Xerography uses scanners, networks and printers for high-speed document facsimile transmission.
1964	IBM	IBM introduces its IBM 360 series of business computers, as well as magnetic tape and Selectric typewriter.
1964	Nike	Phil Knight and Bill Bowerman each contribute US$500 to their partnership, subsequently named Blue Ribbon Sports (BRS). Grassroots promotions are born as runners don BRS shoes, many prototypes of which were designed by Bowerman.

1964	AT&T	AT&T provides telephone service to Asia via the first transatlantic submarine telephone cable.
1964	Hewlett-Packard	H-P gains worldwide recognition for the "flying clock," a cesium-beam standard instrument flown around the world to set international time standards.
1964	Canon	Canon introduces the world's first 10-key electronic calculator, the Canola 130.
1965	Tobacco Warnings	US President Johnson signs into law a requirement that warning labels must accompany all cigarette packaging.
1965	INTELSAT I	INTELSAT I, the first commercial application geosynchronous communications satellite, successfully launched on 6 April.
1965	Motorola/RCA/Ford	In a joint program with Ford and RCA, Motorola designs and manufactures the first 8-track tape players for the automotive market.
1965	Texas Instruments	TI invents semiconductor-based thermal printer.
1965	Boeing	Boeing designs the 737 aircraft, which would later become the world's best selling jetliner. First flight is in 1967.
1966	Siemens	Siemens & Halske, Siemens-Schuckert and Siemens-Reiniger merge to become Siemens AG with headquarters in Munich.
1966	Boeing/Pan Am	Boeing announces the 550-seat 747 jetliner; Pan American places a US$525 million order for the new 747 almost immediately, and the first flight is just one year later.
1966	Danone	BSN, later named Danone, is founded in France.
1967	Motorola	Motorola introduces the "Quasar" line of color receivers, America's first all-transistor color television sets.
1967	PAL Color TV	W. Bruch of Germany develops the PAL standard for color television. The United States uses the NTSC standard.
1967	Heart Transplant	First heart transplant performed by Christian Barnard in Cape Town, South Africa.
1967	Texas Instruments	TI invents electronic hand-held calculator.
1967	Rockwell	Rockwell Standard and North American Aviation merge, forming a new company named North American Rockwell.
1967	Boeing	Boeing installs 1,000 Minuteman missiles across the United States.
1967	Daewoo	Daewoo is founded in South Korea.
1968	General Electric	First flight of C-5 military transport with GE TF39 engines.
1968	Black & Decker	Black & Decker develops a unique power head for the Apollo Lunar Surface Drill to remove core samples from the moon.
1968	Hewlett-Packard	H-P introduces the first desktop scientific calculator, the HP9100A.

1968	Intel	Intel, maker of computer processors, is founded in the United States.
1968	Canon	Canon introduces the VCR industry's first four-track, four-channel recording head.
1968	Evergreen	Evergreen, a container shipping company, is founded in Taiwan.
1969	Space	Astronaut Neil Armstrong is the first human being to walk on the surface of the moon. President Kennedy had a stated goal that the United States would put a man there before the decade was over. Mission accomplished.
1969	Boeing	Boeing designs the 138-foot-high, first stage booster of the Saturn V rocket. The Saturn V rocket, having 7.5 million pounds of thrust, was used in the Apollo Space Program. Boeing also designed the Lunar Roving Vehicle, taken to the moon on the last three Apollo missions. Boeing was also responsible for overall systems integration for the entire Apollo project.
1969	General Electric	Space project Apollo includes 6,000 GE employees.
1969	Siemens	Siemens installs its first nuclear power station at Obrigheim on the Neckar using a light water moderated pressurized water reactor.
1969	IBM	IBM introduces System/3 for small businesses and "mag-card" Selectric typewriter.
1969	Internet	Internet is started. Originally called ARAPNET and designed by the US Defense Department's advanced research projects agency at the University of California at Los Angeles (UCLA).
1969	Texas Instruments	TI announces Silent 700 data terminal, first to use thermal printing technology.
1969	Roche	Dr. Sidney Pestka at the Roche Institute of Molecular Biology begins isolating interferon, which is registered in 1986 in the United States and Switzerland for the treatment of certain malignant diseases.
1969	Glaxo	Glaxo discovers Ventolin, which revolutionizes the treatment of asthma. Ventolin is regarded as one of the most important products ever to emerge from British pharmaceuticals research.
1970	Gene Synthesis	The first complete synthesis of a gene is accomplished by University of Wisconsin scientists.
1970	General Electric	GE announces synthesis of gem-quality diamonds. Also, successful first flights of DC-10 aircraft powered by GE CF6 engines.
1970	Canon	Canon introduces its first plain paper copier, the NP-1100 copier. Canon entered the photocopier field with the introduction of the Canofax 1000 in 1965.
1971	Dollar Devaluation	United States devalues the dollar, while Japan and many European countries revalue their currencies upward.
1971	Tobacco	Cigarette advertising is banned from American television.

1971	China	The People's Republic of China is admitted to the United Nations.
1971	Gold Standard	US President Richard Nixon announces the end of the dollar-gold exchange on 15 August.
1971	Nike	The name Nike (the Greek goddess of victory) is dreamed by first full-time employee (and former track star) Jeff Johnson the night before the shoe boxes are to be printed. A shoe for football (soccer) and American football is the first Nike model to hit the retail market. A Nike T-shirt to promote the shoe becomes the first apparel item.
1971	Texas Instruments	TI invents single-chip microprocessor and single-chip microcomputer.
1971	Bayer	Bayer introduces the herbicide Sencor to the market. With this product it was possible to destroy weeds and grasses without harming the crops. Sencor became the Bayer product with the single biggest sales volume. Bayer gave 33% of its production to DuPont, which claimed previous patent rights. DuPont was also successful with its similar product, Lexone.
1971	Philips	Philips of The Netherlands introduces the first videocassette recorder. With this model the cassette was still almost square and the tape reels were placed on top of each other.
1972	Munich Games	Arab terrorists kill 11 Israeli athletes at the Olympic Games in Munich.
1972	NEC	NEC begins production of the world's first single-chip 10,000-element LSIs for desktop calculators on 4 August.
1972	Hewlett-Packard	H-P introduces the first hand-held scientific calculator, the HP-35, which makes the engineer's slide rule obsolete. In the same year, H-P introduces its HP3000 minicomputer.
1972	Daiei	Daiei becomes largest retail chain in Japan (second is department store Mitsukoshi). Daiei introduced the discount retailing concept in Japan in 1957.
1972	Singapore Airlines	Singapore Airlines is founded.
1972	Volkswagen	The 15 millionth Volkswagen Beetle comes off the line as the world champion, beating the previous production record held by Ford's Model T.
1972	Cheung Kong	Cheung Kong Holdings, Ltd. is founded in Hong Kong.
1972	Boeing	Boeing's AWACS aircraft for military use makes its first flight.
1972	Canon	Canon introduces the world's first plain paper copier with the liquid-dry system, the NP-70.
1972	SAP	SAP, a German software company, is founded.
1973	OPEC	OPEC launches an oil embargo against many Western countries, including the United States.

1973	Dollar Devaluation	The United States devalues the dollar for the second time.
1973	Iran	The Shah of Iran nationalizes all oil assets.
1973	Middle East	Fourth Middle East War breaks out 6 October, and OPEC reduces oil production on 4 November.
1973	World Trade Center	World Trade Center is completed in New York.
1973	Space Station	US Skylab space station launched into earth orbit.
1973	Xerox	Xerox introduces 6500 color copier which makes full-color copies on plain paper and transparencies. Also, Xerox introduces first non-impact xerographic printer for computer output.
1973	Texas Instruments	TI introduces 4K-bit dynamic random access memory (DRAM) chip.
1973	Philip Morris	Oscar Mayer is the first in the food industry to start printing the Universal Product Code on product labels.
1973	Siemens	Siemens begins manufacture of large-scale integrated circuits.
1973	Federal Express	Federal Express initiates its inaugural overnight air express delivery service on 17 April. A total of 186 packages were shipped that night. In 1995 the average volume is 2.4 million packages per night.
1974	Oil Embargo	The oil embargo prompts the US Federal Energy Administration to print 4.8 billion gas-rationing coupons. They go unused.
1974	Nixon Resigns	Gerald Ford takes the US presidency when Nixon resigns.
1974	Philip Morris	Miller Lite® beer is introduced.
1975	Vietnam	The last of the Americans in Vietnam leave quickly by helicopter.
1975	UPS	United Parcel Service is the first parcel delivery service to serve the 48 contiguous United States. The company has come to deliver more packages than even the United States Postal System.
1975	ATMs	Automatic Teller Machines become generally used by banking customers.
1975	CN Tower	The CN tower is completed in Toronto. At 553 meters, this radio and TV tower is the highest self-contained construction in the world.
1975	Philip Morris	Marlboro becomes the top selling brand in the United States and the all-time best seller in the world.
1976	Viking 1	US space probe Viking 1, launched in 1975, lands on Mars and sends data and photos back to earth.
1976	General Electric	World's largest hydroelectric turbine, from Canadian GE, is installed at Grand Coulee Dam.
1976	Apple	Steve Wozniak is working at Hewlett-Packard, and Steve Jobs is at Atari. They finish work on a preassembled computer circuit board. It has no keyboard, case, sound or graphics. They form the Apple Computer Company on April Fool's Day. They raise

		US$1,350 and begin production in Jobs' parents' garage.
1976	British Airways	The Concorde begins supersonic service.
1976	Canon	Canon introduces the Canon AE-1 35mm SLR camera, triggering an SLR boom. Also in this year, Canon enters the fax market.
1977	Xerox	Xerox introduces first xerographic laser printer with capability of 120 pages a minute.
1977	IBM	IBM introduces System/34, a low-cost data processing system with multiple workstations.
1977	Voyager	The US spacecraft Voyager travels deep into space, carrying a message to any extra-terrestrials.
1977	Apple	Apple is incorporated and introduces the Apple II with color graphics, keyboard, power supply and attractive case. It includes 4k of memory and comes equipped with two game paddles and a demo cassette, all for US$1,298. Monthly orders reach a US$1 million annual sales rate.
1977	Glaxo	Glaxo introduces Zantac, a unique treatment for peptic ulcers. In the 1990s, Zantac became the largest selling medicine in the world.
1978	IBM	IBM introduces electronic typewriters with microprocessors.
1978	Texas Instruments	TI introduces first single-chip speech synthesizer; first product is "Speak & Spell."
1978	Airlines	The US airline industry is deregulated, and intense competition begins.
1978	NTT	Nippon Telegraph and Telephone finally completes installation on its backlog of telephone subscribers.
1978	Philips	Philips of The Netherlands introduces the first videodisc player.
1979	Xerox	Xerox introduces 860 information processing system, a multi-functional office information system combining processing of text, business records and data. Also, Xerox introduces Ethernet local area network for connecting workstations, printers and other office equipment.
1979	3M	3M introduces Thinsulate thermal insulation, providing lightweight warmth with much less bulk than previously possible.
1979	Motorola	Motorola introduces the first 16-bit microprocessor, the 68000.
1979	Apple	Personal Software, Inc. releases VisiCalc for the Apple II. The spreadsheet is the first application to make personal computers a practical tool for people who don't know how to write their own programs.
1979	Philips/Sony	Philips and Sony demonstrate the first compact disc (CD), a design which becomes a world standard a year

		later. This product revolutionized the record industry with sound quality and resistance to damage.
1980	Xerox	Xerox introduces Diablo 630 computer printer, a daisywheel printer which sets the industry standard.
1980	3M	3M introduces "Post-it Notes," an invention of scientist Art Fry.
1980	CNN	The Cable News Network (CNN) is founded 1 June.
1980	Motorola	Photographs of Saturn taken by Voyager I are returned to Earth over a distance of one billion miles using Motorola equipment.
1980	Chrysler	US President Carter provides Chrysler with US$1.5 billion in federal loan guarantees.
1981	Microsoft	Microsoft introduces MS-DOS operating system, which is shipped with the first IBM PC.
1981	Telecommunications	British Telecommunications Act partially introduces competition into British telecommunications in July.
1981	Space	Re-usable US manned space shuttle Columbia successfully launched into space. The first test shuttle, originally named the Constitution, is renamed Enterprise as a result of a letter-writing campaign by "Star Trek" fans.
1981	Frito-Lay	Frito-Lay introduces Tostitos® crispy round tortilla chips, the most successful rollout in the company's history to date.
1981	Xerox	Xerox introduces Memorywriters, electronic typewriters with internal memory.
1981	IBM	IBM introduces the IBM Personal Computer (PC). IBM and its Microsoft DOS operating software quickly become the standard for businesses. Apple greets its new competitor with a full page ad in *The Wall Street Journal* with a headline that reads, "Welcome IBM. Seriously."
1981	MTV	MTV music television is founded 1 August.
1981	FMC	FMC's first Bradley Fighting Vehicle rolls off the production line. Ten years later during Operation Desert Storm in the Middle East, the Bradley is hailed as the best performing weapon system in the history of the United States.
1981	Nomura	Nomura (NSI) becomes a registered member of the New York Stock Exchange.
1981	Canon	Canon introduces the world's first bubble jet printing technology.
1981	Siemens	Siemens is the first European manufacturer of the 64-kb memory chip.
1982	Canon	Canon introduces the PC-10 and PC-20, the world's first personal copiers with replaceable cartridges.
1982	Apple	Apple becomes the first PC company to reach US$1 billion in annual sales. *Time* magazine's "Man of the Year" issue is devoted to "The Year of the Computer."

1983	Apple	Apple enters the *Fortune 500* at 411 in under five years. The millionth Apple II rolls off the assemblyline.
1983	Microsoft	Windows operating software is introduced.
1983	Boeing	Boeing's "Dyna-Soar," designed in the late 1950s, re-appears in the form of the space shuttle.
1983	Chrysler	Chrysler introduces the minivan, which becomes a new market segment. Also in this year, Chrysler pays off federal loan guarantees seven years early.
1984	Apple	Apple introduces the Macintosh PC.
1984	Xerox	Xerox introduces Kurzweil 4000 Intelligent Scanning System, which recognizes a wide range of characters and document formats.
1984	3M	3M introduces medical laser imager, the first imager to make fast, high-quality medical images from digital data.
1984	Motorola	Motorola introduces the first true 32-bit MC68020 microprocessor.
1984	Zenith	Zenith develops the multichannel television sound (MTS) transmission system adopted by the industry for stereo TV broadcasts.
1984	AT&T	AT&T divests its assets to regional operating companies and shrinks from US$149.5 billion in assets and over one million employees to just US$34 billion in assets and 373,000 employees. Until 1 January 1984, AT&T was the parent company of the Bell System, the regulated enterprise that formerly provided the bulk of telecommunications in the United States.
1984	Hewlett-Packard	H-P pioneers ink jet printing technology with intro-duction of H-P Thinkjet printer. Also introduces H-P LaserJet printer, H-P's most successful single product ever.
1984	Videotex	Deutsche Bundespost in Germany introduces Video-tex following field trials in Berlin and Düsseldorf that began in 1980.
1985	Xerox	Xerox introduces the ViewPoint Series, an icon-based, mouse-driven document processing software for the Xerox 6085 workstation. This interface introduced ease-of-use technology to desktop computing. Also, Xerox introduces 1185 and 1186 artificial intelligence workstations, intended for the design, use and delivery of AI software and expert systems.
1985	3M	3M introduces first refastenable tapes for disposable diapers.
1985	Edmark	Edmark begins developing Apple II software programs for special education students, and shortly thereafter expands into the preschool market.
1985	Coca-Cola	Coca-Cola launches "New Coke." Consumers revolt. Coke reintroduces the original formula as "Coca-Cola

		Classic." The original Coca-Cola syrup was produced by an Atlanta, Georgia pharmacist in a three-legged brass pot in his backyard in 1886.
1986	Nuclear Disaster	Major reactor accident in USSR at the Chernobyl nuclear plant.
1986	Xerox	Xerox introduces 4020 color ink jet printer, Versatec CE3400 Series color plotters, 2285 Engineering Workstation, and Datacopy MacImage and PCImage scanning software for PCs.
1986	Sprint	United Telecom and GTE establish a 50-50 partnership to market Sprint long distance service. "Pin drop" television commercials help double the customer base in just a few months. First coast-to-coast US fiber-optic transmission is completed—a videoconference linking New York and Los Angeles.
1986	Roche	Interferon is registered in the United States and Switzerland for the treatment of certain malignant diseases such as leukemia. It is subsequently approved for other forms of cancer as well as AIDS.
1986	Marks & Spencer	Marks & Spencer of England is the first retailer in the world to be awarded the AAA credit rating.
1987	Stock Market Crash	October 1987 sees the US stock market crash to its second worst mark since the 1929 crash.
1987	Xerox	Xerox introduces Voice Message Exchange System V, a voice messaging system for 800 to 10,000 users.
1987	Texas Instruments	TI introduces the first single-chip 32-bit artificial intelligence microprocessor.
1987	Zenith	Zenith patents "flat tension mask" (FTM) technology for high-resolution color video displays.
1987	Sprint	Sprint introduces its FONCARD™ and distributes millions of the chrome-colored cards in the first year.
1987	British Airways	British Airways is fully privatized.
1987	BP/Sohio	British Petroleum acquires Sohio, merges it with other United States interests, and forms BP America.
1988	Marks & Spencer	Marks & Spencer of England acquires Brooks Brothers in United States.
1988	ABB	ASEA Brown Boveri merger is complete. ASEA was founded in Sweden in 1883. Brown-Boveri was founded in Switzerland in 1891.
1989	Berlin Wall	Berlin Wall comes down in November.
1989	China	Protesters are massacred in Tiananmen Square, Beijing.
1989	Xerox	Xerox introduces Encryption Unit, an electronic encryption device that mathematically encodes computer signals so they may travel in top security on ordinary local area networks.
1989	Sprint	United Telecom acquires controlling interest in Sprint from GTE, bringing its ownership level to 80.1%.

| 1990 | Population | Population in 1990 versus 1900 of largest industrialized countries: |

	1900	1990
Great Britain	38 million	58 million
Germany	30	81
France	39	58
United States	75	261
Japan	44	125
Russia	126	147

1990	Germany	Germany reunifies.
1991	Gulf War	Crisis and war in the Persian Gulf region. Iraq invades Kuwait. Other countries come to the rescue.
1991	Hewlett-Packard	H-P introduces HP95LX palmtop PC, weighing 11 ounces and combining Lotus® 1-2-3® software with advanced calculation features and data-communication capabilities. Also in 1991, H-P introduces HP SONOS 1500 echocardiograph system allowing doctors to perform quantitative, non-invasive cardiac analysis in real time by processing ultrasound waves.
1991	Canon	Canon develops the world's first FLCD (ferro-electric liquid crystal display).
1991	European Union	The Maastricht Treaty signals the start of the unification of Europe.
1992	Canon	Canon introduces the EOS5, the world's first eye-controlled autofocus camera.
1992	3M	3M develops blue-green laser for future applications in communications, data storage and imaging markets.
1992	McDonald's	McDonald's now has 13,000 restaurants in 69 countries.
1992	Edmark	Edmark launches a new generation of award-winning multimedia educational software products for young children.
1993	Anheuser-Busch	The Budweiser brand is the best selling brand worldwide, with 1993 shipments of 89.7 million barrels. Second place is held by Heineken of The Netherlands at 47.7 million barrels.
1993	3M	3M introduces Scotch-Brite Never Rust Wool Soap Pads made from recycled plastic beverage containers.
1993	Carlson Companies	Carlson's TGI Friday's restaurants average US$3.4 million each, the highest sales per unit of any US restaurant chain. Curtis Carlson says to his heirs and successors, "All the world will be your territory, whatever you want to sell."
1993	Hewlett-Packard	H-P has now sold over 20 million printers.
1993	Canon/IBM	Canon and IBM jointly develop the world's first notebook computer with a built-in printer.
1994	Wal-Mart	There are now 2,176 Wal-Mart stores throughout the

		world, impressive growth from just one store in 1962. Net sales for 1994: US$82.5 billion.
1994	3M	3M introduces O-Cel-O StayFresh Sponge. The sponge kills germs and their odors, and is the first on the market to use anti-microbial technology.
1994	Hewlett-Packard	H-P introduces HP Color LaserJet printer, HP OfficeJet printer–fax-machine–copier, and HP200LX palmtop PC with built-in Pocket Quicken.
1994	Daiei	Daiei merges three subsidiary companies (Chujitsuya in Tokyo, Uneed in Kyushu and Dainaha in Okinawa) and becomes Japan's first national retail chain, with 348 superstores totaling 2.6 million square meters of floor space. Daiei also has four supermarkets and one superstore in Hawaii, and is struggling to open a super-market in China.
1994	Bayer	Bayer buys back its Bayer aspirin from Sterling Drug for US$1 billion. Bayer aspirin had been confiscated by the United States during World War I, and had been sold to Sterling Drug in 1918 for US$5.31 million.
1995	Eurotunnel	The long talked about Eurotunnel opens for operation. Begun in 1986, the tunnel links England and France (Folkestone and Calais, respectively).
1995	Lotus	Lotus now has 3.5 million users of its Lotus Notes groupware.
1995	Microsoft	To date, Microsoft shipped 100 million units of its Windows™ operating system.
1995	Netscape	Netscape captures 70% of the web browser market on the Internet after offering its web browser free of charge. Netscape Communications was founded in 1994 and has its IPO in 1995.
1995	Sun Microsystems	Sun makes JAVA software available, free of charge, on the Internet. JAVA's appeal is that it will run on a wide variety of operating systems. Virtually all major computer manufacturers endorse the new software before its official January 1996 release.
1996	AT&T	AT&T splits itself into three separate corporations comprising: (1) long distance, cellular, Bell Laborato-ries, (2) switching equipment, and (3) computer equip-ment. AT&T has now come full circle twice, the first time through government regulation and the second by choice.
1996	Coca-Cola	Coca-Cola is served in almost 200 countries, with hundreds of millions of servings each day.

APPENDIX 3

INTERNATIONAL BUSINESS JARGON GLOSSARY

Bootstrap—To succeed on one's own.

Called some excellent shots—Made sound business decisions.

Cat will come out of the bag—The truth will be known.

Caught off guard—Surprised.

Centurions—Commanders.

Coattails—Aided by association with another.

Could not hold a candle—Unable to compare favorably.

Cracked the top ten list—Became one of the "ten best" in a given category.

Crap shoot—A gamble or risky decision.

Dips and dives—Fluctuations.

Dovetails—To join or fit together harmoniously.

Drag them down—To decrease the stature of someone or something.

Duke it out—To engage in fighting.

Feather in the cap—A symbol of a great accomplishment.

Feeding frenzy—To devour.

Flagship stores—The initial outlets of a chain of stores.

Flapper era—A period in the United States characterized by lively music and provocative fashion (1920s).

Foot in the door—An opportunity.

From cradle to grave—Spanning a lifetime.

Gaining more steam—Increasing momentum.

Get off my soapbox—Cease to continuously state an issue.

Getting the steam up—Raising momentum.

Globe galloping mindset—A world view.

Gone sour—A situation which has worsened.

Grabs the brass ring—Achieves its ultimate goal.

Grease monkey—An auto mechanic.

Green grocer—A retailer of fresh vegetables and fruit.

Ground zero—A starting point.

Handing over the reins—The turning over of responsibility.

Hang their managerial hat—Wager their career.

Harks back—Reference to an era long ago.

Hitching post—A post to tie horses to.

Hooking up—The merging of two entities.

Huckster—A retailer of small articles using questionable sales methods.

Iffy—Questionable.

In step—Synchronous, in tandem.

Intellectual property—Data, information and knowledge possessed by a company.

Jazz Age—A musical era of the 1920s.

Jumped in with both feet—Began a process with confidence.

Jumped right on it—Began immediately.

Keener eye—More acute vision.

Kill the goose that lays the golden egg—Abandon one's most successful or promising practices or products.

Knack—A talent or aptitude.

Knick-knacks—Collectible items such as found at gift and souvenir shops.

Largess—A generous bestowal of gifts.

Lean and mean—Operating without waste, with fewer people, and with great vigor.

Leaving in its wake—A result, or an aftermath.

Leitmotif—A theme associated throughout.

Limp along—Move about slowly and ineffectively.

Lock horns—To engage in a power struggle.

Lose big time—To suffer grave consequences from defeat.

Made from scratch—To construct using basic materials.

Made lots of headway—To make significant advances or progress.

Marketing muscle—Strong marketing savvy, techniques and capabilities.

Midas touch—To achieve extreme luck or skill; "everything one touches turns to gold."

Mish-mash—A confused mess.

MO—Modus operandi, Latin for "method of operation."

Mom and pop—A very small business.

Move onto their turf—To invade a competitor's established territory or market.

Mumbo-jumbo—Meaningless words.

Muscle—To use aggressive strategies to quell competition.

Muscle the market—To leverage market position using brute force.

Mushroomed—Expand greatly.

Nose-dived—Decrease suddenly, or to go down.

Old hat—Time-tested, antiquated, or commonplace.

Paid for handsomely—To purchase through a large, perhaps too large, financial commitment.

Pass muster—To meet requirements.

Pep them up—To invigorate or increase the determination to succeed.

Peppy—Energetic, vigorous, lively.

Play their card—To make a strategic move.

Pratfalls—Comic blunders.

Put your money where your mouth is—An ultimatum which advises one to back up lofty speech with financial investment; to make a commitment to a stated belief.

Red-hot—Fierce or intense.

Rev up—To initiate or increase action.

Ride the same wave—To continue to benefit from something.

Running in place—Exerting much force to accomplish little.

See-sawing—Swaying from one extreme to another.

Seems to be all thumbs—Clumsy.

Sink their fate—To have a negative effect on one's future.

Slam-dunk—To succeed with vigor; analogy of basketball player slamming ball into net.

Smooth out—To ease relations.

Smorgasbord—A large variety of choices.

Snaking—Winding.

Snapping up—Acquiring.

Snowballed—To have grown or become larger or more intense.

SOP—Standard operating procedure.

Squeeze-outs—To eliminate through competition.

Staying power—The ability to maintain a position or status for a length of time.

Stranglehold—An influence which restricts free actions.

Stumbling block—An obstacle or hindrance to progress.

Stumbling in their own backyard—To struggle in one's own marketplace.

Sunday Best—A person's best clothing.

Taglines—Advertising slogans.

Tinkering—To play around with.

Tip of the iceberg—A small portion of a very large object or endeavor.

Took the industry by storm—Experienced much success quickly.

Trip them up—To cause to stumble, or impede progress.

Two-steps forward, one-step backwards—Slow progress.

Uphill struggle—An extremely difficult endeavor.

Upper crust—The highest social class.

Vacuum-tube tubby—A large number of vacuum tubes used in an early computer.

Warp speed—Extremely fast.

Watchwords—Words or short phrase expressive of a principle.

Wear so many hats—To have numerous responsibilities.

Willy Loman—A failed salesman; a character in Arthur Miller's *Death of a Salesman.*

You do not have a clue—To be utterly without guesses, or you don't know what you're talking about.

Zillion—An extremely large number.

Zoot suit—A suit with baggy tight-cuffed pants and an oversized coat.

INDEX
